Kimberley Walsh is an award-winning singer, dancer, and actress. There's lots more to come from the UK's favourite Northern lass. Just watch this space.

A Whole Lot of History

Kimberley Walsh

headline

This edition first published in 2014
by HEADLINE PUBLISHING GROUP

1

Cataloguing in Publication Data is available from the British Library

Paperback ISBN 978 1 4722 0932 0

Photo credits:
Section 2 page 1 © Ian West/PA Archive/Press Association Images
Section 2 pages 6-7 © David Hogan
Section 3 page 6 [top] © BBC Photo

Typeset in Berling by Palimpsest Book Production Limited,
Falkirk, Stirlingshire

Printed and bound in Great Britain by Clays Ltd, St Ives PLC

Headline's policy is to use papers that are natural, renewable
and recyclable products and made from wood grown in
sustainable forests. The logging and manufacturing
processes are expected to conform to the environmental
regulations of the country of origin.

HEADLINE PUBLISHING GROUP
An Hachette UK Company
338 Euston Road
London NW1 3BH

www.headline.co.uk
www.hachette.co.uk

Acknowledgements

I would firstly like to thank my very talented friend Terry Ronald for writing this book with me. You made it so incredibly easy and I'm thrilled with the result.

Thank you to Sarah Emsley and everyone at Headline for giving me this opportunity and the freedom to write my story. It's been a pleasure working with you.

I want to thank my manager Hillary Shaw, Nikki White at Shaw Thing Management and Sundraj Sreenivasan at Supersonic PR for all your help along the way.

Thank you Richard Bray and everyone at Bray and Krais.

My girls for an incredible 10 years. I'm so proud of our journey and all that we achieved.

Finally I want to thank my loving boyfriend Justin, my wonderful family and all the incredible people that have brought something to my 31 years. There are far too many special people to mention, I feel extremely lucky to have you all in my life.

Enjoy!
Xxx

Contents

Prologue

It was a strange day, that final day of Girls Aloud – 20 March 2013. There was weird energy in the air and I felt unsettled and anxious from the moment I woke up. Cheryl and Nicola both told me that they felt it, too, but they didn't need to because I could see it in their eyes. None of us knew what to think or exactly how we were going to feel when it actually came to the final moment. I wasn't sure if I was going to break down, fall apart or jump for joy when I walked out on that stage; I had so many different emotions flying around my brain. I suppose it's not all that surprising, really. This was a big deal for us whatever way you looked at it. It was the end of an era.

It had been ten years since the five of us had come together as strangers on Saturday night TV talent show *Popstars – The Rivals*. Ten whole years. I could hardly believe it. We'd had twenty-one top-ten singles, sold four million albums, and we'd become the twenty-first century's biggest-selling girl group. Now here we were at the end of it, about to leave it behind for good. And there was a lot to leave behind, too: a whole lot of history, as the song says. The first time the five of us watched the video montage of ten years of Girls Aloud moments that was to accompany the song 'I'll Stand By You' on our tour, every single one of us broke down in tears because it was all right there in front of our eyes again. I suppose I was worried about our fans as well, and how they were going to react. We knew that we were going to have to announce that Girls Aloud were no more after the final show, and we knew that there were going to be a hell of a lot of sad, disappointed people to contend with – fans who'd supported us since the beginning. They'd undoubtedly be asking the same question – why?

For most of the day I told myself that I wasn't going to get too emotional. I actually felt quite strong and I thought that I might get through the night without too many tears. During the penultimate show, Cheryl had completely lost it during 'I'll Stand By You'. She'd just gone, suddenly, crying her eyes out as soon as the song and the accompanying video had finished. At the time I thought, What are you doing, Cheryl? You're never going to get through 'The Promise', which was the next song. Hold it together, Chezza. The fans don't even know this is the end yet, we haven't announced it and there you are crying like a baby. That's me, I suppose, always the practical one, but I knew how much this meant to her. We'd given everything to the band, and now we were saying goodbye.

Then something strange happened while I was getting my hair and make-up done for the final show. Our choreographer, Beth Honan, walked into the dressing room, and as I looked up at her I began to think of all the times we'd spent together. Beth had been with us right from the early days. She'd directed all of our tours, and she'd choreographed most of our videos and TV appearances over the years. In fact, she was almost like another member of the band. All of a sudden I felt as if every memory I had of her had flooded my mind at the same moment, as though there was a little movie playing in my head, with scenes and moments from all our tours and TV shows flashing in front of me. Quite unexpectedly the tears came, and suddenly I couldn't stop them. Beth saw what was happening and she turned away, hastily.

'Don't you look at me,' she said. 'Don't you dare look at me.'

In the end she had to leave the dressing room in case I started her off as well. I don't even really know why I chose that particular moment to lose it. Perhaps it was the realisation that I wasn't just saying goodbye to the rest of the band. I was also saying goodbye to everyone we'd worked with over the last ten years, and to the memory of all the things we'd done together – things that we would never do again. We'd all felt it at some point during the tour, I suppose. Our hair and make-up stylist, Lisa Laudat, had had a near breakdown after watching one of the shows from the side of the stage one night. She was a friend who'd also been with us for years, creating some of Girls Aloud's most memorable looks. It was as if a family was breaking up, not just a band.

After I'd pulled myself together I really had no idea if I might break down again but by the time we got on stage the sadness had passed and I felt a lovely mixture of happiness and relief. I also felt very grateful to have been part of something so special. I enjoyed that last show as much as, if not more than, any show we'd ever done. To me it was a celebration rather than a death, and looking back I'm really glad I felt that way. When it came to 'I'll Stand By You' I was expecting tears again from Cheryl, but there were none. While we were performing the song she looked at me as if to say, look, I'm not crying. I think she was quite surprised that she wasn't because she's usually very emotional. At the end of the song we just smiled at one another. It was such a knowing smile that said, 'This is right. It's been amazing but now it's over. It's time to move on.'

As we took our final bows as Girls Aloud at the Echo Arena in Liverpool that night, there wasn't a doubt in my mind that we'd made the right decision and that it was time for the band to end. In fact, I've never been as sure of anything in my life. The five of us had had such a fantastic run, and although there'd been some difficult times along the way, we were finishing on an amazing high at the end of a wonderful and really successful tour. But I was done. I'd given everything I could to the group and I didn't think I had any more to give.

It had been different the first time we spent some time apart because that felt like unfinished business. There was no big announcement, no lavish farewell show. We all just sort of wandered off to pursue our own various projects – and it was only supposed to be for a year. And even though that one year eventually turned into three, I always knew that we'd get back together again, and that's what I wanted at the time. I wanted to finish it all off properly and go out with a bang rather than just drifting apart, and that's exactly what we finally did. We ended on a high. If we'd carried on any longer, I'm not sure that would have been the case. I think we might have spoiled what we had and I didn't want that. It was time for that chapter in my life to end and that night, as the lights went down on our final show, I knew it.

1

The Entertainer

'Let's do raindrops on roses and whiskers on kittens!' From the moment I could string a sentence together I was a proper little performer. My older sister, Sally, was the same, and once the two of us started stage school there was no stopping us. We would sing and dance for anyone and everyone, friends or family, whether they liked it or not. We were the only kids I knew who actually got up early for school, jumping out of our beds at the crack of dawn so we could practise our routine for 'My Favourite Things' from *The Sound of Music* before we went down for breakfast. We were dead serious. And as for annoying the hell out of everyone, well, we were oblivious to that. We just loved to perform. We were obsessed.

There was always music in our house as far back as I can remember. My mum, Diane, was a schoolteacher, her first subject being music, and as well as playing the piano she taught it to some of the kids who lived on our estate in Bradford. That was just one of the things she did to earn a bit of extra money. We had a piano in the house, and various local kids would come round each day for their lessons. I remember it used to get on our nerves because we kids always had to keep quiet while there was a lesson going on, and that was never easy for us. Still, Mum was brilliant like that. She was always thinking up ways to earn a bit of extra cash and she had to work hard at it, especially after my dad left home when I was just six.

My mum's mum and dad were both quite musical, too, so I guess it's no real surprise that we eventually turned into a sort of Yorkshire version of the von Trapps. My grandma, Joan, could play the piano and my granddad, Tom, was a fantastic singer. He always said that he wished he could have done it professionally and I reckon he could have, he was that good. We loved going round to their house when we were little because we always ended up around the piano with Grandma playing and Sally, my younger brother, Adam, little sister Amy when she was old enough, my cousins and me singing along with her, and dancing around the living room like lunatics. It just seemed so exciting to us that our grandma was able to sit down at the piano and bust out a good old tune – we were in heaven. She played 'The Entertainer' and she taught us how to play 'Chopsticks'. She had a really good repertoire of songs and, of course, we got to know them all by heart.

Sally was the real showbiz child of the two of us, and although we both loved performing, I was always slightly in her shadow when I was very young. We were like chalk and cheese. Sally was more highly strung than I was, so she'd be more likely to throw a tantrum or play up. I was always very chilled out, like my mum, and whenever she gave me to one of her friends to look after, I'd end up sleeping right through. I was a babysitter's dream. I never really minded being the one in the background, though. I really looked up to Sally. She was the perfect big sister and I was always happy to follow her lead.

There were seven grandchildren altogether – my mum's sister Helen had three children – and sometimes we'd all be at my grandparents' house at the same time. On these occasions we could put on a really big show, and we had a captive audience with my auntie and uncle there as well as my grandma and granddad. I recently found a picture of all seven of us kids standing in a row and singing at the adults. We would meticulously organise and rehearse a full show and then perform it in front of them all in the living room. Sally was the bossiest one, so she was the one who called the shots. She would take the role of director, with the rest of us falling into line. I was always happy to do as I was told as long as I was performing. We'd re-enact scenes from *The Sound of Music*, *Annie*, *Seven Brides for Seven Brothers* – all the old classics. We knew them off by heart because from a young age my mum and dad would sit down with us and watch them on television or on video. Of course, if we had them on video, Sally and I would watch them over and over again until we'd virtually worn the tape out. We actually knew most of the scripts as well as the songs.

Whatever show we did at my grandparents' place, my little sister Amy would join in, playing the younger characters, including Molly from *Annie*, and I remember when we were a bit older doing scenes from *Grease*, starring my brother, Adam, as Danny and me as Sandy. Adam wasn't always quite as enthusiastic about performing as we were, but the poor boy didn't really have much of a choice. Sally and I were deadly serious about the whole thing.

My granddad loved ballroom dancing as well as

singing, and often while my grandma was playing the piano I would hold his hand and stand on both his feet while he glided gracefully around the living room, teaching me the right steps to all the different ballroom dances – moments like that felt magical to me at that age. He was so thrilled when I did *Strictly Come Dancing* in 2012, and to be honest he was one of the reasons I did it when I did. He was quite ill by then, and we lost him not long after the series ended.

John and Diane, my mum and dad, had four kids before they eventually separated. Sally was born in July 1979, followed by me in November '81, Adam in February '84 and Amy in March '87. We weren't too far apart in age and we have always been extremely close. I think when your mum and dad split up or get divorced when you're young, that's what tends to happen – the kids latch on to one another and look out for one another. Well, that's the way it was with us, anyway. It wasn't long after Amy was born that my parents split, and although my dad always remained a big part of our lives afterwards, the four of us were very close to our mum, too. It was as if we felt we had to look after her as well as one another once Dad had gone – just like she was looking after us.

My mum is a really soft, warm lady, and lovely looking with it. When she was younger, people used to say she looked like Debbie Harry with her fine features and her bleached blond hair. She has always been well liked. She's one of those people whom nobody ever has a bad word for. And although when we were little she was often run ragged with four kids, she was naturally very beautiful and she always looked great with her stone-washed jeans and her eighties perm.

Dad was always very well turned out, too. In fact, I can't remember him wearing anything other than a suit with a shirt and tie until I was at least sixteen. He is a handsome man with dark hair, and a real charmer who likes to make people laugh. As dads go, I think he was pretty cool. He was certainly a lot cooler than all of my friends' dads, who seemed a little bit old-fashioned in comparison. I guess that's why my friends all liked him so much, because he was always joking around and not as serious as most of the grown-ups we knew. Dad would take us to the snooker hall with him – which probably wasn't an ideal environment for kids, but we loved it – and he always had what we thought of as a flashy car, although looking back they weren't really all that flashy. He liked to go out with the lads and gamble, and I suppose he was a bit of a bad boy in some ways, but he was always loving towards us kids and he did whatever he could to make us happy.

When Sally and I were young, the family lived in a small, three-bedroomed, semi-detached house in Allerton, Bradford. It was on a main road and not the nicest of places. After Adam was born we moved to a bigger house in a really nice cul-de-sac in Sandy Lane, which was a lot more rural than where we'd been used to. Sandy Lane is a lovely village, heading out towards Haworth, where the Brontë sisters lived. It had a church and a post office and a small school, which I eventually attended. The house we lived in there was still a three-bedroomed place, but it had so much more space. It had a proper garden and was very close to a gorgeous wooded valley called Chellow Dean, so it was like a whole new world for us – quite a step up from where we'd just left.

I don't think I really appreciated it at the time, but looking back now, Sandy Lane was a great place to grow up in and we were quite lucky. The village was small and friendly, and as there were loads of other kids on our estate we were never short of someone to run around with outside. Mum was always quite relaxed about us playing out on the street or in the nearby woods. She's never been a big worrier in that respect – she knew we would never go too far and she trusted us to behave ourselves. I suppose all the kids kept an eye on one another, and she knew that. Dad was the complete opposite. He was always worrying about where we were and what we were doing. Luckily, though, Mum was the person who generally set the rules in our house, so we often got to play out for as long as we wanted to, which was all day if we could get away with it. We'd be in the woods, swinging on homemade tree swings, running around and climbing – the fun that we had. I just can't imagine children having that much fun these days because people wouldn't think it was safe to let their kids run wild in the woods. Maybe it wasn't then, but at the time we never saw any danger. There were usually too many of us to be scared of anything.

As we got older, Adam and I played together a lot and because he was quite boisterous I usually ended up being led astray and doing all the daring, daft things that he did. He was the naughtiest, most mischievous little boy you could ever hope to meet, but gorgeous with it. He took after my dad, and loved being the centre of attention, and he was always playing jokes. I can't count the number of nights he lay under my bed for up to an hour, just so he could jump out and scare the hell out of me with the maximum effect. One night he locked poor Amy in the loft with her hands tied behind her back and an apple in her mouth. When we eventually found her, she was laughing. My mum was so run ragged I don't think she had any idea what was going on half the time.

Chellow Dean has two big reservoirs and in the summer Adam and I would climb the surrounding walls and throw ourselves off, plunging down into the water. It was probably extremely dangerous – people have drowned in those same reservoirs, and we had no idea what was in the water – but to us it was just good fun. In the winter, we used to go sledging down a huge hill behind our garden, which was fantastic, and the two of us used to love building our own tree dens, too.

One day we were playing near the house of a scary family who lived at the bottom of our road. I call them scary because they used to scream and shout at kids who went anywhere near their garden or touched anything that they thought belonged to them. So that day, Adam thought it would be hilarious to shove me over their wall, right into their garden, and, of course, they were out there in a flash, yelling and shouting at me. I got a proper telling off and I was gutted. Not only that, but I'd caught my coat on the fence as I went over and it ended up covered in varnish. This was a coat that my mum had lovingly made for me because she didn't have the money to spend on a shop-bought one. She made a lot of our clothes to try to save money and she was good at it, although we didn't always appreciate it at the time. We did later on when we wanted her to design something special or a bit fancy for us, but when we were little, I think we'd as soon have been wearing ordinary stuff from the shops, just like all the other kids. Anyway, my homemade coat was pink on the outside and flowery on the inside, and it was reversible so you could wear it either way. A lot of work had gone into that coat and Mum was none too pleased when I went home and she saw the state of it.

I didn't get into trouble very often. I normally knew where to draw the line. This was mainly out of respect for my mum. I thought she had enough on her plate without having people knocking on her door saying, 'Your kid's done this, your kid's done that.' I didn't want to put her through that, so I always tried to keep on the right side of any mischief that might be going down. If ever Mum was angry with us, she had a really calm way of making us see that what we'd done was upsetting her. I don't know how she did it, but she made us care about our actions.

Even though I did hang out with my brother and his mates a lot of the time, I certainly wouldn't have called myself a tomboy. I still had a very girly side, and I met my best girl friend, Alix Walker, when I was four or five – in fact, she's still my best friend today. We met on the very first day of primary school when poor Alix was crying her little heart out, she was so distraught about her mum leaving her. I was absolutely cool with it and didn't shed a single tear, which is probably why the teacher suggested that we sit together so I could look after her. It's funny, both my sisters and my brother absolutely hated the first day of school whereas I skipped up the stairs and through the door quite happily – I was really laid back about the whole thing. I loved school. I wasn't particularly studious or anything, I just enjoyed being there.

My first school was Sandy Lane Primary – a really lovely small village school. Even right back then I was singing my head off in all the school concerts and plays. My first-ever public performance was at a Sandy Lane school show, singing 'Hand Me Down My Silver Trumpet'. One of my teachers, Mrs Kay, said that she wanted to give me a special bit in the show because she thought I had a nice voice. When I asked her what I should wear, she said I could choose whatever I wanted to and that I could perform the song however I wanted to perform it. This turned out to be a big mistake on her part as I plumped for a black Lycra cat suit, swathing myself in tinsel over the top of it and finishing it off with a flashy cape. My idea was to dance around with the trumpet for a while before ripping the cape off for a big reveal. I remember thinking that it was so exciting and so grown-up that I was going to do this big 'strip' in the middle of the number, while pretending to play the trumpet. I'm not sure that all the mums and dads were quite ready for it, but I certainly enjoyed myself. I guess I started my whole 'showbiz, showtime, showgirl' obsession with that very first performance.

For our family holidays we went to Filey, Bournemouth or Scarborough, and we usually stayed in my Auntie Helen's caravan. With the two families together there were seven children, so the adults slept in the caravan and the kids bedded down under the awning, which was like a tent that attached to the side of the caravan. I suppose I was aware that other kids in my class went abroad for their holidays, and that seemed quite glamorous to me, but I wasn't envious. We always had a really good time wherever we were, playing in the arcades or swimming. I think when you're a kid, you don't mind where you are, as long as there's a beach to play on or a pool to swim in. I never once felt deprived or hard done by just because we were on a caravan holiday.

I do remember us having one holiday abroad when I was little, and that was to Ibiza, which must have been while Mum and Dad were going through a good patch. It was an all-inclusive holiday with plenty of organised activities to keep us all amused, including evening cabaret shows and even a kids' talent competition. Of course, this was too good an opportunity for Sally and me to miss, and luckily for us none of the other kids seemed to be that interested in taking part, so the floor was ours. The two of us took it in turns to perform, over and over again. Our repertoire was fiercely worked out and rehearsed – Perry Como's 'A – You're Adorable', 'My Favourite Things' from *The Sound of Music*. Sally did a cracking rendition of 'Catch a Falling Star' while I enjoyed belting out '(I'd Like to Get You on a) Slow Boat to China'. That was one of the songs that my granddad had always sung to me and I loved it. It always felt so good to me when I was singing and performing, and those memories are the happiest of my childhood.

2

A Normal Childhood

Unfortunately, my childhood wasn't just one long chorus line of singing and dancing. My parents' marriage hit a rocky patch when I was about five, and it never recovered.

Mum and Dad had gone all out to buy the house in Sandy Lane and they'd really had to stretch themselves financially. Looking back now, I think that was part of the reason they started to row all the time – it was probably the beginning of the end for their marriage. As I said, Mum was a full-time teacher, and she made pretty good money. Dad had his own business, selling kitchens and windows, and for a while he did really well, too. Eventually, though, Dad's company went bankrupt and that was when things got tough. The huge financial commitment they'd taken on with the house put strain on their relationship, and the arguments started to get more and more frequent. Mum had to take on the mortgage practically single-handed, which is why she taught piano to earn extra money, and although my dad tried very hard to keep up with various bits of work, things seemed to go from bad to worse once his business went bust.

It's sad to say, but many of my earliest childhood memories are of my mum and dad arguing, and often it was pretty full-on. When it happened, Sally, Adam and I would huddle together in another room and try to think of ways to entertain ourselves and take our minds off the terrible screaming and shouting coming from downstairs. This was before Amy was born and when she was just a baby. Sometimes, when we heard a row starting up, we'd take it in turns to go down and try to put a stop to it or distract our parents in some way. We knew that if one of us walked into the room while they were shouting, they'd stop, but it was usually short-lived and they'd start up again as soon as we left them alone for five minutes. Once we even went as far as recording the two of them screaming at one another on a ghetto blaster and then played it back to them. 'This is what we're having to put up with,' we told them, angrily. I'm sure they must have felt terrible, but it didn't seem to make things any better.

Sometimes, at night, I would sit at the top of the stairs while Mum and Dad were arguing, when they thought I was in bed. I'd be terrified and I wanted to make sure that things didn't go too far or get too bad between them, although they were bad enough already. We three children would often take it in turns to keep a check on them without them even realising. They assumed we were in bed, sleeping, but how could we have slept with all that going on? If ever we did think an argument was getting out of control, one of us would do our usual trick of going downstairs to try to stop it.

I just don't think Mum and Dad realised that, even though we were little, we were intelligent enough to know exactly what was going on. It's funny when I think about it now, knowing how much they both love and care about us. It's hard to believe that they could have exposed us to all that when we were so young, especially Mum, who is always so calm and hates any sort of confrontation. I guess at the time she just couldn't see any further than all the hurt and anger she was feeling, but for us as children it was quite traumatic. I never wanted to have friends over to stay because I was always scared that my parents were going to kick off in front of them, and even at that young age I'd have hated the feeling of awkwardness that would have caused. In grown-up terms, I'd have died of embarrassment. On one occasion, Sally did invite a friend over but she was nervous about it. 'If I never have anyone over, everyone's going to think I'm weird,' she told me. I so wanted it all to be fine, but it wasn't. Mum and Dad had a big row while Sally's friend was in the house and Sally was mortified. I remember us all being upstairs and turning the music up really loud to cover up the sound of the shouting, but that never worked.

In the end, I just wanted to get away from it as often as I could, so whenever the opportunity arose for me to sleep over at Alix's house, I jumped at it and pleaded to be allowed to go. Then I'd always feel guilty for leaving Sally and Adam back home in the midst of it all. When I think about it now, it seems like a lot for a young kid to cope with.

Nowadays it's hard to imagine that Mum and Dad ever got together in the first place. They were the most unlikely pairing. My mum went to an all girls' school, Belle Vue, and she was head girl there. She studied hard, learned to play the piano, and her childhood was very normal – she had just the one sister, Helen. My dad, on the other hand, didn't go to school all that often, and he was always in trouble. The funny thing was that his father, Walter, was actually a teacher, but he and my grandma had six children to contend with – four boys and two girls – and that certainly can't have been easy. Dad was a rebel. He didn't like to conform and he clashed with his father, my granddad, who was a bit of a disciplinarian. By the time Dad was fifteen, he didn't see himself as a child any more and my granddad just couldn't handle his son's self-confidence and all the confrontation that went with it. Consequently, Dad left home at the age of fifteen. His parents just let him go and I think the fact that his father never came after him to bring him home really hurt him. It's probably the reason he's never been as close to his parents as my mum is to hers, although he did take us to see them a lot when we were children. We always had two sets of grandparents.

My dad was quite a charmer when he met my mum and that's why she fell for him, even though he was a bit of a tearaway to say the least. I remember him telling me about a certain Saturday when I was still very young. Apparently, our house was about to be repossessed if my parents didn't come up with three grand by the Monday, and they didn't have anywhere near that kind of money saved. So on that Monday, my mum had gone to a friend's house, fretting and worrying about the possibility that she might be evicted sometime soon, while Dad took all the money he had, which was about sixty quid, and put it on a horse. As it turned out, Mum hadn't been able to concentrate on her night out because she was so worried, so she came home early. When she got there, my dad was in the living room waiting for her.

'I couldn't relax and enjoy myself, what with all the worry about the house,' she said. 'So I came home early.' Dad smiled.

'Well, you can go back out,' he said. 'I've won it! I've won over three grand. We've still got the house, so go back out and enjoy yourself.'

It turned out that he'd put the sixty pounds on a 16-1 winner, and then turned his winnings into £3,200 at a later meeting. He actually took the cash to the building society in a carrier bag on the Monday morning.

That was the kind of bloke he was.

My parents got married in 1978 in Sandy Lane Methodist church, and I don't doubt that they meant every word of their vows on that day. They were very much in love, but when it came down to it, they just weren't compatible. My mum's parents never wanted the marriage to happen. I think they could tell my dad was never going to be the doting, devoted husband that they wanted for their daughter, and I suppose I can understand how they felt. Dad never played the part very well, so all they ever saw were the arguments and fights and the bad side of my dad. I'm sure that he really loved my mum when they got married, and she loved him. He always said that no other woman in the world could have been a better mother to his kids but sadly, in the end, my grandparents' fears and worries about the marriage turned out to be right.

Just after Amy was born, Dad had an affair and Mum found out about it. A friend of a friend told her, and when she confronted Dad about it, he came clean straight away and admitted that it was happening. After that, of course, the arguments between them were even more bitter and angry. I was five at the time, but somehow I understood what was going on, and I remember thinking that something really bad was happening right in front of our eyes. I was so scared – we all were – because to us it was the most horrific thing ever. I can remember feeling so ashamed and embarrassed about it – afraid that my friends at school might find out what was going on under our roof. I couldn't bring myself to tell anyone what I knew, not even Alix, my best friend, because in my eyes, what was happening to our family was so awful.

Not long after that my dad left home, and the reali-sation that he wasn't going to be around his kids every day tore him apart. We were all really upset about it, because although we knew that what he'd done was wrong, he was still our dad and we wanted to see him as much as we could. Mum was as amicable as she could be with him because she knew how much we missed him, so she let him come around most mornings and take us to school and then pick us up again at the end of the day. She must have been very hurt and angry, but Adam and Amy were still so young and I suppose she knew they needed a father in their lives as well as a mother, even though he wasn't living with us any more. She always put us first. When it came to Christmas and birthdays, we would plead with Mum to let Dad come over and spend the day with us, and she always did. She knew that we still needed him, and however bad their relationship was, she would never deny us that.

In many ways, things were much better after he'd left because the fighting stopped for the most part. Mum has since told me that she was so unhappy with the way things were between them that in some ways his affair had been an easy way out for her. And although I'd felt quite traumatised by Dad's affair and I missed him being around, I felt relieved, too, once they'd split. There would still be the odd row about money when he came round but it was nowhere near as bad as when he was living with us. Suddenly I didn't feel as if I was living on the edge any more, worried that something was going to kick off at any moment. It was still tough, with us not having a great deal of money and Mum trying to look after us on her own, but nothing compared to what we'd lived through while they were together. It's odd when I talk to them about it now because they both appear to have forgotten a lot of what happened back then. They don't seem to remember just how terrible it was. Maybe it was such a bad time for them that they've pushed thoughts of it out of their minds. I've even reminded them about certain times and events and they'll say, 'No, we didn't do that.' 'You did,' I say. 'You did do that.' Maybe those bad memories are more vivid for me because I was so young.

Once Dad had left, Mum really had to pull out all the stops to keep the money coming in. I've always found her ability to turn her hand to so many different things quite inspiring. Right from when we were very young she always had so many different ventures on the go, and they were usually geared towards making some extra cash, which was now in short supply. As well as her full-time job as a teacher and the piano lessons and making our clothes, she had a little side business with my Auntie Helen. They would go and buy clothes from a wholesaler in Manchester and then throw parties for women at which they sold the clothes at a profit. I learned a lot from her about 'getting on with it' no matter what. Yes, things were hard but we still needed a roof over our heads and food on the table, and she always made it happen. I'm sure I inherited my own strong work ethic from my mum. I can't even compare anything I've done to what she did, but through her I learned that you don't get something for nothing. You have to work for what you want, because nothing is going to land magically in your lap.

As well as the everyday cost of living, my mum tried to find the money for all the extra activities we wanted to do as kids. Sally and I went swimming every week, and we did ballet and gymnastics from a very young age. In fact, for a while, when I was about five, I was convinced I was going to be an Olympic gymnast. Unfortunately, after a couple of sprained wrists Dad decided that it would be best if I didn't go any more. He was always the overprotective one, the one who worried about everything a bit too much. I think that's the trait I've inherited from him, because I'd probably be the same with my kids and it's something I think I'll have to fight against. My mum could sometimes be a bit too relaxed, though – a nice balance somewhere in between would probably be the best bet.

We kids did our bit to earn some extra cash. One of the things we loved to do was have yard sales outside the house. We'd raid the loft or my mum's cupboards, and dig out anything she didn't want. Then we'd set a table up in front of the house with hand-made price tags and everything displayed so that passers-by might be tempted. We just wanted to earn a bit of extra pocket money, probably because we could see some of the other kids on the estate with things we simply couldn't afford. For a start we all desperately wanted skateboards, but Dad – being a worrier – wouldn't get them for us in case we ended up breaking our necks or something. By the time he finally relented and presented us all with brand spanking new skateboards, it was about a year after everyone else had got them and most of the other kids were over it. Even the kids who were still doing it had skateboards that looked well used and cool, whereas ours looked all new and cringe-worthy. I can laugh about it now, but at the time I thought I would never forgive him.

The thing I remember wanting most was a bike for Christmas. Not just any bike, though: I wanted a Princess bike – a pink one with a basket on the front. Some of my friends had them, but I never in a million years thought that my mum and dad would be able to afford a present like that for me. There was no way I was ever going to get one. My brother and sister really wanted bikes, too – my sister had her eye on a lilac bike, and my brother was after a BMX. I still believed in Santa Claus at this point, so I asked him to please bring me the Princess bike, knowing that my mum and dad wouldn't be able to.

On Christmas morning that year when we came downstairs we were all completely gobsmacked. Sally got her lilac bike, there was a BMX for Adam, and there in front of me was the Princess bike with the basket on the front that I'd been longing for.

'Oh my God!' I said to Sally and Adam. 'He's definitely real. Santa's definitely real.'

What other explanation could there have been? Of course, we were just very lucky that no matter what a struggle it was, our parents always did their very best to make us happy, even though they weren't together. Dad wasn't around all the time, but they still worked together to make our childhood as normal as possible and we'll always be grateful to them for that.

3

'You Can't Sing, You'll Have to Mime'

It definitely wasn't normal, the way Sally and I carried on when we were kids. It was as if we were living in a real-life version of *Fame* or *Glee*, with one or both of us bursting into song at the drop of a hat. 'Shall we do a death scene?' one of us would suggest. And without further ado we'd launch into a full re-enactment of Eponine's death scene from *Les Mis*. I would always perform my death scenes with real tears and extraordinary attention to detail in an attempt to make my younger sister Amy cry. Yes, it was quite a mean thing to do but if my death was so utterly convincing that it sent Amy screaming and crying to my mum, then I knew

I'd done a good job. 'OK, that was good work,' Sally would say to me, nodding earnestly. 'Very good work, Kimberley.'

Being the youngest, poor Amy had to be tough, particularly as the closest in age to her was Adam, who was sometimes a bit of a bully and often gave her a hard time. She was a chubby little kid, and I think that made her realise that she had to stick up for herself, too. Amy was so cute, though, and a real character. I think of all of her siblings I was closest to her because Adam just wanted to play with his mates, and Sally was that bit too old to be bothered with a baby sister hanging around. They both loved her, of course, but I was the one who ended up looking after her the most, almost becoming a mini-mum to her some of the time – we were very close. Amy's childhood must have been quite hard because she never really knew what it was like to have a mum and a dad living together under the same roof. Although she saw my dad all the time, she never experienced normal family life the way that we had because they'd split up just after she was born. On the other hand, I think in many ways she was the lucky one. Amy has always been the most chilled out and laid-back person in the family, and I sometimes wonder if it's because she wasn't party to all the fighting and arguing between our parents. Unsurprisingly, Amy started performing at a young age, too, and like Sally, she's now an actress. In fact, of the four of us, Adam is the only one who hasn't ended up in show business of one sort or another.

Thankfully, we'd all had an outlet for our crazy obsession to perform from quite a young age. When I was still only about six, my godmother, Jane, who was a close friend of Mum's, suggested that Mum take Sally and me to a stage school that had not long opened on the other side of town. Jane was going to take her two daughters there as well.

'Why not?' Mum said. 'They love singing, don't they? Let's give it a go.'

Well, that was it. The minute my sister and I walked in through the doors of that place – Stage 84 – we knew we'd found our calling. It's a renowned and very successful stage school these days, but at the time it all took place in a hired church hall with about fifty kids and a couple of teachers. I remember getting so excited every week when it was time to go there – we absolutely loved it. The woman who founded and ran the school, Valerie Jackson, was quite a savvy business-woman, and right from the start she made contacts with agents and TV producers with a view to furthering her young students' careers.

I remember finding Valerie quite scary at the time.

She'd been a teacher before she started Stage 84 and she was the archetypal schoolmistress. Still, working with her definitely instilled in me all the right disciplines I needed for the entertainment industry. For a start we were taught to turn up on time for every class – in fact, if you were late for something, you'd usually be chastised and shamed in front of the entire class. Nothing was worth that, even at six years old, so I always made sure that I was on time for everything and I still pride myself on being on time for everything now.

The whole atmosphere of the school was very professional, so you had to take it seriously if you wanted to attend. It wasn't a place for kids who just wanted to have a bit of a laugh and see how things went – the classes were quite intense – but for Sally and me it was perfect. We were deadly serious about wanting to perform and we were in our element. Up till then we'd just been practising and performing like mad things in our bedrooms or for our families, but now we could take all that enthusiasm to Stage 84 and do it all on a proper stage.

Once Valerie Jackson had set up her various connections with agents and TV producers, we were able to go and audition for various different things, so for us the whole notion of performing quickly became something more than just a hobby. When Sally was around ten she got a part in a children's TV show, *Tumbledown Farm*. It wasn't just a small part, either. She was the star of the show and it ran for two series in 1988 and 1989. Not long after that I got a part in another kids' TV show, *The Book Tower*. I was about seven and it was my first time in front of the cameras, but to be honest I just remember it as a fun day out. My mum had done my hair in pigtails and I think I was wearing a dress that she'd made for me. I played a little girl who was a bit fed up with her family, and in one scene I was sitting on the toilet with my knickers round my ankles, doing a monologue about how I wanted to throw my entire family in the dustbin and play on my own. At the end of the scene I shouted out to my mum, 'I'm finished!' That scene has been dug up and shown on various TV shows since, as you can imagine.

After *The Book Tower* I did quite a few voiceovers for Yorkshire TV kids' shows, and a few adverts, too – Barratt Housing, Scottish Bedding, and one for a new game called Fireball. I hadn't been at Stage 84 for all that long, but I was lucky to get quite a few jobs fairly quickly. Now I wonder how, as a child of that age, I even knew how to act. I'm not saying that I was brilliant, but I somehow knew how to learn my lines and deliver them and I enjoyed it. It didn't really seem like a chore to me. It all just came very naturally.

Each week at Stage 84 we'd do a bit of improvisation, and then we'd perhaps learn a song or a dance routine. Quite often we'd be rehearsing numbers and scenes for the end-of-year show, which was the most important event in the school's calendar. The productions started off quite small, but further down the line they were staged at the Alhambra, which is a lovely old theatre with old-fashioned balconies and red velvet drapes. It's one of the North of England's most famous venues. By the time I stepped out onto the stage there, I felt I was really getting a taste of what it was like to be a proper musical theatre performer, and as much as I loved doing the TV shows, I knew *that* was what I really wanted to do when I grew up.

It wasn't all plain-sailing for me as far as performing went. The standards were high at Stage 84, and I can remember Valerie Jackson walking along the line as we were all singing, like some sort of army general inspecting his platoon, weeding out anyone who might not be good enough. If she thought that you weren't up to it, you were told to mime. I remember being horrified when this happened to me, aged six. Valerie went up and down the line and stopped at me, telling me I wasn't to sing because I had such a deep voice.

It was a terrible shock after all my hard work. I was aware that I had a deeper voice than most of the other kids, and although I loved singing, I wasn't sure how good at it I was. I remember standing there thinking oh my God! She thinks I can't sing. I'm not good enough. It was as if my world had fallen apart.

A few years later, when I was around nine, I was given the part of Pearl in a *Starlight Express* section of our end-of-year show, and that was quite a big turning point for me. I had a few solo songs in the show and a duet, and I guess that was when I truly started to believe in myself. All the older kids would come in and watch me while I was rehearsing my bit, and lots of people told me how good I was. Maybe I'm actually all right at this, I thought. Maybe I *am* good enough now. I can remember so well the excitement of standing in the wings at the Alhambra that first time, and I don't think I've ever felt a buzz like it since. When you're young, you don't have the same kind of self-doubts and worries that you do when you're older – you're just dying to get out there and do what you know you can do. I thought there could be no better feeling on this earth when I stepped out on the stage and performed for everyone at that show. Yes, I was nervous, but at the same time I loved it and I'll never forget it.

From that point on, I always got lead parts in the

end-of-year shows, and I was probably hated by a lot of the other kids because of it. I think having a deeper voice must have made my performances sound more mature – particularly when I was belting out big dramatic numbers about love and relationship breakdowns written for grown-ups. People said it made my delivery more convincing, and, of course, I took my performances very seriously and gave every one of them all I had. So in the long run, I suppose, having a lower voice worked out rather well for me.

Adam went to Stage 84 for a while, too, but having three kids at the school was obviously going to be quite expensive for my mum. As I said, the head teacher, Valerie, could be quite strict, but she also had a really good heart and she let my mum pay the fees for just one child even though all three of us were attending. She knew there was no way Mum would be able to manage it otherwise. Adam did really well and got quite a few good parts; after all, there weren't a lot of other boys there who could sing, dance and act as well. After a while, though, he started getting into football and turning up late for classes and rehearsals. Valerie gave him an ultimatum.

'You have to decide what's more important to you, Adam,' she said, firmly. 'It's either the show we're rehearsing or football.'

'Football!' he said.

Adam was dead to Valerie Jackson from that moment on. But Sally and I still made him take part in all the shows that we put on at our grandparents' house, whether he liked it or not.

As well as attending Stage 84 and doing the odd bit of acting, I had to keep up with all my normal school studies. Middle school was my favourite time, when I was aged nine to twelve, probably because I didn't have the pressure of GCSEs and intense studying to worry about. I was always a pretty good student but I never tried that hard to be brilliant. I was just lucky that I managed to get good grades and stay in the top sets for most subjects. The only reason I ever got told off was for singing out loud while I was sitting doing my work. I didn't even know that I was doing it, but suddenly a teacher would start telling me off and demanding that I keep the noise down. I was also a bit of a chatterbox at school, so that sometimes got me into hot water.

As much as I enjoyed school, my main objective every day was to get home as quickly as I could so I could run upstairs to my room and practise my singing some more. That was all I really cared about. I guess I just wanted to get better and better. I was always aiming towards something even though I might not then have known exactly what it was. I'd sing to *Miss Saigon* and *Les Mis* or *Sister Act 2*. I remember seeing Lauryn Hill in that movie and completely falling in love with her voice.

I loved pop music, too, and back then we used to buy cassette singles, which seems quite antiquated now. The first one I ever bought was Kim Appleby's 'Don't Worry'. I played it to death; I couldn't get enough of it. Sally and I also had 'The Hit Factory' album, including all the Stock Aitken Waterman hits. That really was the soundtrack to our bedroom when we were kids. I loved that pure pop sound, and like a lot of girls then, I was mad about Kylie Minogue and Jason Donovan, who were absolutely huge at the time.

Glamour was another important factor for Sally and me, and although we weren't always that fond of our homemade clothes, there were times when Mum's sewing skills came in handy. I remember in the run-up to a Christmas party at Stage 84 one year, Sally and I decided that we wanted to make an impact.

'Right, this is what we'd like, please,' Sally announced to my mum a few weeks before the party.

'Gold puffball skirt for Kimberley, with black lining underneath. I'll have the same but the other way round. Then we'd like matching tops – gold with black spots for Kimberley and black with gold for me.'

Once we'd topped off these outfits with a massive gold bow we were good to go, and we thought we looked sensational. Just like Madonna. We were very much into the fashions back then – palazzo pants, pedal pushers and puffball skirts. I was so into fashion that I asked Mum to teach me how to sew and make things for myself. The first thing she taught me was how to make scrunchies out of old material off-cuts, which I used to sell outside school for 50p. Then, as I got older, I graduated to making wrap-over skirts, denim bags and eventually palazzo pants – which are great big wide trousers. My handiwork was eventually quite in demand on the estate, so it became a good way to make money. An actor friend of Sally's, Nicky Evans, thought my palazzo pants were amazing, and consequently asked Sally if I could possibly make him a pair – I'm not sure why because they were quite girly. Nicky eventually went into *Emmerdale* with Sally, and is now better known for his role as Shane in *Shameless*. I don't really get the time to make my own clothes these days, but for a while now I've been thinking about buying a sewing machine, just to make sure that I haven't lost my touch.

My music teacher had faith in me from the get-go. During rehearsals for a Christmas concert, when I was about ten, she took my mum to one side and spoke to her about it.

'Do you know what a good singing voice your daughter has?' she said.

'No, not really,' my mum said.

She knew I loved performing and acting at the stage school, but I'm not sure she realised how passionate I was about singing. It was only after she watched me in the Christmas concert that Mum considered the possibility that I might actually have a shot at singing professionally as well as acting. My teacher was funny. Sometimes, during a music class, she'd just haul me up to the front of the class and get me to sing.

'Shall we take five minutes,' she'd suggest right in the middle of what was supposed to be a lesson. 'Kimberley, do you want to come up front and sing through a few numbers?'

God only knows what the other kids in the class thought – they must have wanted to kill me. Perhaps they didn't care because it meant they didn't have to do any work for half an hour. Anyway, I'd get up and belt out songs from *The Little Mermaid* or *Beauty and the Beast* or *Aladdin*. I was in my element, but I really don't know what my teacher was thinking because there wasn't much music tuition going on. She always championed me, though, and I'll always be grateful to her for that.

By then, Alix and I were inseparable. She ended up

going to Stage 84 as well. She wasn't a natural-born performer, but she was actually a lot better than she thought she was. She played Sally's younger sister in a TV series called *Children of Winter*. I was really proud of her at the time, but she always preferred to languish in the chorus line while I did my best to thrust myself forward in a starring role. Alix was much more into fashion and magazines, and these days she's the deputy editor of the magazine *Stylist*.

We had another friend from school, Ruth, and for quite some time the three of us were a little team. Ruth was quite different from Alix and me but she was very charismatic and warm and we're still friends now. When we were young, she lived right in the village and her house seemed to be at the centre of all the drama in the area. Alix and I absolutely loved staying at Ruth's place at weekends because there was always something juicy going on in the streets outside her house, and it was much more exciting than where either of us lived. For instance, a woman who was always drunk lived a few doors along from Ruth. Her five sons, who were fairly notorious and frequently in trouble with the police, would be outside causing trouble and making a racket. Consequently, their mother would often be out in the street, drunk and shouting her head off, which Alix and I thought was highly entertaining. It was very different from our environment so I suppose it was a bit of a novelty. We also used to camp out in Ruth's garden and some of the boys from the village used to come around while we were sleeping and scare the life out of us. This all added to the fun of staying round at Ruth's house and we never got bored with it.

As teenagers, Ruth, Alix and I often had sleepovers on a Friday, and then we'd go out shopping in Bradford or Leeds on a Saturday. The three of us went to see nineties girl group Eternal together. It was my first pop concert, and I loved the spectacle of it – the lights, the dancers and the glamorous clothes. I wondered that night if I might ever make it as a pop star and perform in front of thousands of adoring fans. At the time all that seemed like a very distant dream.

When Alix's family suddenly moved away from the estate, I was heartbroken. We'd been the best of friends ever since our first day at Sandy Lane school, and now she was leaving the area. Not only that, but she was changing schools as well. Her dad had inherited his father's printing business and turned it around to become very successful and lucrative. All of a sudden, my best friend's parents were rich, and they were moving into a massive house with a swimming pool on the other side of town. I remember going to look at it with them before they moved in and I'd never in my life seen anything like it. I could never imagine anyone I knew living in a house as grand as that. It was like something I'd only ever seen on TV or in films. Luckily, after they'd moved, both of our mothers helped us to keep the friendship going, ferrying us backwards and forwards across town to visit one another. I counted myself really lucky, because this gorgeous house eventually became like a second home to me, and Alix's mum and dad practically adopted me as one of their own. They took me on holiday to Center Parcs with them, and even Disneyland in Orlando. Her mum and dad were a very generous couple, so as her best friend I got to share in all of Alix's wonderful new experiences and I was really grateful for that.

Sometimes, Alix's mum would generously insist on buying things for me while we were out shopping for Alix. 'I'll just get you some trainers while we're out and about,' she'd say when mine were looking a bit past their best.

She'd once shared a teaching job with my mum, so she knew how hard it was when there wasn't enough money around. Our grandmothers had once worked together in Lister Mills, too, so all in all Alix's family had a long history with mine. They never made me feel like the poor relation, though. I was always just part of the family. Still, I have to admit, after a lovely

46

long weekend at Alix's place – playing in the swimming pool, or with the ever-growing collection of pet rabbits that she bred – going home wasn't always easy. Sometimes it was a case of, oh well . . . back to this again! My brother and sisters would drag me back down to earth if they thought I was getting ideas above my station. 'Just because you've been at Alix's, don't think you're too good to play with us now,' they'd say.

I suppose I got a taste of what life could be like when I was at Alix's house. My eyes were opened up to so many new things and I can remember hoping that one day I might be able to have the kind of house and the kind of life that her family had. It wasn't always the big things like holidays and swimming pools, either. Just the fact that Alix and her family went out to eat in restaurants was a revelation to me. My family never did. We didn't even go to McDonald's unless it was for a big treat, whereas Alix's family went to McDonald's all the time. It's funny the things that touch you as a child.

When I think about it now, it makes me realise how fortunate my children will be in that respect. They'll probably never have to miss out on something just because there isn't enough money around, but it's important to me to make sure they appreciate the fact that it isn't necessarily the same for everyone. When you grow up living with one parent, or come from a broken home, you don't always have that protective cushion around you that kids from a so-called normal family have. Everything seemed clear to me from a young age, harsh even. I'd seen my mum struggling with four kids and no money ever since I was tiny, and I think I knew too much, too young. It's one of the main things I want to protect my children from. I want to let them be children for as long as they need to be children, so they can grow up in their own time. That being said, I think my childhood has made me the person I am, and I wouldn't change that. I've got the most amazing family, who all love each other, and I never forget for a minute how lucky I am.

4

'You've Got the Part'

Whenever I went for TV castings, I'd see a lot of the same young actors and actresses and we all became very much part of the same scene. Samia Ghadie, who now plays Maria in *Coronation Street*, was one person I used to bump into a lot and also Suzanne Shaw, who eventually joined the pop band Hear'Say. You kind of knew whom you were going to be up against and who your main competition was when you went for certain parts. My family used to laugh at me because I was so laid back about the whole thing. If I went for an audition and eventually lost out to someone else, I used to try to shrug it off. 'Oh well,' I'd tell them all. 'Next time, eh.' I definitely got that laid-back attitude from my mum. That's not to say I wasn't disappointed at times when I didn't land a role, and there were plenty of times that happened.

There was never any rivalry between Sally and me when we were auditioning, because she was more the actress and I was the singer. Even when we were both auditioning for TV stuff, there was no jealousy or resentment when one or the other of us got a role. I think because of how difficult our home environment had been we were always supportive of one another, rather than competitive. We both needed that support, too, because the auditions could be quite tense some-times. You'd be given a script to look over as soon as you arrived – or, if you were lucky, it might have been sent to you the day before – then you'd go in with the director and some of the cast and read your part with the other actors reading theirs. Afterwards you might be interviewed as well, which was sometimes a bit nerve-racking for a kid. I remember one audition particularly vividly because I nearly ended up in hospital on the way to it. In fact, I was lucky I wasn't killed.

I was twelve at the time, and once everyone realised that I could sing as well as act, I was put up for the part of the young Cosette in a professional production of *Les Misérables* at the Manchester Palace Theatre. Stage 84 sent a few girls up for the part, and I knew there was going to be quite a lot of fierce competition for the role, but I really, really wanted it.

The night before the audition I stayed at the house of a family friend in Middlesbrough, along with my Auntie Helen, Sally and my cousin Leonie. Leonie also attended Stage 84 and she was going up for the audition as well. The plan that winter morning was to drive back home to Bradford with my auntie, get ready, and then head to the audition in Manchester. We set off quite early to give ourselves plenty of time, and I remember there being a lot of black ice on the road so we had to take it pretty carefully. I was snoozing in the back of the Jeep while we were en route home, when I was suddenly jolted awake by the sound of my auntie's screaming. It wasn't just a quick scream, it went on and on, and as I came to my senses I realised that the Jeep was skidding and spinning around in the middle of the road. Before I knew it we'd tipped over sideways and smashed into a high stone wall. The side windows shattered and as the car finally came to a standstill I looked down to see two or three large boulders that had come crashing through the windows as we'd rammed against the wall. It was terrifying and a miracle one of us wasn't killed. Auntie Helen's face was cut quite badly and she was bleeding, but she seemed OK apart from being really shaken up. I checked myself over, quickly, but apart from a few bumps and bruises I seemed to be fine.

I can see us now, all in a daze, walking down a long country road in search of a house where the people might let us use the phone. We ended up calling my uncle and then we had to wait for him to come and rescue us – the Jeep was a complete write-off.

'I think we'd better just forget this audition now,' my auntie said. 'Perhaps we should go to the hospital and get you girls checked out.'

I wasn't having any of that, though. I was adamant I had to get there.

'No, please! I have to get to this audition. I have to.'

There was no way I was going to miss out on my big chance to try out for a real professional stage production. It was something I'd always dreamed about and I was bloody well going, car accident or not. When we finally got back to my mum's house, Leonie had totally gone off the idea of getting back into a car and going to the audition, but I was still gung-ho, even though I knew that I was going to be really late. Mum rang ahead and told the casting people that I'd been in an accident.

'If we get there in time, can she still at least sing?' she asked.

They agreed that I could, so off we dashed to Manchester.

As I walked through the stage door of the theatre with my mum I was still feeling a little bit shaken up, but I knew that I just had to focus and do the best job I could in front of the casting people. I wasn't dressed up too much – just leggings and a jumper – but I'd had my hair cut in a stylish bob, which was a new look I was trying out. The audition itself was being held on the stage of the theatre, and when I got into the wings I could see lots of other children already lined up on stage, waiting for their turn. Then, as their names were called, each of them in turn would step out of the line and sing for the director and the other people casting the show. I didn't know whether the kids had done anything else that day – a bit of acting or reciting lines, for instance – but I was literally the last child in and I was just going to have to make the best of it.

When it was finally my turn, I was asked simply to walk to the middle of the stage and sing. I can remember being nervous, but my overriding emotion was one of relief because I'd actually managed to get there after almost being killed on the way. I sang 'Castle on a Cloud', which is the young Cosette's featured number in the show. Then I watched, anxiously, as the panel of casting people talked among themselves for a moment. Whenever I'd done auditions in the past for children's TV shows or adverts, I'd had to go away and wait for a phone call before I found out whether or not I'd got the part. With this audition, however, one of the casting people let me know straight away, almost as soon as I'd finished singing.

'You've got the part,' he told me. 'We'd like you to play Cosette.'

Just like that.

I was buzzing. I was actually going to be in a proper professional production of one of my favourite musicals and I could hardly believe it. The part had to be split, because children are allowed to work in the theatre only for a certain number of hours while they're still at school, so I'd be playing the part of Cosette three nights a week and another girl was chosen for the other three nights. It was going to be a big commitment on my part, but I was ready for it – this was what I'd been working towards ever since I started at Stage 84. It was also going to be a big commitment on my parents' part. After all, they were the ones who were going to have to ferry me back and forth from Bradford to Manchester three times a week. I don't think they minded, though. They were proud of me. And I was secretly happy with the prospect of having every Thursday afternoon off school to do the matinee, too.

I didn't seem to have very many rehearsals for the show, which was a bit of a shock as at Stage 84 we'd rehearse, rehearse, rehearse. Normally, we rehearsed everything to death, but for this – my first professional show – I didn't get much time with the director at all. This made me more than a little bit anxious because it wasn't what I was used to, but I've since learned that it's very much the way with a lot of professional shows. You're expected to learn as much as you can on your own, and sometimes you're thrown out there without a lot of rehearsal time, especially if you're stepping into a role after someone else has left. For a twelve-year-old girl, though, it was all a bit scary.

On the first night, the nerves kicked in like never before. I was in my starting position, sat on a chair, ready to get up and start sweeping the floor as the stage revolved, and all I could think was oh my God, any second now I've got to sing. My heart was beating out of my chest as the music started, and to be honest, I wasn't sure whether any sound was going to come out. It was a feeling I'd never had before, but one that I've experienced many times since. As it was, the first couple of notes were a little bit shaky, but suddenly I pulled myself together and my voice just got stronger and stronger. Within seconds I went from feeling dead nervous to experiencing the best feeling in the world. My voice just seemed to lift and soar over the audience – it was amazing. From that moment on I loved every second of it, and afterwards everyone was so kind and complimentary about my performance. I still couldn't believe I'd actually done it.

After the first few nights doing the show I knew that I had the bug. Just walking into that theatre every day was wonderful – the smells, the sound, the atmosphere of the place. And the feeling I had when I woke up in the morning, knowing that it was a show day, reinforced it. I can still feel and smell that whole experience, even now. I knew then that this was what I was born to do, and I wouldn't entertain the notion of it turning out any other way. I really loved hanging out and chatting with all the older professional actors and actresses, as well as working with them. In fact, I'm sure I talked them all to death some nights. I remember thinking how lucky they all were to do this amazing job every day of their working lives. How could they even call it a job? Towards the end of the run I remember some of the actors saying things like, 'Only a month to go – thank goodness for that.' At the time I couldn't believe that they would ever want it to end. Now, after working on *Shrek the Musical* every night for eight months, I know exactly what they meant. At the age of twelve, I obviously hadn't quite grasped how hard an actor's life could be. For me, then, it was all just magical.

Most of the cast seemed happy to keep me entertained

and spend time with me because I was the only kid. In turn, I would entertain them by learning and performing everybody else's scenes. I knew it all off by heart. I even used to do the 'Lovely Ladies' number, which is a song performed by all the prostitutes – hardly suitable for a twelve-year-old but I didn't care, and the other members of the cast seemed to find it highly amusing. I was a very outgoing child. I wouldn't say I was precocious, but I was probably a little bit older than my years. I preferred chatting to adults and having what I considered to be proper conversations. Even when the grown-ups were talking about their relationship problems, I always thought that I had words of wisdom to impart, whether they wanted to hear them or not.

A little while later, I was in *Evita* when the touring version came to Bradford. I was just one of the chorus children, but by now I felt like a seasoned professional. Adam was in that with me, and though he doesn't do anything musical these days, he still knows the entire *Evita* score by heart – that's something not many straight lads can say! I learned all the other parts in that, as well. I was always thinking about what roles I might play in the shows when I was older – Eponine or Fantine in *Les Mis*, or Eva Peron herself in *Evita*, if I was lucky. I'm too old for Eponine now, but I could still have a crack at the other two. I've kept an autograph book from that time, and the messages from all the members of the cast are so inspiring and encouraging. Some of them wrote about me having a bright future if I kept up the same level of professionalism I'd just shown. I was really chuffed about that at the time, and it's weird to think that in the end it came true.

One of the other things we did at Stage 84 was to go up to Edinburgh and perform at the Fringe Festival, just like a proper theatre company. It was during the school holidays, and I did that for six years running. The first time we went I was about seven years old. The production we put on was *Daisy Pulls It Off* and I was the only really young child in the entire company. Sally went with us that year, too, but even though she's a couple of years older than I am, she was the one who got homesick during the time we were away, not me. The following year I ended up going on my own for two whole weeks and I wasn't the slightest bit homesick. I'm not sure why I was so relaxed about being away from home for so long at such a young age. I think I just got wrapped up in the excitement of it all.

Those summer productions in Edinburgh were an invaluable experience for me. It's such a beautiful city, and being in the thick of it with many other actors, playwrights, comedians and dancers made me feel as though I was part of something special and important. As well as that, I was performing with teenagers and older kids from the school, which meant I was learning a lot. Every year we did a different show – *Seven Brides for Seven Brothers* and *Oklahoma!* are two that stand out in my mind – but we always performed at the same venue, the James Gillespie High School. We usually stayed in university accommodation and chaperones – one or two of the students' mothers – kept us all in line. My mum could never come with us, although I'm sure she would have loved it. She was too busy with a full-time job and looking after my other sisters and my brother back in Bradford. My Auntie Helen came with me a couple of times, though, and I loved having her there.

During the day we would go to one of the main squares in the city and put on street performances, in full costume – excerpts from whatever show we were doing – and then hand out leaflets encouraging people to buy a ticket for the show that evening. It was very exciting to be performing at night and staying up late with all the older kids. Again, my eyes were opened to a whole new world. This time it wasn't to do with money or possessions; it was about being part of a working theatrical company and mixing with all different kinds of people, experiencing a cosmopolitan city and seeing life outside of my little village. Everywhere I turned there seemed to be so much to see and so many people to meet, and I wanted to soak it all up like a sponge. I wanted to explore everything and learn as much as I could. I realised, suddenly, that a very big world existed out there beyond Bradford and school and our village. There was so much more to experience. I wasn't ashamed of where I was from, but I knew that I wouldn't stay there once I was older. Maybe I'd have a flat in Manchester, or maybe I'd even live in London one day.

I'm a bit of a scrapbook queen, so I've still got all the reviews, press clippings and programmes from those Edinburgh shows. Those trips to the Fringe helped fuel my ambition to make something of myself – to make it as a performer. It was a magical time for me, and I really cherish my memories of it.

5

'Oh My God! I'm Not Doing That!'

I was quite terrified by the idea of boys and romance when I was at middle school. I had my first nervous kiss when I was about twelve, with Danny, a boy from Stage 84 whom I had a crush on. Then there were other boys I fancied, but the thought of anything actually happening scared me to death.

This anxiety got worse as I got older because I really didn't know what boys expected of me. I was at school with girls of thirteen and fourteen who were already having sex, giving blow jobs and all sorts. I was mature in many ways, but I certainly didn't feel ready for anything like that. I remember one Monday morning at school, a couple of girls were telling me lurid stories of what they'd got up to over the weekend. They weren't good friends of mine, just girls whom I sometimes chatted to in technology class, but they were clearly on a different planet from me as far as sexual matters were concerned. I remember thinking, Oh my God, I'm not doing that! I don't want anything like that – no way! As far as I was concerned, being intimate with a boy was something to be taken seriously. I'd learned quite a lot of the whys and wherefores about sex from having an older sister, but that doesn't mean I actually wanted to get involved in it.

One year when I was on holiday with Alix's family at Center Parcs, I had quite a big crush on a good-looking lifeguard. He was about eighteen while I was fourteen, so I was much too young for him, but that didn't stop me fancying him, especially as he was always so nice to me and made me laugh. Alix and I would strut down to the pool, where I would regularly attempt to attract his attention as I got out of the water. However, there were fast-moving rapids in the pool, and it wasn't always easy to look your best when you'd just been dumped under the water and looked like a drowned rat. After I'd been staring at him for about a week, he told me that I looked like the girl from the Nivea Visage advert, and Alix and I giggled like fools. 'Is he taking the piss?' I said, although I was secretly over the moon.

On one occasion I remember desperately trying to attract his attention as I walked towards the pool where he was standing. I was almost breaking my neck to look over and smile at him as I walked across the little bridge that led to the rapids, but I wasn't really looking where I was putting my feet. Suddenly, I went flying. I literally stacked it down the stairs that led to the pool. Right in front of him and in my bikini! I really hurt myself, too – I was winded, and my back was killing me. But it was my pride that was hurt the most – I was mortified.

Alix and I ended up going on holiday to the same place for the next couple of years and there was always a little bit of innocent flirtation between me and the lifeguard, but by the time I was actually old enough for something to have happened, I'd kind of lost interest.

'He's totally coming on to you,' Alix said to me one day at the pool. 'You should go for it; you've liked him for ages.'

He just didn't seem that attractive to me any more, and I wasn't bothered. I guess I thought quite a lot of myself in those days. I was a bit of a Sandra Dee character. I didn't want to be 'one of those girls'. Maybe I was a bit judgemental, but I wasn't going to bow to peer pressure, and I wasn't going to give it away to a lad for the sake of it.

I suppose I was about fifteen when I started going out at night with Alix, Ruth and the girls. My cousin Leonie often came with us. I was very close to her. We usually went to Kiss or Maestros, or another club in Bradford. For me, it was just about having a bit of a dance and a good time. I wasn't bothered about getting off my face like some of the girls I knew. We shouldn't really have been let in to those places at all, to be honest. Yes, we looked older than we were, but there was no way we looked eighteen and old enough to drink. Somehow, we always managed to swing it, although I took a little while to get used to the nightclubbing scene. I remember quite clearly my first time queuing up to get into a club – I was nearly sixteen and I was wearing a white Lycra crop top that crisscrossed at the back, a white Lycra mini-skirt that I'd borrowed from Sally, and patent leather wedge shoes, like the Spice Girls used to wear. My hair was dyed very blonde and I was made up to the nines. I must have thought I looked so mature and fabulous. Despite the daring outfit, I was sh***ing myself as the queue went down and I got closer to the door of the club, I was so sure I was going to get turned away for being too young. When I finally got to the entrance, the burly doorman looked me up and down and smiled.

'I've got a video camera downstairs,' he said to me.

'What?'

I wasn't sure what he was talking about.

'A video camera,' he said again. 'If you fancy coming downstairs with me.'

I was absolutely terrified for a moment and thinking, Oh my God, why am I here? What am I doing? Then suddenly the guy laughed and winked at me.

'Go on, in you go, love,' he said.

As I wandered, wide-eyed, into the club, I wondered what kind of world I was entering. What on earth was I letting myself in for? I wasn't sure if I could handle it.

Once inside, I saw lots of people I knew from school, and they all seemed to be having a fine old time – really going for it – falling around drunk and getting off with one another. It was as if a massive hormone-fest was raging all around me, and I wasn't keen to get involved. The whole scene made me quite wary about drinking alcohol because I just didn't want to get as out of control as all the other kids were. In fact, I remember thinking that I should be the one to stay sober among my mates, just in case anything bad happened. Leonie was going for gold for a start, so I knew I'd have to look after her at the end of the evening, if nothing else.

Luckily, Alix was a bit more like me, so we were like the two old women on the sidelines, looking on in horror.

When I look back now, I wonder why I was so sensible when most of the other kids were letting loose – maybe I was a bit uptight. It didn't seem right for people that young to be getting drunk and going wild like that. I suppose after that I just kind of fell into the role of looking after people, and it never really left me, especially through my time in Girls Aloud. I was always the one who tried my best to keep a sensible head on when everything was going crazy – somebody had to. I did eventually learn to let my hair down and have a good time when I was out clubbing, but it wasn't until I was a bit older and had people around me whom I knew would look out for me.

One night, I met Martin Pemberton – or Pembo as he was known to his friends – in a bar in Bradford. I already knew who he was because he'd played football for quite a few professional clubs, but when I met him he was working as a security guard while his back healed from an operation. I thought he was quite fit, if you know what I mean, and although I was only seventeen and Pembo was twenty-three, I was quite 'old' for my years, so the age gap didn't seem a big deal. I never really thought anything major would come of it, but we clicked straight away. A weird thing kept happening where I would receive texts from him, but he wouldn't receive the ones I sent back, so for the first few weeks he wrongly assumed I wasn't that bothered. Then, after a few dates, we got pretty close quite quickly, and I found myself falling for him. It was the first time I'd ever experienced those all-consuming feelings – you know the ones, when you can't think about anything or anyone else, and you hardly eat or sleep because you're just thinking about the next time you're going to see him. It was love.

At the age of seventeen I found myself in my first real relationship, and I was glad that I'd waited to fall in love before I got serious with a boy, because in the end it meant so much more to me. All of Pembo's mates were older than I was, and quite a few of them were in couples. This meant that I ended up doing a fair amount of grown-up coupley things, rather than the usual teenage stuff, which I didn't mind at all. We went out for dinner and to a lot of bars and clubs in Leeds, and all that seems quite odd when I look back at it now because I was so young. I was quite happy being in such a committed relationship, though, and back then it didn't seem weird to me at all. The idea of going steady with someone seemed much more appealing than going out on the pull every weekend or having lots of different boyfriends.

Meanwhile, I was still working hard and learning my craft at Stage 84 and by now I was lucky to have been taken under the wing of a brilliant choreographer who'd started teaching there a couple of years before. Deana Morgan had an immediate impact on me when she arrived at Stage 84, and as soon as I started working with her, my whole attitude to performing changed forever. Deana had been a professional dancer in London, but she moved to Bradford after marrying a guy who worked for Adidas and was based there. I remember being fascinated by Deana, by her ripped tights and her battered-up tap shoes. She was in her late twenties and a proper working dancer – nothing like all the forty-something Joans and Jeans that we'd had before, with their boring 'step-ball-change' routines. Deana could really dance, and on top of that she looked amazing. I was completely blown away by her. I took her classes really seriously, and eventually she gave me a scholarship for extra dance lessons because she knew my mum wouldn't be able to afford them. Deana was aware that I could sing well, but she also knew how tough the entertainment business was, and she wanted to make sure I was prepared.

'If you want to make it in this business, you've got

to be the triple threat,' she told me. 'You need to be a great singer, actor and dancer.'

As well as the free lessons, I got to go to her dance workshops on a Saturday, and that's where I got a sense of real professional modern choreography for the first time. It's also where I learned tap, which I put to good use when I performed in *Shrek* years later. Deana ended up becoming a real mentor and role model to me, and she even persuaded Valerie Jackson to organise some extra singing tutorials for me, for free, she believed in me that much. When I think back now, she reminded me of a cross between a young Julie Walters and Liza Minnelli, and I was totally in awe of her. I was absolutely gutted when her husband was relocated to Germany and she had to move.

Recently, I found a letter that she sent me while she was over in Germany, and reading it now it seems as if she was still coaching me from afar. 'You've got such a serious talent, Kim,' she wrote. 'Please let me know what your plans are for training and practising. You really need to push yourself as much as you can in this business.' My mum and dad were never overly pushy about me going into the business, so I guess Deana filled that role. I might have just coasted along if it hadn't been for her, and when I think about everything she did for me, I realise how lucky I was to have someone like that in my corner, spurring me on. She was actually the one who persuaded me to go for the *Popstars* audition.

When I was about eighteen, she came back to Bradford and opened her own school, the DM Academy. Sally and I used to teach drama there. Sally was already running her own weekend drama classes in the church hall, for kids of all ages, and I often helped her out. I never really had a hankering to teach, but it was another way of earning a bit of extra money and besides that, I enjoyed it. Before Sally eventually moved to London, she ended up with a hundred or so kids in her various classes, and she put many of them through their performance exams.

At the DM Academy, Deana was the main teacher. Sally and I helped out and covered the class when she wasn't there. By that time, Sally had done quite a few professional acting jobs. She was the lead in the Disney version of *Little Nell*, opposite Sir Peter Ustinov, which led to a long-running part in *Emmerdale*, playing a character called Lyn Hutchinson. That was when I got my first glimpse of what being famous was like. When you're in a soap opera that's a British institution, and on TV several times a week, people seem to think that they know you. Whenever Sally was out and about in Leeds, which is where the *Emmerdale* film set is, she couldn't move two feet along the pavement without someone coming up and talking to her or asking for her autograph. Of course, that's all part of being a television actor or a pop star, but Sally was never comfortable with it. While she loved being an actress, she hated the fame that came with it. She couldn't understand why people in the street would stare at her or randomly come up and start talking to her. It made her feel uncomfortable and anxious rather than loved and admired. I remember wishing and hoping that the same would happen for me one day. I wanted to get a job as wonderful as the one Sally had, and I didn't think I'd mind people recognising me in the slightest. 'I think you'll be fine with it when it happens,' Sally once told me. 'You'll cope with it a lot better than I do. You're far more relaxed than I am.'

As it turned out she was right. I've always dealt with fame in a very matter-of-fact way, and I think part of the reason for that is that I got to share her experience of it when I was younger. Being exposed to her fame, and the fact that Sally was earning more money than we'd ever dreamed of, gave me an insight into what success might bring. I was also used to meeting other actors and famous people from a young age. My uncle, Simon Rouse, was one of the main actors in *The Bill*, and between us we'd come across a fair few celebrities in our young lives. Maybe that helped prepare me for what was to come. I have to say I've always been very lucky when it comes to meeting fans and supporters, with no bad experiences. When you're in the public eye, I think you have to accept that people feel like they know you and they want to chat to you – it's all part of the business. I've met some lovely people and some great characters over the years, and the feedback I get from them has always been very positive.

I gained a lot of experience teaching at the DM Academy alongside Sally, and Deana continued to inspire me all the time I was working there. She really was my rock during those years, and I'm quite sure I wouldn't be where I am today without her help and encouragement. Years later, in 2006, I was shaken and very upset when I ran into a dancer from Bradford whom I knew, who told me that Deana had breast cancer. Of course, anyone can fall victim to cancer, but I still found it hard to comprehend that someone so full of life and energy should be struck down and suddenly fighting for her life like that. I'd been in such a bubble being in Girls Aloud that I hadn't known a thing about it, and I felt terrible that I hadn't been there to help support her. I called her straight away and she told me that she'd had a double mastectomy and chemotherapy and that she was now doing well.

got involved with various breast-cancer
ⲟming a spokesperson for Breast Cancer
ι provides help and support for women
se at several 'havens' around the country.
re such special places and I know that
L   ot of support from the charity while she
wː   ted to help, and in 2008 the two of us
op   ⲟrkshire Haven in Leeds together. It's a
ch   ʝ ⲓ ⱴⲉ ⲃeen involved with ever since, and something very close to my heart – mainly because of my
amazing dance teacher, Deana, who is now, thankfully,
well past her five-year all clear. We're still close to this
day, and I helped organise a Haven charity event to
mark her fiftieth birthday in 2013.

6

Almost Maria

A nd so the auditions and small TV roles went on.
I did well in my GCSEs (two As, five Bs, three
Cs) and I was now doing A-levels in art, English and
media studies. It was 1999, and I got a part playing
alongside Alun Armstrong in a TV drama, *This is
Personal: The Hunt for the Yorkshire Ripper*. He played
police detective George Oldfield and I was his studious,
geeky daughter. The auditions were held at Yorkshire
TV and then there were a couple of recalls. Some of
the casting directors thought I looked too modern and
not plain enough. In the end, I got the part because I
agreed to dye my hair a very dull, mousy brown and
look as dowdy as I possibly could. That was fine by me

– I was acting, and it was a really great drama to be involved in.

I also did a TV show called *Budz* with Kelli Young, who ended up in Liberty X. The show was about a young pop band, and although it wasn't anything amazing, we got to record all the songs for this show in a proper recording studio. This was where I got the bug for singing and recording pop music, and it got me wondering whether a career in pop might be something I should pursue. After all, singing was singing, and that was the thing I loved more than anything. As well as that, we got a little taste of the pop-star lifestyle while we were filming *Budz*, with make-up artists and stylists on hand to help us look the part. Actually, we looked horrific – and when I say horrific, I really do mean horrific – but at the time I suppose we thought we were the bee's knees. Interestingly, my character in *Budz* was the sensible one who kept everyone else in line, which was the role I later fell into in real life with Girls Aloud.

Once I finished school, I decided that I wanted to carry on studying. It wasn't that I was especially passionate about going to university; I just couldn't think of any job that I wanted, apart from acting or singing. I knew that if I went to uni, it would be easier for me to take time off for auditions and castings than if I was working full time. Pembo was living near Leeds at the time – quite near the university – which made it easy for us to see one another regularly. That was one of the main reasons that I decided to stay at a local uni, rather than moving away, as well as the fact that I was saving money on student accommodation by living at home. I was still utterly driven, although I think by this time I was veering towards singing rather than straight acting. I was also sensible enough to know that the more qualifications I had, the more options I would have if my dream of working in the entertainment industry never came to fruition.

So I ended up at Leeds University – Trinity and All Saints – doing a degree in English and media. The media course was great, because it was looking at the industry from the other side. We studied journalism, and learned how to use a recording studio. In fact, when we had to do a studio-recording project, I was the one in the group who was nominated to do the singing. Yes folks, I always found a way to get a bit of warbling in, whatever I did – even studying at university. That being said, I did find the theory side of the media course a little bit daunting. I went in every day and I did my best, but I found it a struggle. Most of the time I was just holding on by the skin of my teeth and it was even more difficult once I landed an agent. On quite a few occasions she would call me with an audition or a casting at the last minute. 'You've got to be in Manchester at ten tomorrow morning,' she'd say. Even if I had something important going on at uni, I would always put the casting first, because that was where my heart lay. Quite often, I'd end up missing full days at uni and then I'd find it even harder to keep up. Auditioning could be an expensive business, too. If I had to fork out the train fare to London or Manchester, it was a lot of money, and if I went down to London, I had to find somewhere to stay on top of that.

I'd worked ever since I was thirteen, when I got a Saturday job cleaning in a bakery. My mum's friend Pam used to give me £10 to do her ironing. After that, I worked in a café in Ilkley, along with Alix. It was a bit of an old biddies' tearoom, but we ruled the roost there; in fact, it was almost like we were running our own little café most of the time. Then, as I got older, I had a whole string of waitressing jobs, and quite often I'd be working two jobs at the same time. Some weekends I would finish my lunch shift at the Salts Mill diner, and then head over to my other job at the Tapas Tree to work the evening shift.

It was hard and at times I'd be dog-tired, but I enjoyed the freedom it gave me, and I loved earning my own money. That way I could save up for holidays and buy clothes, and the extra cash helped with all the travelling costs that went with auditioning for jobs up and down the country. My mum thought I was a little bit obsessive about work. 'You need to take some time for yourself outside university and work,' she'd say. 'Take a day off this week.' But I didn't see it like that. The more money I had saved up, the more I could do. If an audition came up in London, I didn't have to worry that I wouldn't be able to afford the train fare. That was my priority, and I didn't care how hard I had to work to achieve it. Money had always been a problem when I was a kid, but as soon as I started to work and earn my own money, that problem seemed to go away, and I liked that. Plus, I actually enjoyed being a waitress. The work wasn't at all boring, and the working environment was very social, so I ended up making quite a few friends along the way.

In early 2000 I got a call to go up for an audition for the producers of *Coronation Street*. They were casting the part of Maria Sutherland, and it was tipped to be a major, long-running role in the show. The audition was at Granada Television, like many of the auditions I went for, and I was over the moon when I got a recall. After that, I got another recall, and then another, and by this time I felt quite excited about it and more than a little hopeful. The final recall was a screen test, and that was the most important one. I had to act in a scene opposite Alan Halsall, who plays Tyrone Dobbs. I remember thinking that he seemed like a really nice guy, and I felt like I'd done a pretty good job. By this time, my agent had told me that just two other actresses were in the running, Samia Ghadie and Suzanne Shaw, and these were girls I was used to going up against. It wasn't the first time I'd been in that position. A couple of years earlier I'd got down to the last three for a major role in *Emmerdale*, and I remember that Suzanne was up for that one as well. Neither of us got it! This time I dearly hoped it was going to be different.

I remember that day well, because the producers told us they were going to make a decision in the next few hours. My mum and I headed into Manchester for a wander and to wait for what we hoped would be good news. I knew that my life could literally be transformed with just one phone call, and by that time I was pretty desperate for it to happen. However hard I was trying at university, my heart wasn't really in it, and I knew that doing any other job was just going to be settling for second best.

In the end it was close, but not close enough. The *Coronation Street* audition was one of the biggest and most important things I'd been up for, but unfortunately it wasn't to be, and Mum and I went back to Bradford feeling gutted. Samia got the part. I'd been a breath away from my life changing, and on top of that I was so sure that my final audition had gone really well. It was an awful feeling, and yet another near miss. It was becoming a bit of a running joke within my family that I always got down to the last two or three for everything I went for, but never walked away with the part.

I was nearly twenty years old and I was starting to wonder just how long I could carry on pursuing this dream of mine without having any success. The little bits and pieces I'd done were all very well and good, but they never seemed to lead on to anything else, and they weren't enough for me to build a career on. I also began to worry that if I left it too much longer to think about an alternative, I'd miss out on getting my foot on the ladder for any other type of career. Looking back, I was still young, but I'd been performing and auditioning for so long by that point, it seemed as though it was make or break time. The trouble was that because I had done some acting parts, and I was getting close with the big auditions, it was like I had a carrot constantly dangling in front of me. And every time I considered throwing in the towel, something new would come along. It might not have been a life-changing role, but it was enough to spur me on that little bit further and keep the hunger alive. It was a vicious circle.

To make matters worse, my relationship with Pembo had hit a rough patch. We'd been dating for almost two years and we were pretty serious, but suddenly things just weren't right between us any more. In that first year, our relationship had been quite intense, and thinking about it now, I'm not sure I was mature enough to handle it, even though I thought I was at the time. Sometimes I would give him a hard time about the most trivial of things, and I think he started to see me as a nagging girlfriend rather than someone he was having fun with. If he was a little bit late picking me up to go out, I'd make a massive deal about it, and instead of accepting him for the kind and loving person he was, I think I pushed my luck and expected far too much of him. I always felt as though I had to be in charge and have the upper hand, instead of being in an equal partnership, and I guess Pembo felt that he just couldn't do anything right. It was an immature vision of a relationship on my part, but then again the only real relationship I had to go on was my parents' one, which had been quite dysfunctional.

Still, it was a horrible shock when he told me that he wanted to break up with me. In fact, I was completely devastated, inconsolable. I couldn't believe that Pembo had dumped me like that. It was horrendous. Somebody telling you that they don't want to be with you when you still really love them is the worst feeling in the world. This was my first taste of pure unadulterated heartbreak, and I just didn't know what to do with myself without him. I'd taken our relationship very seriously – perhaps too seriously – and I simply couldn't get my head around the fact that it had come to an end because of me. I couldn't even eat for those first few weeks after we split up, and at uni I was walking around in a daze. I'd put on quite a bit of weight while Pembo and I were together, but now it was dropping off me so fast that I lost about two stone and started to look a bit too thin. My sister Amy was so upset about my inability to eat that she stopped eating too, in solidarity. I thought that was incredibly sweet as she was only fourteen at the time. I didn't even have any exciting work prospects to take my mind off it because I wasn't getting cast or chosen for anything. It was a horrible time.

Eventually, I realised that I needed to meet someone else and put some distance between Pembo and me. He clearly wasn't coming back and there was nothing I could do about it. My friend Jenny, whom I'd met because she was dating one of Pembo's friends, had broken up with her boyfriend around the same time, so the two of us just thought, sod it, and went on a mission to find ourselves new men just as soon as we could. We were out on the pull in Leeds, and there was no stopping us. One night I met a really nice guy in a bar called Norman's, and there were definite sparks. He was gorgeous and it felt really good to be with someone so handsome who fancied me, and although nothing much came of it that night, it helped me to regain a little bit of my lost confidence. The trouble was I knew this guy wanted more than I was ready to give. He called me quite a few times after that night in Norman's, but I just couldn't do it. As much as I told myself I was ready to forget Pembo and move on, it simply wasn't true. After that, it was back to listening to Mary J. Blige singing 'No More Drama' over and over again while I cried in my bedroom.

Sally's boyfriend at the time was a friend of Pembo's, so I often heard stories of what he was up to, whether I wanted to or not. Once I heard a tale about him asking out a girl I knew, and I was devastated. I felt like someone had stabbed me through the heart – it was all so dramatic. At the time, though, it was very real, and I just couldn't bear the thought of him with another girl. I couldn't work out what he was thinking, because as far as I was concerned, we were meant to be together and that was that. I got myself in such a state that Alix suggested I came on holiday to Orlando with her family.

'You can't carry on like this,' she said. 'You're not eating properly and you look terrible. You need to get away from here.'

I expect she lived to regret that kind offer because I was as miserable as sin the whole time I was there and they probably all wanted to kill me. It was a terribly unhappy time.

7

Falling At the Last Hurdle

On Christmas Eve of 2001, just when I was starting to get over Pembo, I bumped into him in a pub. He breezed through the door and I thought, Bloody hell, I still fancy him! WHY? That being said, I knew I didn't look too bad myself. I had lost two stone – mostly through being distraught about the break-up – and was feeling quite good about myself. We eventually got chatting at the bar and in the end we stayed in the pub together for the entire evening. We talked and talked about everything that had happened between us, and eventually he asked me to go out with him on New Year's Eve. I was a bit wary, because I couldn't stand the thought of going through all that heartbreak again. I think he knew that but he could also see how much I'd grown up, and that things could be different between us. In hindsight, the break-up had actually done me good because it made me take stock of the way I behaved and think about the person I wanted to be. I realised that I'd been much too needy, and consequently put pressure on both him and our relationship.

Once we were back together again, Pembo got a flat just outside Halifax, and I moved in with him. It's funny because right away I became quite the little housewife and I adjusted to living life as part of a couple with relative ease. The fact that I'd had to do stuff at home to help my mum stood me in good stead, but I actually enjoyed looking after Pembo and taking care of our flat. He was playing for Stockport County by then and doing really well. I was still at university and auditioning like a mad thing for anything good that came up. It was a happy time for me and I was utterly besotted with him. The only slight niggle I had was that he had broken my heart once, so there was always the possibility that he might do it again. I think for this reason I always had my guard up slightly. I loved him, yes, but there was always a tiny nagging voice in the back of my mind, probably for my own self-preservation. Whereas before I'd thought of him as my everything, now there was an added 'but'. Yes, you're still everything to me . . . but you really hurt me and I can't ever forget that.

By the summer, I'd started to get really despondent about the idea of ever making it as a singer or an actress. I was continually getting close to being given a role, but for some reason I was never quite good enough to clinch the deal. It had started to get to me by then, and there were times when I just couldn't see a glimmer of light at the end of the tunnel. Most of the other girls I knew from doing the constant rounds of auditions had ended up in bands or in major TV roles. Samia was now playing Maria in *Coronation Street*, Kelli Young was in the band Liberty X, and Suzanne Shaw was in Hear'Say. It just seemed like everyone had found their place apart from me, and I often wondered whether it was even worth going on. It knocked my confidence, which ended up making the auditions even tougher than they already were. When I was a kid, I never got very much criticism as far as my performances went; it was mostly praise. Sure, I had a few nerves – like most performers – but I always got out there and gave it my all, but after the knockbacks the nerves started to take over whenever I went for an audition, and self-doubt started to get the better of me. I guess the stakes were higher all of a sudden. I wasn't a cute little kid singing Julie Andrews songs any more. I was a young woman who needed to get a job soon, or give up on her dream for good.

I was in the second year of my degree, and still waitressing as much as I possibly could, but I could always find the time to cram in an audition whenever one came up. On one occasion, I auditioned for Daniel Glatman, who'd had success managing the boy band Blue. He was putting together a new girl band, and after my initial audition he asked me to come back and see him again. The trouble was something else had grabbed my attention in the meantime – an audition for the new series of the TV show *Popstars*, which was being held at the Lowry Theatre in Manchester.

For some reason, I had a positive attitude about this particular audition, and a good feeling. It wasn't as though I thought I was going to walk away with it, but I'd been so beaten down by it all at that point that I just thought, What the hell! Go in there and do your best and it'll be fine. And I really wanted to put myself in front of what I thought to be an esteemed panel of judges – Pete Waterman, Geri Halliwell and Louis Walsh. They were all people whom I admired in the industry, and they would surely be able to tell me, once and for all, whether I was good enough to make it as a singer or not. Even if it was bad news and I didn't

Smiling for the camera, age 1.

Camping in Filey
with cousin Leonie,
age 3.

Acting out a scene as usual – with my brother, Adam.

Family photo, age 6. Check out that fringe!

Showtime! Seven Brides for Seven Brothers at The Edinburgh Fringe Festival.

Striking a pose during another Edinburgh show: The Railway Children.

Minnie Me! Dressed up for our local fair's fancy dress competition, age 7.

Posing for the press, after landing the part in Les Mis, age 12.

As Cosette, with Marius and little Eponine, backstage at the Manchester Palace, age 12.

Sister Act! Me and Sally during our Stage 84 days.

School days, age 8.

On my first TV set, age 6. What a shy child I was.

Daisy Pulls it Off at the Edinburgh Fringe, age 6.

Granddad always played the harmonica at Christmas: with me Sally, Adam and my cousins Leonie and Luke.

All the family, at Popstars: The Rivals.

end up hearing what I wanted to hear, I just needed to know.

I'd already sent in a CD plus my CV, and I'd been told that I had to be at the Lowry on a certain day at a certain time. The producers had been quite specific about my audition slot, so I thought that it surely wouldn't be one of those great big cattle calls that I'd been to so many times before. Wrong!

That day we had quite a stressful time getting to Manchester. My mum and Sally had come along for moral support, and for some reason we ended up driving to the wrong venue, which made us late. Then I spilled an orange drink down my top while we were in the car, and my previously calm demeanour began to crack. For a start, I had to go into a public toilet somewhere and rinse out my top because I didn't have a back-up. Then I had to sit in the car in my bra, waving a soggy white boob tube out of the window as we went along so it would dry. By that time we were all really stressed out, thinking that I was going to miss my designated slot and blow the whole thing. Of course, when we finally got to the Lowry, there was a queue of at least five hundred people and I ended up standing around for bloody hours. I clearly remember Nicola Roberts being about two people in front of me in the queue. Sally and I both thought she had a unique style and looked really striking, with long red hair down to her bum.

'She definitely looks like she could be a pop star, that one,' Sally commented.

Once I got through the initial round of auditions, which were in front of the show's producers, I was finally given my chance to perform in front of the judges. Someone who was really terrible also got through in my group, and I couldn't understand why. These days we all know that half the fun of watching the TV auditions comes from laughing at the people who can't sing a note, but back then I didn't get it. By the time it was my turn to go in I'd been hanging around for so long that I just wanted to get it over with. I sang the Whitney Houston song 'Where Do Broken Hearts Go', and right away Pete Waterman told me I was going through to boot camp. 'You're definitely coming to London, love!'

I was elated. Maybe there was a reason to carry on after all. I still had a long way to go, of course, but my mum, Sally and I were all very happy that day. It was a brilliant feeling after all the knockbacks and near misses I'd had in the last couple of years.

The boot camp in London was quite an overwhelming experience. We stayed at a hotel in Kensington, which is a lovely part of London, and although the hotel itself wasn't overly glamorous, all our travel, accommodation and food was organised and paid for by ITV. It felt very exciting to be part of something so big. The thought of what might come out of it and how important it all was suddenly dawned on me, and I couldn't help looking at everyone around me to see how I measured up. Some of the girls looked quite cool, but I'd had to borrow clothes from friends to make sure I looked the part, because I didn't have that many decent outfits myself. The first person who actually spoke to me was a pretty girl called Cheryl Tweedy.

'Your skin is amazing,' she said. 'What foundation do you use?'

I remember thinking that she looked so sweet, and she seemed younger than I was, but at the time I was just grateful that someone had spoken to me – Cheryl was so warm and friendly, which was just what I needed at the time. I also got close to Nadine Coyle during boot camp. She was a quiet girl, and she seemed to shy away from the cameras. She had been famously disqualified from the Irish version of *Popstars* the year before because she was too young, so I knew who she was. I was quite happy hanging out with her because I tended to shy away from the limelight myself during boot camp. My idea was to stay off-camera as much as possible, and then if I didn't end up going through to the next round, no one would have seen me that much anyway and it wouldn't matter. I really didn't know how to play the game, did I?

One of my boot-camp auditions was bloody terrifying. We had to perform not only for the judges, but for all the other contestants as well, and for the first time in my entire career I had a complete and utter blank. I could not for the life of me remember what the opening lines to the song were, and I froze in front of the judges. I think I'd watched so many of the other contestants sing so many different songs that by the time I came to do mine I'd completely forgotten what the hell it was. Mercifully, Louis Walsh saved my arse on that occasion, blaming my hesitation on the loud drilling noise that was going on somewhere in the background.

'Can we keep it quiet back there, please?' he shouted.

It was enough time for me to compose myself and remember that what I was supposed to be singing was 'End of the Line' by the Honeyz.

I remember getting another call from Daniel Glatman around that time. He was keen for me to come and do a final audition for the girl band he was putting together, which really put a spanner in the works.

'Oh, you don't want to do that *Popstars* thing,' he warned me. 'These things come and go – look what happened to Hear'Say! You should come and be in my new band. The prospects are a lot better.'

It was a really hard choice to make. He was right. There was no guarantee that I would even get into the *Popstars* band, and this seemed like a firm offer. I did think about it long and hard, but decided that I needed to see *Popstars* through. I'd got through several stages of the boot camp by then, so I knew that I was at least in with a chance of making the live shows. I had to say no to Daniel and try to forget all about it, which seemed as though it might have been the right decision when suddenly I was down to the final fifteen girls. I suppose I should have been happy, but by that time my nerves were shot. Louis told me that although I was through, I was going to have to do a lot better if I was going to make the band. I remember I couldn't stop crying that night because I somehow knew that I wasn't going to get into the final ten – I don't know why. My nerves felt frazzled and my emotions were all over the place. I felt like I'd let myself down.

After that, we all had to troop back to our home towns and wait to hear if we were in the final ten, which meant going through to the live rounds. The idea of the 2002 series of *Popstars* was to choose two separate bands, one of boys, and the other of girls. Once the public had chosen the bands, the boys and girls would both record their own singles and compete in a battle of the sexes for the coveted Christmas number one. Pete Waterman was to mentor the boys, and Louis was to look after the girls. By the time Pete Waterman turned up at my house in Bradford to film the 'is she or isn't she in the last ten' part of the show, I'd already told my family that I was quite certain that I wasn't. I was disappointed, of course, but not distraught by any means. At the end of the day it was just another audition and I'd certainly had my fair share of disappointments already. I knew I'd get over it in time.

'Yeah, I've got my head around it already,' I said on camera when Pete delivered the bad news.

I actually felt fine, but that wasn't exactly the reaction they were hoping for, so Pete was told by the producers to keep pushing me until I broke down. They were all there in my house for a good hour, trying to make me cry for the camera, and they really mess with your head while they're doing it. 'I know you think that this is your last chance, but you've got to keep going,' was one of the things I remember Pete saying. 'I'm sure that your mum is still proud of you even though you didn't make it,' was another. They'd say anything to tug on your heartstrings and get you to blub. It was only when they mentioned my mum that I started to get a little bit upset, and they jumped on it.

'Aw! Give your mum a hug,' Pete said.

Then I really did start to cry, and, of course, that was the only bit that they showed on television the following Saturday. I was quite annoyed that I'd been pushed to that point, because it wasn't how I really felt at all. The hardest thing about it was knowing that some of the friends that I'd made at boot camp, including Cheryl and Nadine, were going to be living in a house in London together while they performed on the live shows. That was tough. Once again I'd got so close but fallen at the last hurdle. It was becoming the story of my life.

What else could I do but pick myself up and get on with it? I went back to work at the café and got ready to enrol in my third year at uni. Then suddenly I heard from a producer at ITV that they wanted to do a follow-up interview with me for the *Popstars: The Rivals Extra* show on ITV 2. I must say I wasn't all that keen on the idea of raking the whole thing up again, but a tiny voice inside my head told me that the interview might be something more than they were letting on. When Louis Walsh turned up at my house, I knew that it wasn't just a follow-up interview. They weren't gong to send him to do a quick chat for ITV 2, were they? It turned out that one of the girls in the final ten, Hazel, was actually too old to be a contestant, and her situation was further complicated by the fact that she was eight months pregnant.

I remember so clearly how shocked and excited my family all were when Louis told me that I had been chosen to go into the final ten as Hazel's replacement. In fact, my brother Adam had just walked into the middle of the filming with a towel round him, fresh out of the bath. Mum was elated, but Sally was a bit more wary and protective of me. She wasn't convinced that a reality TV talent show was the right thing for me to be doing, and although she was thrilled for me, I also think she was scared of losing me. All of a sudden everything changed. The next thing I knew I was packing my stuff and getting ready to move to London all on my own. And although I didn't know it then, from that day on I would never really go home ever again.

8

'Kimberley's Going Home Tonight'

London was such an adventure, an exciting mix of anticipation and hope, and it felt right to me that I was there. I felt like I belonged in the house with the other girls, and when I arrived I got a massive welcome from all of them. The house was actually in Surrey and I'd never seen anything like it – not even Alix's parents' house. It was huge and very smart, and it had a pool. I was assigned a room with Nadine, Sarah and another girl, Lynsey, and I was really happy to be rooming with Nadine, apart from the fact that she was impossible to wake up in the morning. Cheryl was sharing with Nicola, and their room was an absolute tip right from the off.

I remember thinking Sarah was completely crazy when I first met her. She just seemed so over-the-top and manic all the time and I was a little bit wary of her. She always seemed to be having a drama of some sort throughout the entire audition process. She was a strong singer, but she wasn't the best dancer, and that was where a lot of her problems stemmed from. She really struggled in the group dance numbers, and she'd usually end up in tears at some point. It was just something you got used to with Sarah, and once you accepted that that's the way she was, it was fine.

For the first few weeks we were confined to the house for the entire time, aside from the odd secret photo shoot. The show where the final ten girls were chosen hadn't aired yet, and ITV wanted to keep us all under wraps until it was time to unveil us properly. We did vocal training and we rehearsed while we were there, but I remember feeling quite isolated from the outside world. It was all very strange. You might think that a house full of young girls let loose on their own for the first time would turn into one big boozy party, but in truth everyone was much more concerned with learning their songs and being the best they could be on the Saturday night show. There wouldn't be just one winner since we were competing to be in a five-piece band, so we all helped each other with the songs, and there was a lot of encouragement going on between us all. Being in that environment was my idea of heaven because I was constantly singing, and on top of that I had a captive audience. There was one little party while I was in the house, which was for my twenty-first birthday. On that day Amy and Sally were allowed to visit me for a couple of hours – and they brought birthday cake! It was quite strange seeing them there, in among all the other girls, but it was wonderful none-theless. It wasn't exactly how I'd imagined spending my twenty-first, but that day was definitely a highlight of the house.

Once the live shows started and I realised that I was going to have to sing in front of the whole country on TV every week, my nerves went into overdrive. On the first week's show I felt quite confident because I was still so grateful for being given a second chance, so I just went for it. After that, though, it all went downhill. With every week that went by I felt more and more pressure heaped upon me and I wasn't enjoying myself at all. Cheryl and I both felt our performances were getting worse as the weeks went by rather than better. In the fourth week of the live shows I sang 'Unbreak My Heart' and when the public votes were in, the girls were split into two groups, with Davina announcing that one girl from each group would be going home. I ended up being the last girl saved before the bottom two were eliminated, and it was incredibly nerve racking. We never really knew how the voting worked back then. Davina never used the phrase, 'In no particular order' when she was reading the results. If you were placed 'bottom three' or 'bottom four' it could really knock your confidence, even though you'd got through to the next round. I think that's the worst aspect of being a contestant on a TV talent competition: the way it messes with your head. After that week, the nerves just seemed to get the better of me during every performance. It's weird because at such a young age I'd performed in *Les Mis* for a couple of thousand people every night, which didn't faze me at all. This was different, though. There was so much riding on it – it was like the last chance saloon as far as I was concerned. Before one of the live shows, Louis walked up to Nadine and said, 'Kimberley's going home tonight,' and she totally freaked out. We actually had to call the nurse to come and give her a tablet to calm her down. Nadine and I had become really close while we were in the house together, and she simply couldn't cope with the thought of me leaving.

All the girls were feeling it by then. It wasn't just that we were being publicly criticised by the panel, we were actually being judged by millions of people watching at home as well. It was a popularity contest as much as anything and the pressure was immense. I hated the idea of being judged. Up until then I'd always looked upon singing and performing as a joy and a pleasure, but suddenly it had become something that was terrifying. On the penultimate week of the contest, when I sang 'Emotions' by Destiny's Child, my comments from the panel weren't that positive. It was Geri Halliwell who helped save me with a little experiment she'd done that week. She'd sent a group of children backstage at the *Popstars* studio to find out who they thought was the nicest girl, and thankfully I came up trumps. If Geri hadn't mentioned that on the Saturday show, who knows if I'd have made it through to the final.

By the last show the whole process had worn me down, and I didn't even feel like myself any more. At least that night I knew that one way or another it would all be over, and for that reason I was a little bit calmer when I performed my final song, which was 'Chain Reaction'. It's not a song I'd have chosen to perform, but I was told I'd already done too many ballads and I needed to do something a little bit more lively.

That night, when Davina McCall announced which girls had made it into the band, I felt strangely confident, I don't know why. When she called my name – I was the fourth out of five – I cried out of pure relief more than anything. I was just so happy it was all over, and I remember thinking, At last! Finally I'd won. Finally I'd jumped that last hurdle and reached the finish line. That was enough for me. It's what I'd been waiting for all my life.

In the run-up to the final show we'd recorded 'Sound of the Underground', which was to be the girls' first single. Six of us were left in the competition by that point – the five who eventually ended up in the band plus Javine Hylton, whom everybody expected to make it into the band. I've since discovered that the people at our record label, Polydor, and the producers of *Popstars* had considered almost every combination of the six but never once considered a line-up without Javine. For them, it was really about her. Consequently, she was over the original recording of the single, and in almost every one of the cover shots for the single sleeve. Apparently, they were gobsmacked when Javine wasn't chosen that Saturday night, and they had to scrabble around to find the best photos of the rest of us together. Then Cheryl was dispatched straight back down to the recording studio to re-record all of Javine's parts, because we were due to shoot the video on the Monday.

When we finally heard the finished single, however,

I wasn't on it at all – I didn't have a single line – so when it came to rehearsing our choreography for the video, I burst into tears in front of everyone. After putting myself through all that pressure for ten weeks and finally getting into the band, it really stung not to have one solo line to sing on our first record. Why had I even bothered? Poor Sarah was going through the mill as well. A lot of stories appeared in the press implying that Javine should have been in the band instead of her, which simply wasn't true. Sarah was a great singer. The two of us were in a right state when we should have been jumping for joy. It's funny – day one in Girls Aloud gave us a taste of the chaos and mayhem that would follow us right through to our twenty-third single. In the end, the producers did a quick remix of the song so that I had some solo lines on it, but who was singing what on our singles was often an issue after that, as it is in many pop bands.

We all absolutely loved the record because it was different and so much cooler than we'd been expecting. Brian Higgins was the producer, and it wasn't your typical girl-band song at all – much more edgy and cool. In fact, compared to the boys' slightly cheesy and fairly typical boy-band pop song, 'Sacred Trust', it really shone out. Once the songs were chosen it was all-out war between us and the boys to see which band would get the Christmas number one, and we were up for the challenge. Up until then we hadn't really seen that much of the boys outside the studio, apart from the odd bit of filming or photo shoots. I thought a couple of them – Daniel Pearce and Anton Gordon – were really talented, and they all seemed like lovely guys. However, nice guys or not, we were determined to kick their arses in the race to number one.

The boys called their band One True Voice, and we went through various dreadful suggestions for names before we finally settled on Girls Aloud. Cheryl wanted to call us Raw Silk, for instance, and Polydor and Granada TV were coming up with such gems as Charmed and Heaven Scent (note the spelling) and In Your Dreams. The story goes that the Appleton sisters, known collectively as Appleton, had an album due out, which was originally called *Aloud*. A few people at Polydor thought that 'Aloud' would make a good name for us, but Appleton were on the same label, so the record company could hardly hijack their name. Then someone suggested 'Girls Aloud', and because by then we had to find a name right away, we were stuck with it.

When the name of the band was unveiled on *Popstars* that Saturday, you could tell that we all thought it was rubbish, but the marketing director of Polydor, Peter

Loraine, assured us that once everyone got used to saying the name, it would start to sound more natural and right. Kimberley, Cheryl, Nicola, Nadine and Sarah were now collectively known as Girls Aloud, and we were off and running.

9

Every Young Girl's Dream

From the minute I was told I was in the band, my feet didn't touch the ground. None of us had any time to do anything for ourselves, and we were lucky if we crammed in three or four hours' sleep a night, such was our mad schedule. The promotional push was massive because we were competing against One True Voice, who were on Jive Records, and the last thing Polydor wanted was to lose out to a rival label. In fact, David Joseph, who was one of the two managing directors of the label, insisted that the marketing department spare no expense in making sure that Girls Aloud grabbed the viewing public's precious votes. This meant that the competition between us and

One True Voice was fierce, but thankfully Polydor came up with a clever slogan, 'buy girls, bye boys', which worked incredibly well and was plastered all around the country on posters, appeared on T-shirts and in radio ads.

On the Sunday before the two singles were released, the boys were doing an interview on Capital FM during the chart rundown. Capital were really supporting the boys, so the promotional department at Polydor couldn't get us a look in on the show. Instead, Polydor bought up the advertising slots that were due to run in the middle of the boys' interview. They even employed Davina McCall, the host of *Popstars*, to record the voice-over for the ad. 'BUY GIRLS, bye boys. This is Girls Aloud, "Sound of the Underground"!' she bellowed over the chorus of our single, right in the middle of the boys' exclusive. Genius.

It's every young girl singer's dream to perform in her own music video – but on the day we shot ours I had no idea what to expect and no real clue what we were supposed to be doing. There wasn't much time for preparation for a start, and aside from the director, we didn't have anyone telling us how they wanted us to act or perform on camera. Still, it was beyond exciting, and the whole thing suddenly felt incredibly real. We all decided to go for the mean and moody attitude on camera, and looking back I think we did a pretty good job because the results were fantastic. The whole thing was shot in what looks like a dank, dark cellar, with the five of us performing the song inside a huge metal enclosure with a band behind us.

I remember how excited we all were that day, having our hair and make-up done in a proper Winnebago – and we heard the first play of the single on Radio 1. We all went absolutely nuts, screaming our heads off. It really was such a special moment, and you can experience it just once in a lifetime.

When the two groups came together to watch one another's videos, it was quite clear that the boys were not happy. Our video looked really fresh and vibrant and had a bit of an edge to it, but the boys' one was just the usual boy-band fodder and didn't stand out at all, much like the song itself. The funny thing was the boys had been so cocky up until that point. 'Girls will buy our record because we're lads,' they kept telling us. They were convinced they were going to take the crown, but during the week of release it was quite a different story. When the midweek chart positions came in, 'Sound of the Underground' was tens of thousands of sales ahead of 'Sacred Trust', but we still thought they might catch us up. We had no idea how it all worked. Of course, in the end they didn't stand a chance, and on the final *Popstars* show, Girls Aloud were crowned the winners, and 'Sound of the Underground' was the Christmas number one. It was an unbelievable feeling.

I could hardly believe what was happening. I don't think any of us could. We'd clicked into a tight unit right away, and already Girls Aloud felt like a real band. Having a number-one record was just the massive cherry on a very big cake. There wasn't a big party after the final show, but Pembo came down and stayed with me at the hotel, and although he was almost as over the moon as I was about our success, I sensed a kind of knowing sadness between us that night. Pembo had always supported me, and he'd never tried to hold me back in any way, but we both knew that this victory would mean me moving to London while he stayed up north to play for his team. It was going to be a lot harder for us to see one another from then on, and I guess neither of us really knew how that would affect our relationship. If it hadn't been for that one niggling doubt, everything would have been just perfect.

Later that week we recorded the Christmas edition of *Top of the Pops*, and I don't think I'd ever felt so excited. That was the one TV show we all watched on Christmas Day in our house, and it was completely surreal gathering around the TV to watch it with my family that year, knowing that I was actually on it.

That Christmas was wonderful. Firstly, although I had so much to look forward to, it was a good feeling to be back home with the family for a few days. During those first few weeks of the band we'd been living at the K West Hotel, which is a renowned music-business hangout, and although that might sound glamorous, it wasn't an easy existence for someone who likes her home comforts. We had nowhere to do our washing, and although we all had our own rooms, there was hardly any room to move, surrounded by two or three suitcases of clothes apiece.

My grandma and granddad were with us that Christmas, just like they were every year. Granddad had a Christmas tradition of playing carols on the harmonica, and we would all sit around and sing along. Ever since I was little, we've had a good old singsong at Christmas. My partner, Justin, thinks we're mad, but we all love it. Granddad was always perfectly rehearsed and he knew exactly which songs he was going to play every year before he got there, like a true perfectionist.

Although he never said a lot, I knew that my granddad was quietly happy that I was doing what he'd always wanted to do – which was sing – but he never once showed me any special favouritism or heaped any more praise on me than he did on any of his other six grand-children. Of course, that's how it should be, but it's not always the case. Some people have treated me differently over the years because of my job or my fame. Sometimes Granddad would almost go the other way, not commenting very much on my achievements and the things I did over the years. I know he was proud of me, of course, but he was quite hard to please sometimes, and he'd always tell you straight if he thought something wasn't good enough.

On Boxing Day I was on my way to a family party when Nadine called me with the most terrible news. Our tour manager, John McMahon, had been killed in a car accident on Christmas Day. John had come on board as soon as the band were formed, and he'd driven us around and looked after us every single day. He was the band's first close companion, and the one person who was with the five of us every minute of the day during those first few weeks of pure madness, almost like a sixth member of the band. John would say, '*We're* doing a gig,' or, '*We're* at number one.' He seemed to love working with us and felt like part of it all, which was good for our morale.

After a few drinks, he'd crashed into a telegraph pole in the black Chrysler people carrier that we'd travelled up and down the country in during those first few weeks of promotion. It had our 'Girls Aloud' logo emblazoned across its side. I remember thinking that because we'd been so tired in the run-up to Christmas, we hadn't been all that nice to him, and then I felt even worse about it. We hadn't really had the chance to get to know John properly and now he was gone. All five of us went to the funeral and cried our hearts out, and I think on that day the bond between us was cemented. It took the wind out of all our sails, and it was a terrible end to everything wonderful that had happened over the previous few weeks.

Once Christmas was over I suddenly found myself immersed in the world of pop, which was very unlike my experience in television or theatre, and also very different from how I'd imagined it would be. For a start, I thought that I'd be singing and performing for the majority of the time, but that wasn't the case at all. In fact, performing seemed to be the thing we did least. Most of the time was taken up with a whirlwind of promotion. I had to get used to the idea that I was just one of five girls who together formed a product that had been created by a TV show. My whole life was being mapped out in front of my eyes with not much time for discussions about anything, but that didn't stop us from putting our two-pennyworth in. All through the duration of the band we never minced our words if we didn't like an outfit or an idea for a video. We always had our own strong vision for the band, and in the early days we united creatively.

Day-to-day life in a girl band seemed to be primarily either sitting in a car, a make-up chair or a hotel room, but the five of us never seemed to get tired of spending time together. Even when we'd spent all day travelling and then rehearsed and performed on a TV show, we would often end up gossiping in one another's hotel rooms. In those early days, we didn't seem to need or want our own space. We just wanted to hang out and talk sh*t all night. It felt like the best thing in the world to be doing an amazing job and getting to hang out with your mates while you were doing it. We got so close that quite quickly I would know exactly how someone was feeling just by looking at them. I could tell the minute one of the girls walked out of their front door towards the car whether they were in a good mood or not. It was an important skill to have, and it helped prevent too many big blow-ups over the years. If someone wasn't feeling it on a certain day, you simply gave her a wide berth until she felt like joining in again.

Everywhere I turned there were hairdressers, make-up artists, photographers and TV and radio presenters, and quite a few of the creative people I encountered seemed a bit over-the-top and unreal to me. Remember, I was just a young innocent girl from Bradford back then! I do remember thinking, Bloody hell, some of this crowd are not exactly what I'd call down-to-earth. They were very arty types. The whole thing was what I imagined the entertainment industry in LA to be like. I thought some of them were trying a bit too hard sometimes, and it took me a while to get used to the way people worked in the pop business. In fact, as exciting as it all was, I wasn't sure it was the most settling or comfortable environment for me to be in. I was quite relieved when we were introduced to Lisa Laudat, a hairdresser who stayed with us right up until the end of the band. She was a breath of fresh air back then, and just so down-to-earth and easy to talk to. Lisa was just as passionate about what she was doing as some of the other creative people we'd worked with, but having been brought up in the East End of London, she was also very grounded and normal. When you're in a girl band, you have to spend a lot of time with your hairdresser and your make-up artist, so it's important that you're on the same wavelength. After all, they're ultimately responsible for how you look when you step out in front of the camera. I needed a bit of comfort and stability from somewhere in among all the madness, and Lisa was it.

The five of us also had one another, however, and we felt comfortable with a few people at Polydor, too, including our marketing director, Peter Loraine, and our marketing manager, Poppy Stanton. Peter had started the Bananarama fan club in the 1980s, so that pretty much gives you an idea of where he was coming from. He had a boyish enthusiasm and he loved pop music, which is why Girls Aloud very much became his baby as time went on. Peter wanted us to succeed almost as much as we did, and he was the person who always pushed for us at Polydor, especially during the tougher times down the line. He became so closely involved with us, and so close to us, that to him we became much more than just another band. For Peter it was personal, and he seemed to spend his whole working life thinking up bigger and better campaigns for each new record that we put out. At the same time, he was straight to the point and always the mediator. A big part of his job ended up being talking the five of us into doing things we didn't really want to do.

Peter and Poppy were the people who did their best to look after us in those early days, particularly because our so-called manager, Louis Walsh, was nowhere to be seen. Louis had opted to manage us after mentoring us on the TV show, but from the minute the closing credits rolled on the final episode of *Popstars: The Rivals*, he seemed to lose interest. He's since admitted to me that he didn't know what to do with five girls and that he was a bit scared of us, but I'm not sure that's the whole truth of it. Louis has just never really been a hands-on type of manager, and back then we suffered because of it.

Whatever the case, Louis's disappearing act meant that we had nobody looking after us, and nobody fighting our corner as far as record company decisions went. We had a tour manager who got us where we needed to be from day to day, but we were pretty much on our own, apart from the help and advice we got from Peter, Poppy and our head-of-press, Sundraj Sreenivasan. Peter was so much more to us than his job title of marketing director, and he was always on the end of a phone when we needed him. In those days, we had no one planning our day-to-day diaries, and no one keeping us in line and organised. These were the things that a manager was supposed to be doing, but Girls Aloud were being left to their own devices and very quickly it became a mess. I remember phoning Peter one day, feeling desperate about the situation.

'What are we going to do?' I said. 'It's all going to sh*t, Peter. We need help.'

10

A Bunch of English Knackers

Quite out of the blue, things took a turn for the worse in January of 2003. While we were still at number one in the UK charts, Cheryl was arrested in a Guildford nightclub after getting into a dispute with a female toilet attendant. She was charged with assault. The first thing I knew about it was when Nicola came back to our hotel in Guildford in a state of shock.

'Cheryl's locked up!' she shrieked.

We'd been staying in a little bed and breakfast in the area while we were working in the recording studio, which was nearby, and I'd been nervous about Nicola and Cheryl going out clubbing together because we didn't know the area too well. Cheryl also had a bad feeling about going out that night, but she'd gone against her gut instinct.

It turned out that Cheryl had taken some lollipops from the toilet attendant's sweet supply, and before she'd handed over some money to pay for them, an argument had broken out between them. Nicola, who'd gone to the toilets with Cheryl, dashed off to get security. At some point during the scuffle, Cheryl had hit the woman and before she knew it she was being dragged out of the toilets and back to the VIP area by the security guy. At first the club manager apologised to both her and Nicola but forty-five minutes later the police arrived and Cheryl was arrested. A few days later things went from bad to worse as the toilet attendant told the police that Cheryl had racially abused her as well as hitting her. The charge was then ramped up from assault to racially aggravated assault. It was a nightmare.

There was never any doubt in my mind that the 'racially aggravated' part of the charge was completely false. Knowing Cheryl as I did, even in those few short months, I didn't even consider it for a moment. To me, it just seemed like a night out that had gone horribly wrong, and Cheryl, unfortunately, got her first taste of the downside of being famous.

The night after the incident Girls Aloud had to

record *Ant and Dec's Saturday Night Takeaway*, and we were mortified. Cheryl was in bits for a start, and we were dreading appearing in front of an audience so soon after the story had broken because we had no idea how the public were going to react. To us, it was a very big deal, and we were all worried about what impact it might have on the band. Geri Halliwell was also on the show that night, and I remember her telling us not to worry about what had happened, that it would all blow over. Then we got a call from Louis, which was probably the only phone call we'd had since the end of *Popstars*. He'd left a voicemail on Nadine's phone, which wasn't very nice. I can't remember exactly what he said, but the general gist was that we were all a bunch of English knackers – apart from Nadine – and that he didn't want anything to do with us. We were horrified because at the time we still had a lot of respect for Louis, but what do you do when your manager tells you that he wants nothing to do with you? I remember thinking that Girls Aloud might be over before we'd even started. In fact, as soon as news of Cheryl's arrest hit the paper I thought, That was nice while it lasted. Short but nice.

There was no animosity or hard feelings towards Cheryl from the rest of us. We all knew that it was just a night out that had gone wrong, and we knew that there was no way she'd have been racist towards anyone. We were going to stand by her whatever happened, but it was a difficult time for us. The following week we just had to carry on recording our album, not knowing how the court case was going to pan out, or whether the public were going to turn against us after what had happened. It was only when our second single, 'No Good Advice', went shooting up the chart in May of 2003 that we were able to breathe a small sigh of relief.

We'd been living like nomads during the whole period before our second single came out. Polydor weren't sure if we were going to take off, so no permanent accommodation had been sorted for us and we lived out of suitcases in hotels. We had no proper home life and we hadn't been out much socially either. When 'No Good Advice' went to number two in the charts, however, things definitely took a marked turn for the better. The sales of the single were strong, and it was the start of a great period for us. For me, it was a relief to know that we weren't just one-hit-wonders, and I finally started to settle into the idea of being in a band long-term. Eventually, the record company found us some nice little flats in Princess Park Manor, a complex in Friern Barnet. Nadine and I were close so we decided to share, as did Cheryl and Nicola. Sarah was happier going solo, so she got a flat to herself. We were still working all the hours God sent, but having somewhere I could call home made a huge difference to me, and it was great finally to have a place where Pembo could come and stay whenever we had some time off together.

Promotion schedules in those days were insane and jam-packed. It got to the stage when the people carrier we drove around in became like a second home. I really enjoyed the long drives to gigs and TV shows up and down the country, and I think that was where the special camaraderie between the five of us began to develop. There was always hilarious banter, as you can imagine, and I loved whizzing around London or up and down the motorway, putting the world to rights with the rest of the girls. I could always talk for England, and Cheryl wasn't far behind, but the girls laughed at my ability to talk about and analyse the same subject in fifty different ways, to the point when no one ever wanted to hear me speak about it again. If I was going through any sort of drama, I would talk the whole thing through with each of them in turn, and once I'd exhausted them I would get on the phone to Sally and go over it all again with her. By the time I got to phoning my mum with the same issue, the girls had usually lost the will to live. I can't help it! I like to get right to the heart of a problem and I can't rest until I find a solution. Whatever was going on in anyone's life was everyone's business, and there were no holds barred. As time went on, we had more privacy because we didn't live together and often got separate cars, but in those early days, nothing could happen to any of us without the rest of us knowing every last detail.

There was never any shortage of strong opinions, either. In fact, right at the beginning I remember thinking, Kimberley, you're going to have to speak your mind and stand your ground if you're going to survive in this band. A soft nature just isn't gonna cut it. An incident early on brought me to that conclusion, when one of the girls snapped at me in front of everyone in a TV studio. It was nothing serious, but she was taking advantage of my nature, knowing that I probably wouldn't snap back. I hated confrontation because it made me anxious, understandably given my upbringing, and I would avoid an argument at all costs. Still, with four outspoken girls surrounding me, especially Cheryl and Nadine, I realised that I was going to have to toughen up to avoid getting pushed around. In the TV studio that time, I remember thinking, Right, that's not going to happen again. My family all noticed the change in me but they didn't see it as a bad thing. I think it was necessary.

As well as finding my feet with the other girls and

settling down in my new home, I realised that I was becoming quite comfortable financially. I don't remember the first time I went to the bank and thought, Oh, that's a lot of money, but it was weird to know that I could suddenly afford to buy the things I needed or even wanted. Having come from a family that always struggled financially, though, I was stuck in a mindset that I had to be careful with money. I was never extravagant for the sake if it, and I always looked out for a bargain. Still, it was quite comforting to know that money was no longer something I had to worry about, and I set about making my surroundings as comfortable as I could.

As soon as we were in the front door of our new pad, Nadine and I got a car to take us to IKEA, and we did a supermarket sweep of everything we needed – rugs, plants, new towels. It was a proper home, and we were like an old married couple straight away, going to the supermarket and cooking decent meals again after living on take-out and hotel room-service meals for so long. I loved looking after Nadine during that time. She was a young girl from Derry, and at sixteen it was quite daunting for her to be away from all her family and friends. I got us a joint bank account and paid all the bills, and I tried to make our home life as smooth as possible for the pair of us. Nadine and I were quite compatible. We both like order and having nice things around us, so the two of us living together was a good fit. However, during the first few weeks in the flat, we both felt a little bit trapped because we never did anything but work. So each night when we got home, we'd open a bottle of wine, put the music on as loud as we could possibly have it, and then dance like maniacs around the living room. It was our own version of domestic bliss.

Whenever Sally and Adam or Alix and Jenny came down to London to see me, Nadine would stick with us wherever we went, and she fast became like family. Then her boyfriend, Neil McCafferty, a professional footballer, came to London to play for Charlton Athletic. Neil was Nadine's childhood sweetheart and a really lovely guy, and he ended up becoming great friends with Pembo, so the four of us hung out together a fair bit whenever Pembo had time to come to London for a visit. For a while, Neil even lived with us, and I felt as though I had a little brother and sister to look after. It was good for me to have that closeness with someone so early on in the band because it helped me to feel grounded, with all the madness going on around me, and having Nadine to take care of helped take my mind off the fact that I was missing my own family, despite all the fun I was having in the band.

Cheryl and Nicola didn't quite have the cosy set up that Nadine and I had. They lived in filth and chaos and I couldn't bear it. My instinct was to go round there with a scrubbing brush and a bottle of bleach to clean the apartment, but they were just kids, so they had no idea how to manage life on their own. Sometimes, when we were all having a night in together, we'd go round to Nicola and Cheryl's place and there would be bin-bags galore in the kitchen and on the balcony, with flies buzzing around them and things literally growing inside them. For the first few months they lived there, it was always freezing cold because they hadn't worked out how to turn the heating on and neither of them bothered to ask anyone – they just turned on the stove. It was my idea of hell.

Sarah, on the other hand, was quite settled. She was dating Mikey Green, one of the boy finalists from *Popstars*, and was already fairly domesticated compared to the rest of us. Mikey stayed at her place most of the time. She'd get in the car some mornings and tell us that she was defrosting a chicken for that night's dinner and what she was going to cook with it. She seemed to have it all together – nothing like the 'Hardcore Harding' we came to know in later years.

After a few weeks, I started to get a little bit of cabin fever. Most of the time we were either at home or in the studio, and I soon decided that there must be more to the life of a pop star than that. That was when we started to venture out on the town – and once we got into the swing of it, there was just no stopping us. I was still with Pembo at the time, but as he didn't live in London, I'd just been coming home from work and watching TV or playing music and going to bed. Suddenly, though, I found myself calling Nicola at 11 o'clock some nights, while I was sitting there in my pyjamas, asking her, 'Do you want to go out? Can you be ready in half an hour?'

Nicola was always up for it. She was my partner in crime, and the two of us could find somewhere to go any night of the week. Of course, we took full advantage of the fact that we were pop stars and could get on the guestlist for almost any club in town. Why not? Ten Rooms was a regular haunt for us in those days, and I remember one night when Jamie Bell from Triple 8 had to carry Nicola out because she'd fallen asleep in the club. Not bad for a Monday night! If I had to be away from my home and family, my friends and my boyfriend, I was going to make the best of it. I was young and I was in a chart-topping girl band. Surely I should be out there enjoying it.

In the end, all five of us became a bit obsessed with going out clubbing, especially at the weekend. We'd be doing a gig at a club somewhere outside London on a Saturday, and as soon as we came off stage we'd jump in the car, yelling at our tour manager to put his foot down and get us back to London as soon as he possibly could. 'We have to get back by midnight to get into Propaganda. Just do the best you can to get us there,' we'd say.

Sometimes we wouldn't get back to London until 1.30 or 2 a.m. if we were gigging up north somewhere, but we'd still manage to go out and catch the last couple of hours at one of our favourite clubs. Propaganda used to finish at about four but then they would start serving breakfast, so we'd stay for that and just carry on partying.

The other exciting thing was seeing ourselves in magazines such as *Smash Hits* and *OK!* So many pop bands were around at that time, including Busted, Blue, Westlife and the Sugababes, all flying high; and there was so much more music on TV – *CD:UK*, *Top of the Pops*, *The Saturday Show* – and we were on all of those shows. Some of my favourite memories from those days are hanging out at the TV studios and socialising with the other bands. We all frequented the same bars and clubs, too, so it was just like one big social scene. It was a brilliant time. We were five good friends who were lucky enough to have been given an amazing life opportunity, and we were living it to the max.

11

Drama Attached

Before we knew it we were doing our first proper gig with a couple of those bands, at the Point Theatre in Dublin, which is now the O2 Arena. It was a charity gig for Childline, and although it was an exciting prospect, we were just not prepared for a live performance on an arena stage. We had one little choreographed routine – the one we did with our microphones for 'Sound of the Underground' – but that was basically it. We had no idea how to work a stage that size or how to speak to the crowd, and unfortunately there didn't seem to be anyone around to show us. We were out of our depth.

When it came to recording our debut album, we

were just as naïve. Like many pop bands of the time, we were teamed with several different producers by the record company, but the one who seemed to be coming up with the best stuff was Brian Higgins, who had written the single. For a time we thought we might be able to contribute to the songwriting ourselves, and I remember some shocking results. Brian wasn't having any of that; he had a very clear idea of how the band should sound and who should be singing what, and he was keen for us to leave the songwriting to the experts.

I loved the process of recording, and I felt very confident in the studio environment. I would have quite happily stayed there day and night, singing away to my heart's content. The trouble was that there still wasn't that much singing going on as far as I was concerned. It was mostly photo shoots and TV shows and radio interviews. There seemed to be lots of hanging about and not knowing what was going on, and the main reason for that was that our manager, Louis Walsh, now seemed to have disappeared off the face of the earth.

Still, we motored on with the recording of our debut album. In those early days we all recorded every bit of the song, so we never knew who was going to be singing what until we heard the final mix. Nadine often seemed to get the lion's share of the lines, and in some ways I understood that because at the time I felt that she was the strongest, most confident singer. The rest of us never made her feel bad or guilty about it. Brian just liked Nadine's voice the best – it was as simple as that.

Obviously, it was disappointing if you had hardly any lines in a particular song, especially after going through the TV competition. We all wanted to show off our best qualities and be a part of the group, so I always felt terrible when one of the girls didn't have any lines in the finished song, despite spending hours singing her heart out. Even if it wasn't me, I felt bad. But the producer makes the call, and we just had to put up with his decision and trust his judgement. Luckily, we were all loving the sound of the finished songs that we were hearing, so we were at least confident that the album was going to be great, whoever was singing on it. A distinct sound was developing, and by now Polydor seemed to have in mind a clear direction for us in the way of marketing, look and attitude.

The atmosphere down at Brian Higgins' studio, Xenomania, was intense to say the least, as was Brian himself. For instance, he instigated a fitness boot camp at the studio because he thought we were all getting a bit chubby. It wasn't surprising we were putting on a few pounds, to be honest, because whenever we weren't singing, we were just slumped on couches, eating pizza. The prospect of exercising while recording was novel, but Brian insisted that looking great was just as important as sounding great when you're in a girl band. I was always very comfortable with the way I looked, right from the start of Girls Aloud. Yes, I'd had a few weight issues when I was younger, but by the time I was in the band I was pretty happy in my own skin. I knew I was a bit curvier than some of the other girls, but that's just the way I'm built. It wasn't a big deal.

At Xenomania, we worked with Brian and Miranda Cooper, who is a genius with melodies and lyrics. Miranda co-wrote many of our greatest hits. You really had to be on the ball when you were recording because Brian would not be happy if you hadn't learned your parts. And God help you if you tried to change a melody or put your own spin on something because that didn't go down too well, either. I remember one time, in the early days, we arrived at the studio, which was in a large but very quaint cottage in Westerham in Kent, and Brian gave us all a handful of random parts of songs to sing that were completely disjointed. They weren't the sort of thing that we thought we would be singing at all, and so we were a bit confused. Some of them sounded like country songs and some were pure hard dance, and the lyrics seemed to be all over the place. In the end, we nominated someone to tell Brian that we didn't like what we were doing. The message was, 'We don't like this one, or this one, and we don't get this one, either.' We did it as a group, but I think Cheryl did most of the talking, backed up by me. Needless to say, we regretted it very soon after.

'Excuse me?' Brian roared. 'Nobody tells me what they should and shouldn't be recording.'

We were all stunned.

'This is absolutely disrespectful and disgusting,' he went on. 'Who the hell do you think you are to question *my* judgement?'

He literally unleashed a tirade on all five of us, as if we were naughty schoolgirls, and collectively we thought, Oh sh*t! We've properly messed up here, girls! The next thing we knew we had someone from Polydor on the phone demanding to know what the hell was going on.

'What have you done to upset Brian like that? He's fuming. What's going on down there?'

It was all so over-the-top, and we couldn't quite grasp why us having an opinion was such a big deal. After ten years of recording with Brian, we've come to understand how he works, and we now know that with a Xenomania song, you never know what it's going to sound like until it's completely finished. We might sing something over one piece of music, but those vocals might end up going across something that sounds completely different. Brian was interested in the melodies and what our voices brought to those melodies. It was a strange way to work, but it's ended up achieving some pretty spectacular results over the years. Still, that day we learned that Brian Higgins could be quite an intimidating character, and it was probably best never to question him.

Despite the massive hiccup that day, we soon realised, as did Polydor, that the tracks we were recording at Xenomania were so much better than anything else we were doing with other producers. Brian created a unique pop sound for us, and it was mostly due to the bizarre way that he had of putting songs together. Sometimes we would spend hours recording a whole heap of ideas, looking for that one special line or hook, and suddenly one of us would sing something and Brian would say, 'OK, that's it. Let's pursue that idea.' Of course, this meant that a huge amount of material never saw the light of day, but the stuff that did reach fruition was of a very high standard. Consequently, we ended up working exclusively with Brian for the entire duration of the band.

In that first year, we travelled around doing a lot of gigs at universities, radio roadshows and nightclubs. They'd usually be booked and organised between Peter and Poppy at Polydor and our tour manager, who would be the one to sort out all the necessary equipment and transport. Our first gig at the famous gay nightspot G-A-Y was particularly special because it was the first time we were able to put on a bit of a show. We hired American telephone booths and performed a cover of Blondie's 'Hanging on the Telephone' dressed as schoolgirls. The next day one of the Sunday papers singled me out as 'the fat one' in Girls Aloud. Surprisingly, it didn't really bother me at the time, but I sometimes thank God that Twitter and Facebook weren't around in those early days of the band. We'd probably have been crucified! Nicola, in particular, got a lot of negative comments in some of the press about the way she looked in those days. We tried to hide it from her as much as we could, but it would have been awful if that kind of rubbish was being blogged and tweeted all over the Internet every five minutes.

That was the first of many shows we did at G-A-Y, and I remember one in particular when the mostly male audience really got their money's worth. The five of us were in giant beds for the start of one song, wearing tiny little bra tops and not that much on the bottom either. When we emerged, ripping back the bedclothes, we revealed five male dancers between our legs. We were always quite cheeky with our performances and tried never to take them too seriously. On another occasion, at the club's New Year's Eve celebrations, we went on as Christmas fairies, pissed out of our heads. We were so drunk we couldn't even do the dance routines properly – it was a mess. Still, we wanted to have fun bringing in the new year together, and Alix, Jenny and Sally were cheering us on from the wings, ready to party on into the night.

On the whole, the roadshows and the club gigs were a good laugh, but we weren't quite as fond of the university gigs we did back then. They were often very rowdy and not always friendly, either. We had all sorts thrown at us – plastic cups full of beer, small change. Sometimes we'd drive miles to do one of these shows, doing our hair and make-up in the car because we didn't want to go into the building until we absolutely had to. Plus the dressing rooms were usually pretty disgusting. Eventually, we started to do our soundchecks from the safety of the car. The tour manager would bring our radio mics out to us, and we'd sing into them to make sure they were working without even setting foot in the building, let alone on stage. When it came to the gig, we'd jump out of the car, run on stage, perform two or three songs, and then run back to the car and drive three hours to get home again as fast as we could. We weren't experienced performers, and we didn't know how to handle a difficult crowd, but one night Cheryl had a bloody good try.

We were performing at a uni gig when some idiot decided to throw coins at us. The crowd were quite lairy and drunk as it was, but seeing money hurtling through the air towards you at speed just wasn't funny.

'Oh sh*t, this isn't good,' I said to the girls. 'Are we just supposed to stand here being pelted with money throughout the entire performance?'

At the end of the next song, Cheryl picked up one of the coins and got on the microphone.

'Which wise guy threw this?' she yelled, holding it up, angrily. 'Yous could have had one of our eyes out wi' that! It's really dangerous and really stupid.'

The whole crowd went quiet, and I fully expected them to start throwing even more stuff at us.

'Right!' Cheryl said, and we carried on with the show – and no more coins came at us.

The other problem about doing these gigs was that we had no guidance from Louis whatsoever. Nobody organised hair and make-up, costumes, styling or anything like that, so consequently we looked absolutely horrendous most of the time. It was shocking, really. Press and media people were always at the radio roadshows, some of them quite high profile, and there we were, this fabulous new girl group with two top-three singles under our belt, turning up in T-shirts, jeans and trainers, or whatever we happened to be wearing. Sometimes we'd step out on stage looking like a complete hotchpotch of uncoordinated horror. We were so naïve about everything then; we simply didn't know any better.

As time went on the management issue got worse and worse. Louis was still nowhere to be seen, and he wouldn't even take our phone calls. After the death of John McMahon, we'd been assigned a new guy, Paul Higgins, and luckily he was very organised. He would tell me where we had to be the next day and I would pass the information on to the rest of the girls. There were no diaries, no schedules and no management office for us to call if we had any problems or issues with anything. The only people we had to turn to were Poppy Stanton and Peter Loraine at the label, and although it wasn't Peter's job to manage us, that was often what he ended up doing. Louis did nothing apart from take his commission on everything we earned. We tried to get Nadine to contact Louis, as she was the closest to him, but that didn't work. After that, I took it upon my shoulders, because I was getting pissed off by that point.

'This is ridiculous,' I said to the girls. 'He doesn't answer his phone; he doesn't manage one single aspect of our career. We need to sort this out.'

I did my best to get through to him, but I didn't have any luck, either. So I went to Peter Loraine again in desperation.

'We can't do this on our own any more,' I told Peter. 'We don't even know what's going on from day to day half the time.'

Poor Peter. We were all so young and inexperienced. Nicola and Cheryl would ring him up to sort out their gas bills; either that or Nicola would be calling Poppy to tell her that she needed a load of dry cleaning done. No one seemed to know what they were doing or what was happening next.

Paul Higgins had taken on the job of tour manager with no idea of what he was letting himself in for. Instead of coordinating our daily appointments and driving us where we needed to go, he was practically babysitting five girls – dragging us up out of bed in the mornings, running around after us and making sure we had everything that we needed the whole time. One night Nadine stayed over at her boyfriend's house, so she wasn't at the flat when Paul came to collect us. That was the straw that broke the camel's back. He just couldn't cope any more, and after a big row with Nadine he quit. After Paul left we had Greg, but the same thing happened. He couldn't handle the disorganisation either, so he threw in the towel as well. That was when Drew Lyall took up the challenge.

Drew was our tour manager throughout most of our career, and like most people who worked with us and for us, he always went above and beyond the call of duty. He became like 'one of the girls' and would happily collect our laundry if we asked him to, or pop to the shops if we needed something. Nothing was a problem, and he really looked after us. I have to say that I wasn't always comfortable with the situation, though. I try to be very organised myself and I don't like the idea of someone else doing everything for me. For one, it's not real life, and secondly, I feel as though it takes my independence away. Justin often says that I'm too independent, and I sometimes wonder whether or not I'm a bit of a control freak. Whatever it is, I've always preferred to look after myself as much as possible, so having Drew running around after me wasn't something I wanted to come to rely on. The rest of the girls, however, loved having Drew at their beck and call, and they made the most of it. I mean, the number of Starbucks runs that man did in his time with us defies belief. He should have shares in the company. So many times he would be driving us through London when someone would spot a McDonald's in the middle of a red no-stopping zone. Drew would just pull over and leave the car, hoping to God that he didn't get clamped or get a ticket, run in and do a massive food order for all five of us.

The whole thing was chaos due to our lack of management, and we hadn't got a clue what to do about it. Louis Walsh recently said in the press that he didn't enjoy working with us and that we hated him. He said that we never got on and we were all obsessed with who was the skinniest and going out with footballers. That would be almost funny if it wasn't such an embarrassing lie. The man knew nothing about us because he was never there. I remember him randomly turning up at the studio when we were doing the video shoot for 'Love Machine' the following year, and everyone was quite shocked to see him there. We later found out that during the short time he was at the shoot, he'd approached someone from Polydor in a bit of a flap.

'Quick, quick, tell me,' he said. 'What's the ginger one's name again?'

Such was the level of his involvement. Eventually at the shoot, he came over and spoke to us for the briefest moment.

'Oh! None of you are fat any more!' he said – I'm pretty sure that was directed at me – and that was that.

In May 2003, the *Sound of the Underground* album went to number two in the charts, and in August of that year we released our third single, 'Life Got Cold', which went into the top three. Despite this success, our future at Polydor Records was hanging in the balance by that stage, and from what Peter was telling us, we were on the cusp of being dropped from the label altogether. I think some people within Polydor thought that Cheryl's upcoming trial for assault was going to damage the band, but the reality was that sales of pop records were down generally. The public suddenly seemed to be craving either dance music or guitar bands, and quite a few pop acts fell by the wayside during that period. Our first album had done OK, but it hadn't sold anywhere near the number that Hear'Say's album had sold after the first *Popstars* competition. Yes, we'd had a couple of hits, but we weren't exactly the Spice Girls, despite all the exposure. Polydor were worried and we knew it. It was quite a scary time.

Out of the blue, in August of 2003, director Richard Curtis phoned David Joseph – who was one of the managing directors of Polydor – to ask if we would like to record a cover of the Pointer Sisters song 'Jump' for the movie *Love Actually*, and before we knew it, it was all agreed. However, Peter Loraine wasn't all that keen on us recording an old disco song that soon in our career. He didn't think that was what Girls Aloud were about, and neither did we. Peter went in to bat for us, and ended up rowing with David Joseph about it, but David laid it on the line.

'You don't get it, do you?' he said. 'If this doesn't work, it's over for them.'

In the end, we had to get our heads around the fact that having our next single in a movie that was bound to be a worldwide hit wasn't such a bad thing – whatever it was.

The night before we shot the video for 'Jump', I broke up with Pembo. We'd found it really difficult, trying to make our relationship work long-distance, and the previous few weeks had just been one long, sad phone call after another, with both of us desperate to find a solution to the problem. The trouble was that we hardly saw one another any more, and it felt like we were both living the lives of single people, even though we were meant to be a couple. The way things were, neither of us was having a good time and something had to give. Looking back at those last few weeks of tearful phone conversations, I think we were already grieving for what we were about to lose. I knew it was coming to an end, and I think he did, too. I'd been tormenting myself about the whole situation for ages. Was it just because I'd moved away? Had I fallen out of love? I really didn't know, but I knew that it had to come to an end. Still, I don't know why I chose the night before a major video shoot to say goodbye to Pembo, but I guess sometimes that's just the way life happens.

I was at home on my own and we were talking on the phone as usual. 'This just isn't going to work,' I told him. 'I can't do it any more.' I felt sad, as if I'd failed in some way to keep it going. He knew I was right and I knew he felt the same, but that didn't make it any easier. By the end of that phone call it was over between us and I just felt hollow inside. As if something precious I'd held on to for a long time had suddenly been snatched away from me. It was such an awful, gut-wrenching feeling and I'll never forget it.

I didn't sleep a wink that night, and on the way to the video shoot in the morning I was on the brink. When I got into hair and make-up at 5 a.m., my eyes looked like two piss-holes in the snow where I'd been crying so much. Caroline Barnes in make-up had to do some of her best work just to make me look human again. After she'd finished, I still felt incredibly emotional, and within ten minutes I'd cried all the make-up off again. Then I had it redone and cried it all off for a second time. The rest of the girls were quite shocked to see me in such a state, because I hardly ever got emotional in front of them, but that day I was beside myself. The worst part about it was that 'Jump' is such a cheesy, happy and up-tempo number, and the video called for us to be jumping and running around what was supposed to be 10 Downing Street, and it was cut together with clips from the movie. Needless to say, I wasn't really in the mood for that, but the girls all knew what was going on, and they did their best to get me through the day – they were brilliant. I suppose it would be the same with any job. Sh*t happens and you have to do your best to get through it. If a record company has spent fifty grand organising a video shoot, it has to happen and it has to be good. It was a truly awful day for me. I knew I'd done the right thing, but I wouldn't want to have to go through that again.

I'm not sure what I would have done without the girls while I was going through the break-up with Pembo. My sisters and my brother hadn't moved down to London but I felt like I really needed them. Martin Pemberton had been such a big part of my life. My family loved him; my bandmates all loved him. It felt as though he was breaking up with everyone, not just me. I think that was when I realised that Sarah, Nicola, Nadine and Cheryl were true friends and not just four girls I worked with. They knew I was suffering and they were there for me. We were all there for one another through every relationship drama or break-up, not only because we wanted to be but also because we had to be. We were working together every single day, and when one of us went down, the rest of us had to pick up the reins and forge ahead. We had to hold it together for the girl who was hurting, and give her the space and time to heal while we all kept going. When you think about five young women over ten years, it amounts to a hell of a lot of broken hearts. And we went through every one together.

On the night of the premiere of *Love Actually*, Cheryl and I were late because we'd been at *The Frank Skinner Show*, recording an interview about Cheryl's recent assault trial. The whole trial period had been really strange for the rest of us, because although we'd wanted to go to court and support Cheryl, we'd been advised not to in case the whole thing erupted into even more of a media frenzy than it already was. Work stopped while the trial was going on, and I really felt for Cheryl all the way through it. She was this young girl who'd been caught up in something that was very serious, and potentially very damaging. She was found guilty of assault, but not guilty of racially aggravated assault. It had been a scary couple of weeks, but it was finally over and we were all very relieved. That's one of the reasons why Cheryl and I did the interview on Frank Skinner's show that night – to draw a line in the sand and move on.

By the time we rushed from the interview to the *Love Actually* premiere, we were so late that our press officer, Sundraj, was in a complete flap. Everyone else had gone in and the film was about to begin. We practically had to tear down the red carpet, with Sundraj hustling us inside like mad. What we didn't know was that the entire cinema audience were inside watching our frenzied late arrival on the big screen. It was very embarrassing, because they were all killing themselves laughing when we finally appeared in the theatre. Meanwhile, Nicola had somehow managed to cut her toe in the toilets and was busy bleeding all over the place. She'd walked down the red carpet looking fabulous, then ended up leaving the cinema with a massive bandage on her foot. I don't think we ever went anywhere without some kind of drama attached.

Still, we were all dead excited to hear our song in the movie, but when it came to the scene where 'Jump' is played, we heard the original Pointer Sisters version instead of the Girls Aloud track. What the hell was going on? Unfortunately, no one had warned us that our song had ended up as the second song on the tailend of the credits. It sort of defeated the object of doing the record in the first place, and we were all gutted.

My evening didn't get any better at the after-party

at the In & Out Club in Mayfair. I'd been very excited about the prospect of meeting the star of the film, Hugh Grant, but that turned out to be a bit of a disappointment. 'Next time you need help having a hit record, give me a call,' he said, when we all went over to say hi. He seemed to be saying that the success of the song was due to him appearing in the video. He came across as arrogant and we were all a bit deflated.

Eventually, we decided to go somewhere where we could let our hair down and have a bit of fun. Someone suggested a bar but the trouble was that, because we had no one organising anything for us, there were no cabs or cars booked to drive us anywhere.

'Let's just walk,' I suggested, not realising that the bar was quite some way away.

So off we trotted – all five of Girls Aloud in tiny little 'red carpet' dresses and killer heels, plus Nicola with her bandaged and bloody foot . . . in the middle of November.

The following week, 'Jump' shot to number two in both the UK and Irish charts, and was eventually certified silver. It turned out to be more than just a number-one record for us, though, because its success meant that we were no longer in danger of being dropped by Polydor. We'd turned things around, which was a massive relief to all of us. We were also able finally to put the nightmare of Cheryl's arrest and trial behind us and move forward into the future. Although I was still quietly nursing a broken heart, things suddenly seemed a hell of a lot brighter. It felt as though we were back on top.

12

Turning into Tigers

One of the hardest things to cope with in the beginning was being detached from my family, knowing that they were all together and I wasn't part of their day-to-day lives. One day I was in the car, en route to work somewhere, when my mum called me and told me that she had a large cyst on her ovaries, and she didn't yet know if it was cancerous or not. The fear and shock that engulfed me when I realised the potential of what she was saying was horrific, and the fact that I hadn't seen her for a while made it much worse. It turned out not to be cancer, but she did have to have a hysterectomy, so she was in hospital a lot and quite unwell. It was hard, not being there with her through all that, because those are the times when a family needs to come together. It was one of those moments that really smack you back to reality, and it brought home to me how disconnected you can become if you don't take care. I knew my life was never going to feel right without my family in it, so whatever happened to me in Girls Aloud, I just had to make sure that they remained a part of it.

In the summer of 2004 we were busy recording our second album *What Will the Neighbours Say?* The first single from the album, 'The Show', had received fantastic reviews in the music press and reached number two in the charts, but as a band we all still felt as though we were a bit of a joke. Everything we did was a shambles, and as far as we were concerned, it was like amateur hour whenever we performed a show or appeared on TV, which I found really difficult. I wanted us to be the very best we could be. So many times we'd turn up to record some major TV show, only to find that we didn't have the right backing track, or if we did have the right track, it would be a different edit from the one we'd rehearsed to, or the wrong mix completely. It was so embarrassing to hear a track start while you were ready on stage, only to realise with a sinking feeling that you were going to have to stop the whole thing and apologise – 'Sorry, this isn't the right one.' We felt like fools. There was nobody overseeing anything, and we were constantly left with egg on our faces with no one to help us sort it out. To be honest, I think people must have thought we were a bunch of jokers rather than the professional outfit we were striving to be. Eventually, the other girls would get me to listen through the backing track with Drew before every TV performance, just to make sure it was right. Then if it wasn't right, I was the one who called up the record label and yelled at poor Poppy down the phone.

By this time, quite a lot of the decision-making and general running of the band had started to fall on my shoulders. It was in my nature to take it on, plus the other girls saw me as the most sensible and business-like of the five of us, so they looked to me for guidance. I'm not saying I always knew what I was doing, but somebody had to deal with the accountants and lawyers and the people at the label. I tend to like harmony and order in my life as much as possible, so I suppose it was only natural that I would assume that role, but at times it felt quite pressured. After all, it wasn't just me I was responsible for; it was four other people – my friends. It got to the stage where the other girls would rely solely on me to know what the hell was going on.

'What are we doing tomorrow?' one of them would ask.

'OK,' I'd say, 'we're doing this and we're going to need that, and we need to be there at such and such time.'

I wasn't trying to take over, but I was really the only person who could have done it. Cheryl, Nadine and Nicola were so young. They'd only just got used to being away from home and looking after themselves, and although Sarah was completely capable, she wasn't the most organised girl on the planet or the best time-keeper. It had to be me.

The trouble was it was hard for me as a bandmate to keep some of the girls in line when I needed to. 'We can't keep turning up late for things,' I'd say to them. 'It looks really bad.' In the end, if we had to be somewhere for 9 a.m., I'd tell them we had to be there for 8 a.m., just to get them up a bit earlier. We'd still end up being late, just not *as* late.

I was also aware that we weren't really earning enough money. I'd seen other pop stars getting endorsement deals to advertise various products, so I thought that might be something that Girls Aloud could do. I set up some meetings at my flat with some agents, but all that sort of stuff is quite tricky when you don't really know what you're doing, so it didn't come to much. At the end of the day, I just wanted to enjoy being part of a girl band, without the pressure of running it. I was still trying to be a young girl, living as normal a life as possible – we all were. It started to wear me down after a while and I wasn't sure how long I could keep it up. I loved being in the band more than anything in the world, but it just didn't seem right for us to be dealing with all the day-to-day stresses on our own.

We knew that we had to get new management, or should I say *some* management, but Louis wasn't going to walk away easily. This was somewhat of a surprise, given his lack of any communication with us, or interest in us, and even Louis himself couldn't argue the fact that he wasn't doing a single thing on our behalf. The problem for us was that even if we did get rid of him, he would still insist that we pay him commission.

Eventually, I initiated a meeting with our lawyer, Richard Bray, to see what we could do about getting shot of Louis, and to find out if there was any way we could sue him for breach of contract. After all, we'd had no choice but to sign the contract with him at the end of *Popstars*, and even if we'd had a choice, none of us knew any different back then anyway. Surely Louis couldn't possibly be holding up his side of the contract, which was to represent us to the best of his ability. I waltzed into Richard's office with my little notebooks full of all the reasons why Louis had no right to his management commission, but I was out of my depth. Louis basically told us that if we tried to sue him, he would take us to the cleaners. He said that we didn't have enough money to take him on, and he was right. We didn't have the kind of money needed for a long legal wrangle. We were caught between a rock and a hard place. We couldn't take on a new manager because we had to keep paying Louis, and if we kept him on, he'd just continue to do nothing for us. It was a nightmare, but it did mean that we learned a lot of valuable lessons very early on.

It was a strange world to be living in – intense and pressurised – and the fact that at the same time we were growing from girls into women made it even tougher. I think that's why we all became so close, because we needed one another to get through it all. We had to grow up fast, and we had to do it together. We also had to protect one another as much as we could, especially Nicola and Nadine, who were so young when we first started. Most days we were literally together from the moment we woke up in the morning until the moment we went to bed. We were in TV studios, we were in hotel rooms, and we were in a car together for hours at a time almost every day. We were breathing one another's air the whole time, and that's all there was.

By that time, we'd moved into our own rented flats

in Princess Park Manor, but we were all still in close proximity – Nadine lived directly below me – and were hanging out together most of the time, although Sarah was sometimes slightly detached from the rest of us, through her own choice. Sarah's always had a very strong identity of her own, and for that reason she was a bit of a loner when it came to life outside the band. If someone suggested that all five of us hit the town for a night out, Sarah would be the one who'd decide not to go. Then when we all fancied a night in, Sarah would be up for a party. That was just the way she was. I don't think she's ever been one to follow the crowd, or worry about missing out on something.

That being said, we *all* loved going out on the town. It was a fantastic way to shake off all the pressures of work and let our hair down together. The clubs that we loved most back then were Propaganda, Trap and Pop, because so many of the other bands that were around at the time would hang out at those places, too. As soon as we walked into Trap, the manager would hand us a bottle of bubblegum shot to get us in the mood, and we'd be off. We'd quite often bump into Westlife while we were out. They were proper Irish party boys, and they loved a drink. We did, too. One night Cheryl actually got turned away from the door at Pop because she was too pissed. No matter how much she objected, the doorman just refused to let her in. Busted and Blue would be in the clubs, too, all hanging out together. It was a fun scene and it's just not the same these days – there's nowhere like that now.

What was so great about those days was that there was nothing like Twitter or Instagram, and not too many high-tech phones with cameras. That meant that you could indulge in a private, fun night out without people secretly snapping you, or writing posts about what you were up to. I loved those nights, glamming up and going out, and sometimes we'd even compromise what we looked like for a TV performance, designing our hair and make-up to match the outfit we were going out clubbing in later, rather than the one we were wearing in front of the cameras.

'Don't do my hair like that, Lisa,' Cheryl would say. 'I don't care whether it goes with this dress; I want something that's going to match what I'm wearing to the club. And green eye shadow, please . . .'

A couple of times one or another of us went straight from a club to a morning TV studio, still drunk. It might seem irresponsible, but we were learning the ropes. We were often on a live TV show early on a Saturday or Sunday morning, so having an hour's sleep – or no sleep – was the only way we could have a normal life outside of work sometimes.

Nicola used to go up to Liverpool even when she had just one night off, so she could go out partying with her friends. Like all of us, she really missed her friends and family back home, and being so young that really got to her. I felt much the same, but I would usually persuade my brother and sisters to come to London to go out clubbing with me and the rest of the girls. Then, if we had a TV show to do, they would hang out with me at the TV studio as well. It was very important to me to have my family with me as much as possible throughout the madness of those early years. It kind of kept me sane. I also surrounded myself with the same friends I'd had since I was a kid, so Alix and Jenny were often around. I loved and needed that. More than anything, while I was going through the unusual and extreme experience of being in a famous pop band, staying firmly connected to my life before the band gave me the normality and consistency I needed.

Meanwhile, the recording of the album was going really well, and with Brian Higgins producing the entire record, we really started to find what would become 'our sound'. We began to realise that we could pretty much do any kind of song we wanted as long as it sounded new and fresh and had that increasingly unmistakable Girls Aloud vibe about it. The campaign around our second album was geared towards defining our individual personalities, especially with the video for 'The Show', which had us all working as different characters in a beauty parlour full of gorgeous male clients. We got to perform that song on the Royal Variety Show in December 2004. Everything seemed to be falling nicely into place until we heard one particular song that was tipped as a potential single, 'Love Machine'. We hated it! It didn't even sound like a pop song to us when we first recorded it; it was more like something a guitar band would do. And as for the lyrics – 'Gift wrapped kitty cats, turning into tigers . . .' What the hell was that about? We just couldn't get our heads around it, and even when it was finished, we all had a bad feeling about it.

Colin Barlow, who was the managing director of Polydor, loved the song, and he decided that it was going to be our next single. We were appalled, and we told him loud and long. I must admit, Colin did listen to our objections, but he decided that 'Love Machine' was a hit and that was that. We just had to take it on the chin and hope to God he was right. And sure enough, once we did the choreography and shot the video, it finally started to make sense to us. 'Love Machine' eventually became one of our favourite singles, and when we perform it live, it's always one of the most popular moments at a Girls Aloud show.

I guess that experience was a double-edged lesson for us as a band. We learned that we couldn't be right all the time, and also that it isn't always just about the song but sometimes the whole package surrounding it – the video, the choreography, the marketing. It was the right song at the right time for us. 'Love Machine' took Girls Aloud to a whole new level of success.

13

New Man, New Manager

I'd known Justin Scott ever since we signed to Polydor
Records. He was in an all-male pop-R&B band called
Triple 8, who were also signed to the label, and who
were launched around the same time as we were. He
caught my eye straight away, but at the time I was still
with Pembo, so I just thought of Justin as a friend and
label-mate. Girls Aloud and Triple 8 worked with a lot
of the same people – hair and make-up artists, stylists,
radio and TV promoters – so our working lives were
very much intertwined, and after a while we started
hanging out and socialising with them quite a bit.
We'd go to the same clubs, and did several promo trips
abroad together. After I broke up with Pembo, one

stylist, Chloe, introduced me to Justin properly, at Propaganda. She knew that we quite liked one another, so she was doing her best to match-make. There was a definite spark between us straight away, but at the time I didn't feel that I was in the right frame of mind for romance. In fact, it was so soon after the break-up that I felt I would be betraying Pembo somehow – it made me feel uneasy. That was another time the girls were there for me, because as much as they'd loved Pembo, they also wanted me to be happy. They could see what a good guy Justin was and they could see that he brought out a new light in me, a fun side. They all told me that if I liked him, I had to embrace it and go with it. I had to move on.

The more we hung out with the Triple 8 boys, the more I realised there was a strong connection and a growing attraction between Justin and me. He later admitted to me that he'd had a thing for me from the minute he saw me on *Popstars*, and that once Girls Aloud were signed to the label, the Triple 8 lads would always try to find out which club we were going to be at, just so they could come and hang out with us. He was a quiet character, someone who sat back and took everything in. He wasn't bothered about being the centre of attention, and I liked that. I've always preferred a guy who has quiet confidence, rather than someone who's in your face the whole time. If he was trying to be aloof, it certainly worked on me. We chatted for a while and one of the first things I discovered was that he had a little girl of about four. I suppose he seemed quite young to have a child, but he was obviously proud of her and wanted to let me know about her as soon as possible. It didn't bother me in the least, so we ended up chatting away for ages that night, exchanging phone numbers before we went our separate ways.

After that we were texting one another several times every day and this progressed to spending most evenings on the phone, talking for hours. Justin is from Bristol. He is very different from me and had a completely different upbringing. He comes from the perfect 2.4 family. His mum is Irish, his dad Jamaican, and they have always had a fantastic relationship, and he has an older sister, Helene. Although financially Justin's family was no better off than ours, his childhood was carefree in comparison to mine. Justin can't ever remember his mum and dad arguing in front of him. Somehow, though, we'd both ended up doing the same thing in the same place, and he just seemed to 'get' me in a way no other man had before. Some nights we would be on the phone till three or four in the morning, and on a couple of occasions I had to be up to do a morning TV show. It was mad, but I just loved talking to him so much that I never wanted the call to end. It was also much easier for us to talk on the phone because we were a bit nervous about being seen in public together at that stage. We were both in pop bands on the same label and we didn't really want any media speculation about our relationship before we even knew what it was ourselves. It was far too early for all that. Looking back, I think the fact that Justin and I always kept our relationship really private has worked in our favour. The press has never been that intrusive, and I'm thankful for that, especially after seeing what Cheryl went through. I'm not sure I would have been able to handle that kind of scrutiny about my private life.

By the time Justin and I went on our first proper dinner date we were already quite emotionally connected after all the texts and late-night telephone calls, and I felt like I knew him quite well. It's weird, really, because he never even officially asked me out; it was just a slow-burning thing that happened naturally, and it felt right. After that first date he started coming over to my flat, and I would go over to the house in Chiswick where he lived with the rest of the Triple 8 boys and hang out there. I didn't drive so I spent a fortune on taxis back and forth.

I was comfortable around him and I loved the fact that he was always so positive and funny. He made me laugh a lot, and he brought out the fun side of me a bit more. Up until I met Justin I think I was always a bit too serious or 'old before my time', and somehow he managed to break through that and unleash the more carefree girl that was hidden in there somewhere. We'd go out together to nightclubs and have the most brilliant night – just the two of us – dancing with one another or in a crowd of people. He was an amazing dancer, and to be honest, I think that might have been one of the things to seal the deal.

I've been trying to think of a romantic story from around that time, but Justin wasn't the most outwardly romantic boy I'd ever met. Still, he did have his own version of what romance should be, and that was good enough for me. I remember around the time of the 'Love Machine' video I was trying to lose a few pounds, so I was doing the Atkins diet. On the nights when I went round to Justin's for dinner, the most romantic it would get would be Justin thoughtfully buying in all the correct Atkins food for our evening. There'd be cheese dip and chicken dippers – he'd research it all thoroughly. He wasn't always one for roses or chocolates, but that sort of sums up what Justin is like – caring and incredibly thoughtful. He did surprise me with some flowers on the anniversary of our first meeting, which I hadn't even remembered, so he can pull it out of the bag when he wants to.

The love between us was something that just blossomed. Neither of us had to work at it too much, and we were both really happy for a while. Then suddenly Justin broke the news that Triple 8 were being dropped from Polydor. It was a bombshell because they'd had a couple of top-ten singles, but they became another casualty of pop music's decline at that time. I don't think Justin really wanted to open up to me about how he was feeling. I think he'd known about the band being dropped for some time before he told me, because I virtually had to force the information out of him. I knew he was gutted, though, as were all the Triple 8 boys. After all, Justin had his little girl and all the responsibilities that went with that. It made me realise just how fickle the music industry could be and that, at the end of the day, nobody was really safe. Justin and the band had worked so hard to get a record deal, and then, having got one, they'd been quite successful. They were bloody talented, too, with all the right components for success, but it wasn't to be. I was devastated for him. The rug had been pulled out from under him, and all I could do was be there for him as much as possible. He never showed it, but it must have been hard for him to watch my pop career taking off after that. To me, it seemed so unjust.

Following the success of 'The Show' and 'Love

Machine', Girls Aloud seemed to go from strength to strength. Then one day Colin Barlow announced to us that we were going to be recording that year's Children in Need single, which was 'I'll Stand By You'. We had to travel to every single BBC radio station up and down the country, and by the end of it we were dropping like flies we were so tired.

On the day before the actual Children in Need broadcast, we were like five zombies and fit for nothing, but our TV promoter, Rachel Cook, suddenly announced that we had to go and do *BBC Breakfast* at stupid o'clock the next morning. Up until that point, we'd never said no to anything, but on that occasion we all refused to do it, and had a massive row with Rachel about it. It was a horrible situation, because we all got on well with Rachel, and she was only doing her job. Still, we didn't feel that it was fair to push us like that. Nicola and Sarah were ill, and Nadine, Cheryl and I had already had to do several TV appearances without them, singing the song a cappella.

'We need to rest so we can do the show properly tomorrow night,' I told Rachel. 'We're half dead!'

It wasn't just the early TV appearance itself we had to consider. Getting five girls in and out of hair and make-up and ready for 7 a.m. would surely mean a 4 a.m. start the next morning. The BBC weren't happy, though, and later that afternoon the head of the BBC called David Joseph to say, 'They won't come tomorrow, it's not on!'

Everyone assumed we were just being awkward, but that wasn't the case at all. Peter Loraine ended up getting screamed at by his boss, and poor Rachel ended up in tears because we were giving her such a hard time. Eventually, Peter called me to explain why it was so important for us to do the programme, and then I was expected to relay that to the girls. It was always me the label phoned when the girls needed talking round about a certain point, or something needed organising, because they thought I was the 'sensible one'. Peter told me that we could say 'yes' to fifty things, and the one time we said 'no' to something would be the only thing people in the industry would remember. I knew he was right, and I knew that I was going to have to talk the girls into doing it. Our compromise was that we did our own hair and make-up that morning, and although we ended up looking horrendous, at least we all had an extra hour in bed.

The song eventually became our second number-one single in November 2004, and right after that our second album, *What Will the Neighbours Say?*, was released to a great response from the critics. It was a wonderful time for me, but it had a bittersweet edge. Justin and I had started off in exactly the same place, but now my dreams were flying high, while Justin's had been shot down. He's a proud man, though, and it wasn't in his nature to be down or depressed, and certainly not in front of me. I knew he was struggling with it, but he did it internally and mostly on his own. I have to give him credit for not letting the whole thing bring us down as a couple. Even though he was hurting, he didn't want to spoil my success, and so he held his feelings inside.

For a while Triple 8 tried to carry on and get new management, but I knew his heart wasn't in it, and for a while he wasn't sure what to do with his life. He did try out for a few dancing jobs, which I felt he could have done, but Justin didn't feel like he fitted into that world, and eventually he decided that dancing wasn't for him. Then Sally's husband, Joe, offered him some work in his promotions company, which turned out to be the perfect solution. It gave Justin something to focus on while he decided exactly what he wanted to do next.

In January 2005, Girls Aloud were nominated for best pop act at the Brits, and although we didn't win, we were all chuffed with the nomination. We were still so excited about everything back then, and quite starstruck, too. I remember we spotted some of our favourite stars

Buy girls bye boys – our first press picture together as Girls Aloud.

Me and the girls in Zurich.

The first ever 'CHIM' pic.

Girls Aloud go to work!

A promo shot
for our single,
The Show,
at CD:UK.

Girls Aloud:
'middle-ancient'.

Some daring outfits for the opening of our Greatest Hits tour.

How do I look? A costume fitting for the Long hot Summer video.

Holding back the tears. Our final performance of I'll Stand By You on the Ten tour.

at the awards – Snoop Dogg and Pharrell Williams. God, we psyched ourselves up so much to go over and say hi to Pharrell. When we did, he just said, 'How old are you girls? I'm thirty-two.' And that was it. We were devastated. I guess we were still quite wide-eyed, and we really hadn't been groomed for stardom and acting like celebrities.

We were happy and relieved when Louis Walsh was finally forced to accept the idea of a co-management situation. The last straw for us had come while we were trying to organise our first-ever tour. Louis didn't come to one single meeting, and there was nobody to organise any travel or accommodation for us while we were on the road. Since it was a tour rather than a record promotion, it wasn't really the record company's responsibility, so Peter ended up trying to book it all using his personal credit card. It was then I got a desperate phone call from him.

'Kimberley, I can't do this,' he said. 'It's fifteen grand. What if you don't pay me back? I just can't do it.'

Poppy and Peter were already run ragged trying to do the jobs that a personal management team would normally do, and their bosses at Polydor weren't too impressed. Someone once asked Poppy what was in the envelope she was holding, and it turned out to be Sarah's urine sample that Poppy was having biked to

169

her doctor. On another occasion, everyone at work was looking for Peter while he was out buying a Hoover for Cheryl. It was just getting ridiculous. In the end, Polydor were insistent that we sort out our management situation, and so I had to go and lay it on the line to our lawyer, Richard Bray, again.

By that time, Louis had earned hundreds of thousands of pounds from us for doing absolutely nothing, but our initial five-year agreement was up, so at least we could bring in someone else to look after us properly, if they were willing to settle for half the usual commission – Louis would still be taking half his commission. Peter suggested that we meet his best friend, Hillary Shaw. He knew that we needed somebody who was used to dealing with women, and Hillary had managed Bananarama, Dannii Minogue, and a few other female artists, so he thought that she might be a good manager for us. We did meet a few other potential managers, but as soon as we all turned up at Hillary's house – which was just around the corner from where we lived – we knew she was the right person for the job. We drifted in like five lost souls, and Hillary had put out a lovely spread with nibbles and fancy cakes. She understood all the dramas we'd had, and she understood what we needed as women far more than any of the male tour managers ever had. As I sat talking to her, I felt she was someone who would look after us. It was comforting. The other managers we'd met seemed like serious businessmen, whereas Hillary seemed a bit more nurturing. She was exactly what we needed, and she agreed to share the commission with Louis, even though we were no longer going to have anything to do with him.

I later found out from Hillary that she'd been fuming when she found out that Louis was managing us after *Popstars*. She'd called Peter and shouted down the phone at him. 'What does he know about managing a girl band? I should be managing them!' It turned out she was right.

Hillary told us that we needed to build a brand. She said that we needed to move to the next level and aim to be the biggest and the best. She wanted to change the appearance of the band – the hair, the make-up and the clothes – and she wanted us to be more groomed and stylish, with each one of us having her own individual identity within the group. She found us a stylist, Victoria Adcock, who really put her stamp on the way we presented ourselves. Working with Victoria marked the point where we started to look like a well-turned out, sophisticated group. It was an important step for us, because we wanted to inspire girls as well as entertain them, and we felt as though we needed to be setting trends and pushing forward with our image. Victoria created the chic red and black style that we adopted for the whole 'Biology' campaign, among so many more of our iconic looks over the years.

Hillary's other challenge was to get more money from Polydor to do all this, and she then set about strategising a career that would build and build. She also knew that as young girls we needed nurturing rather than bullying, and that she would be able to handle that better than most of the more business-driven male managers out there at the time.

Hills could have her own TV show, I think. She's upbeat and hilariously funny, even though she doesn't know it some of the time. She loves designer clothes, and is immaculately turned out *all* of the time – and she's a proper princess. Her fans on Twitter call her Dame Hillary. However, in among all that fabulousness, she's very grounded and a very good businesswoman, and it said a lot to me that she was still really good friends with all the artists she'd managed before us. Down the line, Hillary was always there for us when we needed her, and it didn't matter how personal the problem was. We went through certain things over the years that weren't really Hillary's responsibility, but she always came through. Sometimes she was more like a counsellor than a manager. We've had our

Breakfast in Paris – on a promo trip with the girls.

Dirty Girls! Quad biking for CD:UK.

Having fun on the summer roadshows.

professional disagreements over the years, but she's always able to put them to one side and get on with looking after us. She's thick-skinned, and in the job that she's in, you have to be. The whole entertainment industry is made up of contrasting opinions and disagreements. That's what makes it tick. One person says, 'I think it should be like this,' and another says, 'No, it should be more like that.' And out of all that comes something brilliant. Having a manager with whom I was able to have those conversations was so important to me, especially in the early days. We needed someone who could push us forward and have an opinion without discarding our own ideas and creativity. Hillary did exactly that.

Finally, we had a proper management team with an office. As soon as we signed with Hillary's company, Shaw Thing, things started to change for us. A weekly diary was set up for us and someone accompanied us to TV studios and gigs. If Hillary wasn't around, her right-hand woman, Angela O'Connor, would be there. We'd never experienced anything like that before, and it was a breath of fresh air for all of us. We also started getting some endorsement deals, including Sunsilk and Kit-Kat, and most importantly, we had someone to call whenever we needed to. It was quite a personal relationship we had with the team at Shaw Thing, and it worked for us. We were even assigned our own Girls Aloud personal assistant, Lily England, who could help do all the bits and pieces that we didn't have time to do while we were working flat out. Lily was a young girl herself, and she certainly had her work cut out looking out for all five of us at once, but she was a great person to have around and a massive asset to the day-to-day running of the band.

I can hardly express what a relief it was finally to have proper management. I felt as if the hugest weight had been lifted off my shoulders and I was so happy to let someone else take the reins. That first year of having proper management was probably the happiest for me as far as Girls Aloud went. We were flying high, I'd fallen in love again, and at last I could hand over the business of the band to someone I trusted, and just enjoy myself.

14

I Can't Feel My Legs

Hillary and the team at Shaw Thing had come on board just in time to set up our first concert tour, which was the most exciting thing we'd done to that point. We were set to play twenty-two dates in theatre-sized venues across the UK and Ireland, starting in Nottingham on 4 May 2005. And as soon as we got out there in front of that audience, who were there to see just us, we realised that we were a lot better than we'd been giving ourselves credit for. We were a live, performing band, and we were good at it.

Beth Honan, who had choreographed the 'Love Machine' video, arrived for the tour, and she stayed with us as our creative director right through to the end of the band. Beth just understood us in a way that no other choreographer ever had. She focused on style and spectacle, and we all responded to that. The first time we worked with her she'd made us strut around in circles wearing stilettos because she thought none of us could walk in them properly, let alone dance in them.

'We normally prefer to dance in trainers,' we told her, but she wasn't impressed.

'No you don't,' she said. 'They don't look good and you're just gonna have to get with the programme.'

From then on we had to rehearse in our high heels whether we liked it or not.

Beth was a really big part of the group's ultimate success, and just like Hillary and Victoria, she had her own vision for us that made sense completely. It was glamorous and fresh, and it suited us and our style. Before Beth and Victoria came along we'd been performing in baggy jeans and Timberland boots, trying to emulate the cool All Saints look, but that wasn't really a style any of us liked very much. We just hadn't known how to achieve anything else. Beth thought that our songs had a fun, sexy, kitsch element, and she believed that our performances and what we wore should reflect that.

I think we got away with a lot of the sexy stuff we wore over the years because there were five of us, and because we always tried not to take ourselves too seriously and to have fun with it. For us, it was never about 'see how hot we all look'; it was about 'look how much fun we're having, and we hope you're having fun, too'. We never wanted to be overtly sexual or intimidating to other women. We were girls' girls, and it was always very important to us that we projected that.

Beth understood that, which is why she and Girls Aloud were such a good fit. She was from Manchester and had had a similar upbringing to some of us. She wasn't 'showbizzy' at all. Beth was a grafter who was passionate about dance to the point that it was seeping out of her. Often she'd do a whole day's rehearsal, and then go home and dance around her kitchen all night until she'd worked out the next routine. I admired that in her, because it was exactly where I'd come from, and what my childhood dance teacher, Deana Morgan, had instilled in me. We trusted Beth's opinion implicitly, because we knew that her main aim was to make us look fabulous and perform like pros. As far as she was concerned, Girls Aloud wasn't about standing there and singing, it was about creating something visually amazing that complemented our music, and she did that with every show and every TV appearance we ever did. She quickly became one of the family, and we all loved her to bits.

I loved being on tour. I loved sleeping on the tour bus and waking up in a different city every day and I loved hanging with Beth and our dancers. The whole way of life on the road really suited me. I remember that Cheryl and I took the two bunks opposite one another at the end of the bus on the very first night, just so we could gossip once we'd bedded down for the night. We kept that tradition on all the tours after that. We weren't very rock-and-roll as a touring band, however. We were more tea and biscuits in our bunks than sex and drugs.

Still, whenever we travelled anywhere to perform, we always managed to have a lot of fun, especially when we went abroad. At the TMF Awards in Rotterdam in 2005, we won the award for best UK act, but as usual it was hilarious chaos. When we arrived at the Ahoy arena for the camera rehearsal, our costumes hadn't arrived – they'd got lost somewhere en route – so there was this whole big drama about what the hell we were going to do about outfits for the actual show. It was quite a prestigious thing for us to win the award, but when our name was announced at the ceremony, the next thing I heard was someone shouting, 'Sarah's in the toilet!' Such a Girls Aloud moment! Someone had to leg it to the toilet to drag Sarah out as we all descended the stairs towards the stage, looking as calm and unfazed as possible. Eventually, Sarah tore down after us, but it was yet another moment of panic.

On that trip we met the group Destiny's Child. We were huge fans of theirs. Mathew Knowles, Beyoncé's father and manager of the band, seemed to like us, and he invited us to come on tour as a support act with his girls, which, of course, we were well up for. It never happened, though. They didn't want to pay us anything to do it. In fact, we would have had to pay to support them, so that was that dream out of the window.

On another trip to Holland – Amsterdam, this time – some people from the Dutch label thought it might be fun to take a few of us first to the red-light area, followed by one of the city's famous coffee shops to buy some space cakes and a joint or two. Of course, I'd never tried anything like that before, and when we got back to our hotel I was more than a little nervous about trying it. I could see Cheryl and Nicola looking at me, thinking, Is she for real? They knew what a goody-two-shoes I was, a case of Sandra Dee eat your heart out, but that's me. I've never been interested in drugs or even cigarettes. Still, after watching them have a go for a while, I decided that one little puff wasn't going to do me any great harm, so I took hold of the joint and gave it a try. Then, after much coughing and spluttering, I finally worked out how to take it back, but by that time I'd smoked a lot more of it than I probably should have.

I don't remember too much about the next couple of hours, but apparently I started to lose the use of my limbs quite quickly, and suddenly I had no grip on reality whatsoever.

'I can't feel my legs,' I said, in the thickest Yorkshire accent. 'I can't feel my legs.'

'Oh, don't be daft,' some bright spark said, 'you're fine.'

I was surrounded by record company people and all I could think was, I'm gonna spew. I am going to spew. I started to freak out, but the more I panicked, the more Cheryl and Nicola laughed. The colours in the hotel room were green, and I felt as if my face was blending in with it all. By now, everyone was stoned and screaming hyserically. And as they laughed, I got more and more paranoid – it was awful.

'I'm scared. Will you take me to the toilet?' I pleaded with someone. 'What if I wee myself?'

I didn't know what was going on or what was happening to my mind and body. Once I got into the toilet I splashed some water on my face, and then I had a thought. If I could just get back to my room and lie down on the bed and close my eyes, everything would be all right, wouldn't it? The next thing I knew,

I was running down the corridor like a mad person – I actually did a runner from the room – and when I got to my own room, I just collapsed face down on the bed and passed out. I was so relieved and happy to wake up the next day feeling normal again, and it was quite a while before I ever tried anything like that again.

After the 'What Will the Neighbours Say?' tour, we carried on working non-stop. We were straight into the next album, *Chemistry*, and that was pretty much the pattern for us over the next four years – tour, album, tour, album. We didn't really have any time off, and I never felt as though I could take time out or book a long holiday because there was always so much going on. We were always fighting to stay on top and to stay relevant. If you dropped your guard for a minute, someone would be along to replace you, or that's what it seemed like. We never got complacent and we never saw ourselves as invincible. All five of us knew that it could all disappear at any time, and that's what gave us the drive to work as hard as we did. By the time we made the ITV2 fly-on-the-wall series, *Girls Aloud: Off the Record*, in 2006, I was completely knackered. The cameras followed us to Australia for a promo tour, but while some of the girls went out and enjoyed themselves, and Nadine was out conquering the heart of *Desperate Housewives* star Jesse Metcalfe, I don't think I made the most of it at all. I felt run-down and tired, and in pictures taken during that time, I look washed out. Even when the other girls wanted to go out and party I couldn't be persuaded. 'You go out,' I'd tell them. 'I just need to go to bed.'

None of us had really wanted those cameras following us around day and night. We simply wanted to get on with our jobs without the worry of having our every move recorded for the nation to watch on TV. We'd already done the reality TV thing with *Popstars*, but that was the way the industry was going at that time. Doing a show like that was another way to let the public peek behind the scenes and get to know us as individuals, and it worked. I think the only reason we went for it was because Peter told us we'd be travelling to Australia to film some of it. That was how he sold it to us.

I do regret not making more of some of our trips abroad, but that's what happens when you're on the same promotional treadmill for such a long time. It catches up with you.

However brilliant our success was, it could all get a bit much, and there were times when I'd rather have been at home watching *Friends* with Justin. He was always very understanding when it came to my hectic and erratic lifestyle. Sometimes we hardly saw one another at all, because on the odd weekend when I had a bit of time off, he would be visiting his daughter, Chloe, who lived in Bristol with her mum. It must have been hard for him being a dad at such a young age. He was only sixteen when she was born and still doing his GCSEs. He was a great dad, though, and he always did everything he could for her. Back then I just had to accept that I could never be the number-one girl in his life. After all, you're never going to match up to someone's daughter, are you? It didn't faze me, to be honest. Seeing him with Chloe just showed me what a brilliant person he is, and if anything made me love him more. I didn't even meet her until we'd been going out for quite a while. Justin wanted to make sure that our relationship was a good solid one before he introduced us, and I was fine with that. Then when we did meet, I was more like a big sister or auntie than a 'wicked step mum'. She'd sit and watch me put my make-up on, and I'd do her hair for her. She's always been a really lovely girl.

It's funny – before I met Justin I think I would have found the idea of my partner having a child who wasn't mine a bit hard to deal with, but when you love somebody, it doesn't matter. Now Chloe is nearly fifteen, and she comes down to London a lot to spend time with us. I've seen her grow up over ten years, but I've never felt as though I had to play a motherly role. She's always treated me with such love and respect, and I don't see it as my job to be another parent to her. I like to think that I'm there for her for any problems she has, or any girly stuff she needs to talk about, but more as a friend now than a mother.

15

Is There Anyone There?

I finally bought my own apartment towards the end of 2005, and not long after that Justin and I moved in together, officially. He'd been virtually living with me for quite a while, but he'd never actually moved all his possessions in. I wasn't that keen on being on my own anyway, and the two of us under the same roof just seemed to work.

The new place was still in Princess Park Manor, and it was beautiful. The building is actually an old mental hospital with four huge towers, and my apartment was in one of them. My bedroom was like a proper princess tower, with windows all around it, and when I saw it I fell in love with it right away. It had a big roof terrace, and lovely bright rooms, and although I knew I was stretching myself a bit financially, I decided to think positively and go for it. I've got nothing but happy memories of living in that place. Members of Busted and McFly lived there, too, as did a number of famous footballers. I remember it being a fun time, because we'd often all hang out at the same nightclubs, and then we'd all end up going back to someone's apartment for an after-party at Princess Park Manor.

It was around that time that Cheryl met Ashley Cole, who lived in the next block to me, and when they started dating, Justin and I spent a lot of time with them. Cheryl had grown up so much in the time I'd known her, and I thought that Ashley brought out the best in her. I'd always been fairly close to Cheryl, but from that point on we became even closer. I felt such a strong bond with her, and I knew that whatever happened within Girls Aloud, our friendship would last and carry me through. When you're immersed in that sort of madness, day after day, you need someone like that, someone who's completely on your level and on your side. When Cheryl eventually moved in with Ashley, we were like two settled, happy couples together, and it couldn't have been more perfect because she was virtually living next door.

This close proximity came in very handy one night

when Cheryl called me at 1 a.m. while Ashley was away – she was totally freaking out.

'There's a ghost on my stairs,' she said. 'It's definitely a ghost. Please come round.'

I don't know why on earth she called me, because she knows that I'm very sceptical about anything vaguely supernatural. The rest of the girls are all suckers for a psychic or a tale of the afterlife, but I'm just not interested.

'Really?' I said, half asleep. 'A ghost?'

I went over anyway, because she sounded so hysterical, but I wasn't too thrilled, and I wasn't expecting to find anything even remotely ghost-like. When I got in there, however, Cheryl's dog, Buster, was going mental, barking its head off, and staring up at some strange orb of light that looked as though it was floating on the staircase. I couldn't work out what the hell it was, and although it didn't look anything like I imagined a ghost might look, it was definitely weird. Cheryl, meanwhile, was literally frozen to the bed, not daring to move.

'There's nothing there,' I tried to reassure her, but Buster was incensed, and I could clearly see this hovering smoky light on the stairs, and for the life of me I couldn't tell where it was coming from. Actually, I decided that I didn't like it much, either.

'Sometimes ghosts or spirits can just appear as light or a shape,' Cheryl informed me, wide-eyed.

So was that it? Was I looking at my first spirit, just chilling at the top of Cheryl's stairs?

'Well, it's not going to do anything, is it?' I said to her. 'It's just a blob of light.'

I was trying to be tough, but as time went on and the dog kept going nuts, I wasn't too happy about hanging around.

'Will you stay with us?' Cheryl begged me.

'Er . . . why don't you and Buster come and stay at mine instead?'

And that's what happened. We left the spirit light on its own and went to my place for the night, with Cheryl in a state of panic.

'See! See! You saw it, didn't you? You saw it!' she said. To this day she still has the picture on her phone of that strange orb of light, and she still goes on about it.

In 2006 we were approached by the *Ghosthunting* TV show and, God knows why, but Cheryl was really keen to do it, so before I knew it, we were filming *Ghosthunting with Girls Aloud*. I thought the whole idea of the programme was a bit ridiculous, and poor Nadine was just too terrified to do it at all. The premise of the show is that you wander around buildings that are frightening enough without ghosts, and then the producers do their best to scare the life out of you.

The show's host, Yvette Fielding, took us to various places over two nights, including a supposedly haunted house in North Wales, and a hospital morgue in a long-abandoned and derelict sanatorium. I did my best to get into it, but, as I said, I'm fairly sceptical about that sort of thing, so when Yvette encouraged us to take part in a séance with a Ouija board, I wasn't too impressed.

'Can you feel that?' Yvette whispered spookily as Cheryl, Sarah and I stood around the board with our fingers on a tumbler. 'Did you feel that breath on your shoulder?'

'Nah,' I said. 'Not at all. I didn't feel a thing.'

'Something's playing with my coat,' Yvette said.

Really?

I had to keep a straight face on camera, but I wasn't taking it on at all. Cheryl and I ended up in a very dark room at the end of a long corridor, and then I felt something hit my finger. When I think about it now, I assume it was one of the bats I'd spotted as I left, or maybe one of the crew just threw something at me. At the time, though, I think I'd done so much intense ghosthunting that it started to play tricks on my mind. That night, Nicola, Cheryl and I all slept in the same bed – just to be on the safe side.

I guess the programme must have been quite funny for people to watch – the fans loved it – but I don't know whether I came away from the experience believing in ghosts any more than I did when I started. That being said, I've never been able to come up with a proper explanation for the funny blob of light on Cheryl's stairs in Princess Park Manor. There are loads of tales about that building being haunted, and although I remain a sceptic, it was definitely one of the strangest experiences I've ever had.

16

Walk This Way

The last part of 2006 was like a whirlwind of work and promotion, and by then Girls Aloud seemed like an unstoppable force. Our single, 'Something Kinda Oooh', became the first British single to reach the charts on downloads alone, and this was followed up with our greatest hits album, *The Sound of Girls Aloud*, which went to number one and went on to sell over a million copies. It was hard for me to believe that we even had enough material for a greatest hits album, but 'Something Kinda Oooh' was actually our thirteenth top-ten single. At the time, I didn't even take in all these facts and figures. I don't think any of us did. When you're in the midst of something so fast-moving and crazy, some of your achievements and the accolades you receive along the way can pass you by, because you just move on to the next thing without even thinking about it.

At the start of 2007 I was offered the chance to visit Africa for Comic Relief and I jumped at the chance. We didn't have much time off in Girls Aloud, and I knew that making the trip would have to be done while we were having a break, but I really wanted to go. I thought that gaining some insight into life in a third-world country – what it was actually like to live there – would be worthwhile. It seemed like another world to me – not really real. If I could get up close to the people, maybe I'd have a better chance of raising more money for them on Comic Relief and Children in Need, and I wanted them to be real to me, not just faces on a TV screen.

I travelled to South Africa with two of the girls from the Sugababes, Heidi and Keisha, and we had a full week of visiting various projects that had been set up by Comic Relief. Some of them were centred on helping people with HIV and AIDS, and being there gave me a true sense of just how bad that situation was. I met small children who were living with disease and who really had very little hope, and I developed such a huge respect for all the people who were working there.

What they were doing was nothing short of amazing. We met elderly people who were living in poverty, we visited a housing charity – there was just so much work going on that it was hard to take it all in within the space of just one week.

What amazed me the most was that so much severe poverty could exist literally ten minutes outside a perfectly developed city such as Johannesburg. It was insane to think that people were living in shanty towns with no real houses, no running water, nothing, just a few miles from what we know as civilisation. When we think about people starving in Africa, we don't imagine that it's happening a stone's throw from a major city where most people are living normally. That really blew my mind.

I was touched by the pride that some of the people took in the homes they'd built in one particular make-shift town, which was under threat from big developers. To us, the houses were shacks with a bit of metal for a roof, but to them each one was a real home, with shelves and pictures on the wall, and the people who lived there were grateful to have it. The inhabitants of the town had built up friendships and relationships over twenty years. This was their estate, and they were proud of what they'd achieved. Comic Relief had set up a charity to support them in trying to keep the town they'd built by providing them with advice and money to help them fight their cause. Without it, these people couldn't even afford to organise a lawyer's letter, and I was very proud to be part of the effort to raise the funds that might help them stay in the homes that they were so proud of.

It was so amazing to see exactly where the money raised was going. I saw food packages being delivered, and AIDS medicine being distributed, and it made all the difference to the way I thought about things. It felt refreshing to be taken out of the superficial world I'd been living in for ages, and dropped into the middle of what seemed like such stark reality. I know you hear celebrities on TV saying things like, 'Oh, the experience changed me,' but it really did change me. It was one of the most eye-opening and fascinating experiences I've ever had, and when I came back, I felt the need to explain to everyone exactly how it was, exactly what I'd witnessed. I actually found it quite difficult coming back into my own world, and into the world of Girls Aloud. I started to question things about my lifestyle that I'd taken for granted. I'd look at my five different bottles of perfume and think, Really? Do I need all of them? Ten different body lotions – do I need all of them? Do I even need one? I certainly don't need ten!

I spoke to Heidi about it and she felt the same. We'd seen it now. We couldn't pretend it wasn't happening because we'd seen it with our own eyes. There are people I met on that trip whose faces I'll never forget, and I felt privileged to have been able to take part. When Comic Relief asked me, I just thought it was too good an opportunity to turn down because however sad it makes me, it's also a really rewarding and enriching thing to do.

The plan was for Girls Aloud and the Sugababes to make a record together for Comic Relief – a cover of Run DMC and Aerosmith's 'Walk This Way'. As a band, we'd always had a lot of respect for what the Sugababes were about, and we all got along, despite stories in the press about us being rivals. We decided that all those girls together on one record as a supergroup was a force to be reckoned with, and the novelty of it would push up the record sales and make money for the cause. Of course, it was bad enough trying to get five girls together for a recording session, so getting all eight of us in the same room was a near impossible feat. Consequently, we recorded our bits separately, and even in the video we're superimposed to make it look as if we're all together, but we never actually were. Sarah and Nadine did their shoot completely separately, Cheryl, Nicola and I did one together, and then there was a third shoot for the Sugababes. The record did brilliantly, going straight to number one, and we performed the song together on Comic Relief night. We also performed the song on the TV talent show *Fame Academy* a few days before, and that really was a night to remember, although I don't remember it at all.

It was the first live TV we'd done for a while and we were a little bit nervous, so I hadn't eaten very much all day, which was my first mistake. By that time, my good friend Jenny had moved to London, and that day was her thirtieth birthday, so I knew I was going out after recording the show, and assumed I'd grab some food then. I remember being in quite a fun and light-hearted mood by the time I reached the Embassy Club, where Jenny was celebrating. Everyone was well on their way to being drunk already and for some reason I decided that it would be a good idea to try to play catch-up, alcohol-wise. So I started knocking back the champers – in fact, I drank shedloads – and that's when it all went wrong. I've since realised that Champagne and me don't really mix, but at the time I was having the best night and I didn't foresee any problems.

At some point in the evening I must have hit a wall, metaphorically, because I can only tell the rest of the story from what Justin and my sister have told me since. Personally, I haven't a clue what happened. One of the last things I actually remember was feeling very, very tired. 'Jesus Christ, I really need to sit down,' I said to someone. I found a seat and flopped down in it. A little while later, Sally apparently came over to me.

'Kim, seriously, you need to get up.'

By this time I was lying down, and I wasn't having any of it. I simply wouldn't move or speak. After that I was unconscious.

'Sh*t! What are we gonna do?' Justin said in a panic. 'How are we gonna get her out? There's no back entrance, she won't wake up, she can't even stand up. What the hell are we gonna do?'

Sally and Justin both realised that even if they did wake me up, getting me out of the club in that state without all the paparazzi outside getting some choice shots of me was going to be a near impossibility. That wasn't an option. I suppose they were quite drunk themselves, so I can't blame them too much for the decision they eventually made, but that doesn't mean that it was a good one.

'Let's carry her out,' some bright spark suggested, 'with a coat over her head!'

For some insane reason this was the idea that they went with, so I was literally carried out of the Embassy Club with Justin's coat over my head. Of course, the paparazzi outside knew exactly who it was, coat or no coat, because Justin was carrying me, so it wasn't such a great plan after all. Plus the fact my arse was hanging out, and they all recognised that, too.

Poor Justin had to get me home, look after me while I was violently ill, and then wash sick out of my hair before putting me to bed. It was bad and I'm not denying it. We've all been there, but Justin had never seen me anywhere near as drunk as that. He likes a drink, too, but he seems to be able to handle it and to this day I've not seen him in a state like that.

The next day I woke up, having slept for hours, and I couldn't remember a thing. Why was I in the spare room? Where was Justin? How did we get home? I could not for the life of me answer any of these questions. When I found Justin, he was not happy at all.

'What happened?' I said, innocently.

'Are you takin' the piss?' Justin said. 'Babe, you need to look at this morning's paper. Have you got any idea how pissed you were? We had to carry you out of the club with a coat over your head.'

'What?'

I was furious and I immediately turned the whole thing back on him.

'What the hell were you thinking? Why would you do that? I'm not bloody Christina Aguilera! What an idiot I'm gonna look.'

I could just imagine people's reaction. 'What the hell is she doing? Thinking she's big-time with a frigging coat over her head.' I was horrified, because up until that point I'd always managed to retain some level of decency and integrity within the band. Justin pointed out that the alternative to having the coat over my head really wasn't all that pretty, and that I should be grateful that he'd covered me up. It wasn't just me I worried about, either; there was also my friend, Jenny. Way to upstage someone's thirtieth birthday!

The girls were beside themselves with hilarity, of course. I picked up the phone to Nicola and all I could hear was laughter. Then I had Cheryl on the phone, wetting herself. It was all so embarrassing. Those photos, which did appear in the press, have gone down in Girls Aloud history as the best-ever paparazzi shots of any of us leaving a club looking the worse for wear, and there have been a few. To this day Cheryl still likes to bring it up in conversation when we meet new people.

I really don't know why or how I got so drunk. I guess it was just a combination of no food and working really hard, and then letting loose in an environment where you feel comfortable and safe with all the people around you. Some of my friends who were there suggested that my drink was spiked that night.

Apparently, I was so out of it that they were convinced someone had put some sort of drug in my Champagne. Personally, I think I just drank too much and got arseholed!

17

Hardly Pete Doherty

Sundraj Sreenivasan had been with us from the very beginning, and these days he has his own successful PR company, Supersonic. He'd turned up at the *Popstars* house to give us media training when there were still ten of us. I remember thinking, Who is this posh bloke? Well, that's the way he seemed to me, coming from Bradford, anyway. He asked us a ton of questions as if we were being interviewed by the press, but none of us had a clue how to behave or what to say in an interview. That's the sort of thing that only comes in time and learning from your mistakes.

There were no frills with Sundraj and he's straight to the point, which is good given the job he does. He was ultimately responsible for all of the Girls Aloud press. Everything we did that went in any magazine or newspaper went through him, even the bad stuff. Whenever I saw his name flash up on my phone, my first thought was always, Sh*t! What have I done? What have they got on me? What am I in the papers for? It was the same for all of us, that feeling of dread on seeing his name on our phones. This was especially true on a Sunday morning when we'd been out on the Saturday night and been caught on camera somewhere, rotten drunk. 'OK, well this is what it is,' he'd say, in his singsong, matter-of-fact way. 'Chill out, 'cause it's not that bad.'

Usually the five of us tended to be over-dramatic about any dodgy press stories, but Sundraj could usually talk us down after a while. He always kept his cool. That's probably the reason that he represents Cheryl, Nicola and me to this day.

When he called me one evening to tell me about a photo of me that was about to hit the newsstands, my blood ran cold, but my initial reaction was disbelief. It couldn't possibly be me in the photo, it just couldn't. 'It's a shot of you smoking a joint,' he told me. 'And it's coming out in the press tomorrow.'

What? Was he kidding? My mind was suddenly all over the place. I mean, it wasn't like I'd never had a puff on a joint, but after the last time in Amsterdam, it certainly wasn't something I made a habit of. Plus, I couldn't for the life of me think who on earth might be in possession of a picture of me actually doing it. What was going on? I suddenly went into panic mode.

'Look, let me send you the picture,' Sundraj said. 'It certainly looks like you, and it's pretty obvious what it is you're doing.'

I was freaking out for the first few minutes after the phone call. Then, as it started to sink in, my next concern was how my family would react – my mum, my grandma and my granddad. They just weren't going to understand this at all. It was a nightmare. My mum had always been a good girl when she was younger, responsible, sensible – she was head girl for God's sake. She was never going to be able to get her head around me 'doing drugs', especially in a photograph in the national press.

When I eventually clapped eyes on the picture, I knew exactly where it had been taken. I'd been at a New Year's Eve house party the previous year with a group of very close friends, and there I was, joking around, holding a big fat spliff up to my lips. I don't think I was actually smoking it when the picture was taken, but it was New Year's Eve and I was quite drunk, so I probably had been at some point in the evening.

It's funny because I looked like I was having a really good time in the photograph, but as I stared down at it in the cold light of day, I was horrified. I knew there was no getting around this one.

Now you might think that a little puff on a joint is not a big deal for somebody in the music industry. After all, you hear much worse things than that on a weekly basis, don't you? However, I was one fifth of the biggest girl band in the country and many of our fans were just kids or young teenagers. This wasn't really the message Girls Aloud wanted to send out to them – that it was cool and funny to get drunk and smoke cannabis whenever it took your fancy. And of all of us, I couldn't believe that it was *me* who got caught doing something like that. I was supposed to be the good girl, wasn't I? At least, that's the impression the public seemed to have of me. Everyone was going to think it was so out of character, and I guess it was really, but that's what happens sometimes when you drink too much, I suppose.

I think I knew deep down that it was never going to turn into some massive scandal but that didn't stop me panicking at the time – mainly because I knew my mum was going to go off on one. I really wasn't looking forward to *that* conversation. However, while I was mid-panic, Cheryl suddenly gave me a call. Sundraj had told her what was about to happen and suggested that I might need calming down, and he wasn't wrong. By the time she called me I was crying my eyes out and I was all over the place.

'Oh my God! How did this photo get out?' I sobbed. 'These were supposed to be people I could trust, my close friends. What am I going to do? This is so embarrassing.'

'Just breathe and calm down,' Cheryl said, sympathetically. She knew exactly how I'd react to something like this. 'It's going to be fine. It's you, so it's going to be fine. If it were me, then I reckon it might turn into some massive press frenzy, but I think you'll be OK. It'll all be forgotten by next week.' I desperately hoped she was right, but at that moment I felt terrible.

I decided to call my dad first because he's a little bit more chilled out about that sort of stuff, and I knew that he wouldn't really think it was that big a deal. My mum was going to be a different story. I knew that she wouldn't be able to grasp the fact that it was just me letting my hair down and having a bit of a laugh at a New Year's Eve party and nothing more. She's always been so straight down the line and I knew she wouldn't understand – she'd be shocked and probably angry, too. When I called my dad, he didn't seem that bothered, as I'd suspected.

'Oh, don't worry about it, love,' he said. 'It'll most likely give you a bit more street cred.'

He made me feel better right away, and that gave me an idea.

'Dad, can you tell Mum?' I pleaded. 'I just don't think I can face speaking to her about it. It'll be far better coming from you.'

The two of them had been separated for fifteen years, but I knew my mum would take the news better if my dad broke it to her gently rather than me ringing her up in a state of hysteria. He agreed to call Mum and I was relieved, but eventually, of course, I had to speak to her myself, and although she wasn't too angry, it was quite clear that she found the concept of me being a 'bad girl' quite hard to grasp.

'What were you doing?' she said. 'I mean . . . what were *you* doing, smoking a joint?'

I tried to explain that it wasn't that big a deal, and that it was just a bit of fun on New Year's Eve, but at the same time I felt sort of protective towards her, and towards my grandma and my granddad, too. It just wasn't the sort of thing they were used to dealing with, and that made me feel guilty. Also, it was still pretty early days as far as the band were concerned, and I was worried that my actions might tarnish the image of the group somehow. I felt responsible. After all, it wasn't just me it affected; there were five of us to consider.

When the story broke under a headline that rather amusingly read, 'Kimberley: I'm a big dope', I publicly apologised. The last thing I wanted was our younger fans thinking that this was the norm for me, or that it was OK to go out and get drunk and run around smoking drugs. When you have young fans, like we did, you do have a responsibility towards them and there's no getting away from that. In a statement to the press I said that I'd got caught up in the moment and that I was sorry, and I meant it. In the *Sun*'s 'Bizarre' column, the journalist wrote, 'Squeaky-clean young Kimberley has been caught being a bit naughty – it's hardly up there with Pete Doherty, is it?'

I suppose that was how most people thought about it, really, but the whole experience certainly taught me a valuable lesson, both about trust and about the way someone in the public eye is perceived. That New Year's Eve party had been quite a small, private affair – it was Justin and me together with a few close friends and their partners. It was clear that someone at the party betrayed my trust and deliberately went to the press with the photo. This was in the days before Facebook and Twitter when people can just lift private photos from a web page. To this day I don't know who put that photo out there, and it's always bothered me. The thought of it is quite upsetting and it's made me a lot more guarded, and it certainly made me much more aware of my actions while I was out in public. I mean, if that could happen within a small group of close friends, imagine what the consequences might be if you were out getting drunk off your head in a nightclub full of strangers with cameras on their phones.

18

Calling the Shots

By 2007 Nicola, Cheryl, Sarah and I had grown incredibly close, while Nadine and I had drifted apart somewhat. After Nadine broke up with her boyfriend, Neil, our lives outside work went in different directions. I still had the same friends but she was hanging out with a whole new crowd, and it just wasn't the same between us any more. Then, when she started spending more and more time in LA, it was bound to affect the dynamic of the group, especially as she wasn't around for band meetings and nights out. There was a definite change in her, which became more evident each time she came back from LA. In the end, I felt like there was no common ground between us, and I just didn't know how to relate to her any more – none of us did. It was quite disconcerting because the rest of us wanted more than anything to keep the band together, but after a while we started to worry that it might not be possible.

Around the time when Girls Aloud filmed a cameo appearance for the movie *St Trinian's* things really got tricky. We were playing the school band, performing the theme song to the film, dressed as unruly St Trinian's girls, but on the day of filming we got a bit of a shock. Cheryl and I were in the Winnebago, getting ready, when Hillary took a phone call. We didn't have any idea who she was talking to, but when she hung up, she was all in a panic.

'What's wrong, Hills?' Cheryl said, slightly concerned.

'Oh nothing,' Hills whispered. 'It's just Nadine's bloody manager.'

'What? Nadine's what?'

It turned out that Nadine had taken on someone to represent her as a solo entity, and we knew absolutely nothing about it. We felt like we'd been sucker-punched, and we couldn't believe that so many people we knew and trusted had kept this piece of news from us, including Nadine herself. Even now we knew about it, there was very little information to be had. What we should have done was confront Nadine about it right away, but we were so shocked we didn't know what to say to her without causing a huge row. Nobody wanted that. So we decided to say nothing, which, looking back, wasn't really the right thing to do because after that day we were on edge the whole time.

We started hearing all sorts of stories from people around us that Nadine was on the verge of doing a solo deal, and at one point we really thought she was going to leave the band. It was around the time of our single, 'Call the Shots', and at the time we all felt that the band couldn't survive without all five of us. It was quite a worrying time, but we were too afraid to confront her about her plans in case she went off the deep end and it pushed her away even further. She was living in LA full time by then, so we decided to shoot the video for 'Call the Shots' out there, hoping that might help things along a little bit. It was a ridiculous situation, to be honest, but we just had to do what we could to keep the band running as smoothly as possible.

This uneasiness about the future of the band continued on to the 'Tangled Up' tour. By that time, Girls Aloud were really in their groove, so the thought that it all might fall to pieces was awful. During that hectic tour our new PA arrived. Up until this point, Lily had been looking after all five of us, but with Cheryl's full-on schedule on *The X Factor*, she needed Lily all to herself. It's funny, despite everything that was going on, none of us felt threatened by Cheryl's job on *The X Factor*. However hard she worked on the show, she always managed to put the group first, and she was always there for everything she needed to be there for as far as Girls Aloud went. I'm not sure how she made it all work, but I never once worried that it would affect us in a negative way. The lovely girl who took over from Lily was Nikki White, who'd been working for George Michael's office at the time of the tour. Hillary had heard how great she was, and quickly poached her to come and work for us. Talk about being thrown in at the deep end! Still, Nikki mucked in right away and very soon became part of the family.

We all loved touring, and however excited we got about videos and albums, it was nothing to the buzz that came from preparing for a live concert tour. The first day of tour rehearsals was always the best day of the working year for me. We'd all be running around and jumping up and down like mad things the minute we got in the room. For a start, it was the most exciting and creative part of our job, because anything was possible. Also there was the camaraderie we built up with both the dancers and the band. You really do become like an extended family unit when you're on the road – and singing with a live band as opposed to a backing track is on another level entirely. Most of our tours were under the musical direction of Joseph Ross and his band, Jerry, Stuart and John, and usually, by the time we joined in, they were already well rehearsed. Beth would get the band to play something while running through the choreography with the dancers, and by the time they'd finished, we'd all be wetting ourselves with excitement. Suddenly, a song we'd heard a hundred times would come to life in way we couldn't have imagined, and we couldn't wait to get in and put our stamp on it. It was hard work, but I didn't mind the long hours and fact that I went home exhausted, having worked my arse off all day. For me, performing on a stage was what it was all about. It was why I'd started singing in the first place.

The other thing I enjoyed about touring was the fact that we got to perform some of our incredible tracks that hadn't been released as singles, songs such as 'Models', 'Waiting' and 'Miss You Bow Wow'. There was often a lot of shared vocals on those tracks, and I loved adding extra harmonies to the songs wherever I could. Coming up with concepts for those tracks was always a great part of the preparation for me, because it gave us so many opportunities to create something visually amazing. The entrance we made on the 'Tangled Up' tour was epic, and, to be honest, I don't think we ever topped it. An eerie extended intro of our single 'Sexy No No No' was played while we were all behind a Kabuki drop – which is a drape of fabric that falls quickly to reveal the stage – suspended in mid-air on invisible wires, with the wind blowing our super-hero style capes. It literally looked as though we were flying in and slowly landing at the front of the stage. Then, when the first chorus of the song kicked in, the Kabuki dropped and we belted out the song. It was an amazing entrance and we felt *so* good every single time we did it. In fact, Beth had tears running down her face the first time she watched it with all the lighting. We knew how fantastic it looked, and there was no better feeling than that at the start of a show.

19

'Oh! You Can Sing, Can't You?'

The craze of reality TV was well under way by the time we made the TV series *The Passions of Girls Aloud* in 2008. The idea behind the show was that each one of us – in our own episode – would work towards achieving a personal goal or dream. Mine was a no-brainer. I love musical theatre and I wanted to be in a West End musical. At the time we were all a bit nervous about doing the series because everything else we'd done had been within the security of the band, but at the same time it was an amazing opportunity to spread our wings and try our hands at some of the other things in life we were passionate about. Still, this would be stepping away from the band and standing or falling on my own, which was something I hadn't really thought about up until that point. At first the producers wanted me to be in *Mamma Mia!*, the ABBA musical, for a two-week period. It wasn't exactly what I'd had in mind but I went along to watch it anyway, and straight off I knew it wasn't right.

'I'm sorry, but I don't think *Mamma Mia!* is enough of a challenge,' I told Hillary the next day. 'Yes, I would be taking part in a West End show and it would work for the TV series, but I already sing in a pop band. When it comes down to it, *Mamma Mia!* is a show full of great pop songs, not musical theatre songs. If I'm going to do this, I want to be pushed and challenged. I want to do proper musical theatre or there's no point in me doing it at all.'

The producers were a bit flummoxed. It had been quite hard for them to find a current show that was prepared to let me be in it, but I was determined that if I was going to make a TV show called *Passions*, then what I did had to be exactly that.

'Well, what's your favourite show?' they asked me. 'What would you like to be in?'

I didn't have to think for very long.

'*Les Misérables!*'

I knew I wasn't going to be able to step into a lead role, of course, but the producers of *Passions* managed to get me an audition, and I was told that if – and only if – I was good enough, they would find a part for me in the show somehow. That was when I started having proper singing lessons with well-respected singing teacher Mary Hammond. She's a really lovely woman, but when you first meet her, she's quite terrifying, and she has the reputation of being quite tough. I think, initially, she was fairly sceptical about the idea of a pop singer taking on a big show like *Les Mis*, and she certainly didn't hold back in that first meeting at her grand house in North London, either.

'You're coming from a pop band, so what makes you think you can sing musical theatre?' she asked.

'Erm . . . well . . . I did it as a child, and I've always loved singing musical songs. Maybe I could sing something for you.'

I sang something from *Miss Saigon*, and Mary went quiet. I thought God, was I that bad? Finally, Mary spoke again.

'Oh! You can sing, can't you?'

Phew! From that point on Mary took me a lot more seriously, and that's when the hard work began. She had to get me to a stage where I could audition in front of the show's resident director, Mariano Detry, and the musical director, Stephen Brooker. I'd been singing exclusively in Girls Aloud for the past six years, which is a completely different way of singing, and not such a stretch for my vocal chords. I had a lot of catching up to do, and I realised that my confidence as a solo performer was pretty shot. In fact, a big part of the challenge of doing this TV show was getting some of that lost confidence back. Once I was in the swing of it, though, I really got the taste for musicals again.

I went to New York and did a workshop with the Broadway Company of *Les Mis*, and I fell in love with the idea of singing my heart out in big dramatic musical scenes all over again. I hadn't been part of that world since I was teenager, but I secretly started to wonder what it might be like if I could do it as a career. I don't think I realised it then, but doing *Passions* was actually a real turning point for me. My priorities were still 100 per cent with the girls, but at the same time something clicked with me. Musical songs suited my voice much better than pop songs ever did, and it was something I wanted to pursue – one day.

For the time being, though, I got to go on stage for the 'Lovely Ladies' section of *Les Misérables* in London and I thoroughly enjoyed it. At the end of that night's performance, I took to the stage again to sing my favourite song from the show, 'On My Own'. This was arranged especially for the *Passions* TV show, but it was such an amazing feeling stepping out in front of the audience that night. I felt like I was rediscovering myself somehow. In terms of Girls Aloud, *Passions* was just supposed to be a fun TV show, but the experience sparked something in me, and it became so much more than that.

Sarah's passion was to play polo because she loved horse riding, and in her episode of the show she trained with British and Argentinian polo teams. It was a million miles away from what I was doing, but then again the two of us always had been like chalk and cheese. Sarah and I didn't always see eye to eye, and I sometimes worried about her life outside the band, but over the years I'd learned to accept and understand her for the person she is, and I loved her like a sister. That's not to say she didn't drive me mad at times. You never know what you're getting with Sarah until she opens her mouth on any given day. One day she'll be on a real high and the next she'll be in a foul mood, but that's just something you get used to. I've always felt very protective towards her, and at that point she was very happy with her boyfriend, Tom Crane, whom she'd been dating for the past few months.

Cheryl wanted to learn hip-hop street dance for her *Passions* show, and Nadine wanted to conduct an orchestra. After one lesson with the conductor, though, she decided it wasn't for her and didn't go back. The rest of us weren't really very shocked by this as she hadn't shown much interest in the idea of the show from the start. The programme's producers, however, were fuming, and we were worried that it was going to damage our good relationship with ITV, but there was nothing Hillary could do to change her mind, and ITV agreed to continue making the series with just the four of us.

Nicola's episode of *Passions* was really fascinating. In her show she set out to create her own foundation for girls with pale skin, like herself. She's always been very fair-skinned, and although she embraces it now, back in the old days she couldn't bear it. Nicola has always been 'the baby' in Girls Aloud. Cheryl and I have always looked on her as a little sister, and despite the fact that she's blossomed into a really strong and confident woman in the last few years, we probably always will.

At the start of Girls Aloud she had a really tough time. There were always comments flying around in the press about the way she looked or came across. Some people even described her 'the ugly one', which was ridiculous and untrue, not to mention hurtful. Looking back now, I feel quite guilty about the way I handled all that. We never really addressed the subject while it was happening. I suppose we didn't want to draw even more attention to the negative comments and make her feel worse. We never saw Nicola as any less interesting or beautiful than the rest of us, so we never took those comments on, and because of that we never really confronted the people who were saying them or stood up for her. Now I realise that Nicola *did* take all that negativity on her shoulders, and I know how hurt she was by it all. In hindsight, I wish I'd been more supportive.

The funny thing is I was always very envious of Nicola's figure and the fact that she could eat whatever the hell she liked without putting on a single ounce. God, that girl can eat, even now. Back in the early days of the band, her culinary tastes weren't all that sophisticated, but she just couldn't ever seem to eat enough. Whenever we went anywhere in the car or on the tour bus, we'd have to stop at McDonald's – not just one McDonald's, though: at all of them.

'I've got to get to a Maccy's, Drew,' she'd wail in her broad Scouse twang. 'I've got to!' So at every possible opportunity Drew would stop at a McDonald's for a Big Mac, which was hardly conducive to my dietary requirements, because I was constantly trying to avoid putting on weight.

'Oh my God, you're gonna make me fat,' I used to moan at her. 'Stop bloody eating all the time!'

Nicola couldn't seem to grasp that I couldn't eat as

much as she could, but I suppose that was my particular issue. We each had our own hang-ups and insecurities within the band and they were all different.

Nicola has always been such a hilarious character. Right back from the early days she would have us in stitches with some of her off-the-cuff remarks and her crazy antics. Her fixation on fake tan was out of control, for a start – she was obsessed. She hated her skin tone so much that she developed the most ridiculous habit of self-tanning, which was a daily ritual. It was almost part of the Girls Aloud calendar that Nicola had to be back home in time to shower, exfoliate and apply her fake tan for the next day. It was actually a problem! I totally get it now, of course. She was being singled out for being different from the rest of us back then, and this was one way she could combat those criticisms. No matter how many times we told her she looked amazing as she was, she wanted to stay as bronzed as possible. I guess it's something you just have to work out for yourself, which is what she did. She's also the messiest person I've ever met. She could literally walk into a room and create pure chaos and disaster within seconds, and then leave again. She's like a human tornado.

I think of all of us, through the years, Nicola is the person who has blossomed the most. I don't just mean in the way she looks, either. She's transformed in so many other ways. We're talking about a girl who only ever ate McDonald's or chips and gravy, but who now eats sushi and will try just about any kind of food. These days she's more likely to be found eating at Scott's or the Dorchester. She's embraced her pale skin tone, and her make-up range for girls with fair skin, Dainty Doll, has been very successful. She's also very knowledgeable about fashion and has become a great songwriter. As she's grown over the last few years, she's also become such an important part of the group. Whereas before, Cheryl and I had mainly been the decision-makers in the band, eventually Nicola started to come into her own, and she was really good at taking the reins. I think all this comes from being in the entertainment industry, travelling and meeting so many different kinds of people. It's quite a privileged position to be in, and having an open mind and learning from other people is all part of it. The same was true for me when I first visited Africa for Comic Relief I suppose – certain things change you for the better. Nicola has grown into a really amazing woman, and Cheryl and I are a bit soft about it. It's almost like we're saying, 'Oh! Look at the baby, all grown up.'

20

'That Night'

When Hillary called in January 2008 and told me what was about to be published in the newspapers about Ashley cheating on Cheryl, I could hardly believe my ears, but suddenly the story was everywhere. A young woman called Aimee was claiming that she'd slept with Ashley after a drunken night out.

'You need to give Cheryl a call,' Hillary said.

Cheryl and Ashley always seemed so happy. The day they got married in July 2006 couldn't have been more perfect. All the rest of us girls were bridesmaids, and we were all truly happy that Cheryl had found someone wonderful to settle down with. I knew what a tough life she'd had, so it was comforting to know that she was getting the happy ending she deserved. Ashley was the man of her dreams and she was totally in love with him, and although it was a whirlwind romance, there was no doubt in any of our minds that she was doing the right thing.

Their entire wedding day had been beautifully planned perfection. At one point in the proceedings, John Legend was playing piano and singing their favourite song, when suddenly the entire stage rotated to reveal a full nightclub within a gorgeous marquee. It was unbelievable. Thinking back to that, it was hard to get my head around the awful story that was all over the papers. Of course, my disbelief was nothing compared to the shock that Cheryl had suffered. As far as she was concerned she'd met and married the perfect man, and I know that she 100 per cent believed they would be together for the rest of their lives. When I called her she didn't pick up, and soon after that I got a text from her: 'I can't pick up. Sorry, I can't speak to you. I can't even see you.' I think if she had spoken to any of her close friends, it would have made the pain even worse, because the whole thing would become even more real.

The next day, however, we had a video shoot for 'I Can't Speak French'. None of us thought that we'd be able to go ahead with it. We thought that we should

225

simply pull the video and reschedule, but Cheryl wouldn't have it. 'No. I'll do it,' she told us. It was a horrible day. We all felt it. Cheryl looked like she was in shock for the entire duration, and it was a real effort to stay bubbly and enthusiastic for the long day of shooting.

Over the next few days I spoke to Cheryl's mum, Joan, but I had no idea what was going on between Cheryl and Ashley. All I did know was that there was no way she was going to be able to think straight while she was still living under the same roof as he was, particularly with the absolute press frenzy around the whole situation. I thought that she needed to remove herself from all that and get away from her house, so I called and told her as much.

'Come and stay at mine,' I said. 'Once you get in the building the paps can't get into the complex. You'll be safe here.'

'If I can physically smuggle myself out of the house past the paps over to yours, I will,' she said. And that's what she did – head down in the car, incognito, she managed to get to me safely.

Cheryl ended up hiding out in our flat for a week or so, and she was in a really bad way. I think she was in shock more than anything, we both were, and she couldn't do anything much more than lie on the couch, crying. At that point, it was just too painful for her even to try to make sense of it all because she felt like her whole world was falling apart in front of her. It was terrible to watch one of my best friends in that much pain because I just felt so incredibly helpless. Justin and I made sure that she was never on her own at any time. We organised our timetable so that if either one of us was out at work, the other would stay at home with Cheryl. I was too scared to leave her, and I remember feeling that I'd been through it all before. Some years before, Sally had been in a serious relationship with a footballer who had cheated on her with some wannabe wag, and then the woman in question sold her story to the press. Sally was devastated, and all I could do was try my utmost to support her. Now here I was helping my best friend deal with the same thing. The most tragic thing about the situation was that Cheryl had been through so much already in her life and she truly believed that Ashley was her reward for all that. Now it had been ruined in an instant.

I couldn't keep Cheryl locked up in my flat forever, though. We needed to get the hell out of there and leave the country, just to get away from all the press attention and constant speculation. Nicola and I came up with the idea of whisking Cheryl off to Thailand on some sort of 'Sex and the City' girls' holiday, although we knew that wasn't going to be a piece of cake, given the way she was feeling. We found a really private villa, but we still heard tales of journalists and photographers hanging around the area, even though they didn't quite manage to get to us. For that reason, we hardly left the sanctuary of the villa during our holiday, apart from going on an elephant ride that terrified Nicola. Other than that, we just chilled out and relaxed.

Cheryl seemed to be a little better after a few days, and at least she was away from all the madness. She still appeared quite distant, though, like she wasn't quite with us, and so both Nicola and I had to keep a close eye on her. The hardest thing for us was that we just didn't know what to say to her. We couldn't rationalise or explain what Ashley had done any more than she could. In fact, we couldn't imagine what the hell he must have been thinking. We both thought that Cheryl was a brilliant wife, and that she'd done everything right. They got on well, and they enjoyed one another's company. Why would he do something like that? All we could do was distract her as best we could, and that's what we tried to do.

Straight after our holiday in Thailand we all flew to LA, where Cheryl was due to film the final bit of her *Passions* documentary. She'd learned hip-hop style street dance for her episode, and for the last section of the programme she was going to be dancing in a video for will.i.am's new single, 'Heartbreaker'. By the time we got to LA, Cheryl seemed to be functioning on pure adrenalin more than anything else, and although we were all tired from the journey, we were still very much in holiday-mode. Cheryl had lost all her cases somewhere between Thailand and LAX airport, so Nicola and I had to go out and buy her a dress, so she could go out that evening. In all honesty, she should have just gone to bed, because a big night out on the evening before she was due to shoot the video was the last thing she needed. And that's when things turned a bit pear-shaped.

We originally went out with will.i.am and some of his friends that night, and we had a really good evening. Then, when we arrived back at our hotel, the Mondrian, a gang of paparazzi photographers and cameramen spotted us and made a beeline. Well, by that time we were all quite drunk, and for some reason we thought it might be a good idea to dance and sing Mary J. Blige songs into the camera at them. What we were thinking, I don't know. We'd never have done that in the UK, but Cheryl had actually enjoyed herself for the first time in ages, and I guess we were just happy that she seemed to be having a good time.

Then Nicola and I ended up in the Mondrian bar

where we got chatting to four burly black American guys. They seemed really friendly and they told us they were the nineties R&B band, Jodeci, which impressed us loads because we'd all been big fans of Jodeci when we were younger. Cheryl, meanwhile, was in the hotel lobby with our hairdresser, Lisa, who had come over to work on the video shoot. Cheryl was in a bit of a state by that point because she couldn't get into her room. 'I've lost me room key,' she told the people at the desk.

They asked her name and if she had ID, but she was staying at the hotel under a pseudonym, so her registered name wouldn't have matched her passport, even if she had been able to get to it. She tried to explain what her real name was and why she wasn't using it, but it all got very confusing and suddenly she was in floods of tears in the middle of the lobby.

She was obviously more emotional that night than I'd realised, and the staff at the front desk must have wondered why the hell someone was making such a fuss about a key. What Nicola and I didn't know was that one of the Jodeci guys had witnessed the whole thing and had taken poor Cheryl under his wing.

'What's a pretty girl like you crying for?' he said. 'I'm from Jodeci!'

Once Cheryl had convinced the hotel staff of her

identity and finally got back in her room, the guys from Jodeci persuaded Nicola and me that we should all go up and join her for a drink. It didn't seem all that weird to us because they didn't look at all dodgy or sleazy, so off we all went. Up in Cheryl's room we had some more drinks – as you can imagine we were pretty drunk by now – and the guys started filming us on their phones and asking us questions about London, while we sang and danced around like fools to the music, which was blaring out of the music system. It was just a bit of fun, and the guys told us that they were shooting some backstage footage for their tour. Luckily for us, Lisa wasn't drunk, so she was running around trying to make them delete as many of the videos and pictures as she could.

Suddenly, Cheryl was sobbing again, but when she explained about Ashley and why she was so sad, Jodeci went all religious on us. They started doing prayer circles with long speeches about God and goodness and worship. We were a little bemused, but we really were too drunk to know what was going on by then.

'You should come to church with us in the morning and pray with us, Cheryl,' one of them suggested.

'Yeah. Yeah, I think I should,' Cheryl said, nodding furiously with her eyes full of tears.

'Yeah, we should all go,' Nicola and I both agreed.

We didn't know what we were saying. As if we were going to troop off to church after a night out drinking. I don't even know how Cheryl made it out of bed and to the video shoot the next day, because the three of us had terrible hangovers. Nicola and I were sharing a room, and in the morning we woke up and looked at one another through a blurry haze.

'Oh my God! How is she dancing around on a video this morning?' I croaked. 'How is she doing that?'

Nicola just shook her head and then we both went back to sleep.

After that we flew back to London for the 2008 Brit Awards. We were nominated in the Best British Group category. It was hard for Cheryl to appear at such a high-profile event so soon after her public separation from Ashley, and at the height of that drama. The rest of us were there to support her, though, except Nadine, who told Hillary she'd lost her passport and was stuck in LA. On that same day, she told a journalist at an LA party that the Brits just weren't her thing. It was a bit of a kick in the teeth, especially as three of us had flown back from LA especially for the ceremony, and we were all trying to put on a united front for Cheryl. I think Cheryl's attitude that night was to suck it up and get it over with. I thought it was courageous of her; I thought she had balls. It's hard to imagine how hard it is to brave a red carpet under those circumstances, and I'm not sure I could have done it. Perhaps the holiday in Thailand and her time in LA gave her the boost she needed to carry on, I don't know, but it was certainly a relief, because all this had happened just before we embarked on the aforementioned 'Tangled Up' tour.

As far as I was concerned, that tour was the best distraction that Cheryl could have had at the time. It's like living in a bubble when you're on tour, and there are so many people around you all the time, you really have no chance to get too lost in your own problems.

A few weeks into the tour I was completely gobsmacked when Sundraj alerted us to a story in the *News of the World*. It turned out that those stand-up, God-fearing Americans we'd met in LA weren't Jodeci at all. Worse than that, it transpired that they'd been making a *Punk'd* style TV show called *Parking Lot Pimps*, where they picked up as many pretty girls as they could and captured them on camera chanting PLP, which, unfortunately, we had done. They'd also sold a video and some photos of us, partying in the hotel room, and there it was spread all over the papers and on the Internet. It's not like there was anything that bad on the video – we were just being drunk and a bit foolish after a night out. Still, we were in a hotel room with four strangers, which, apart from being dangerous, must have looked fairly incriminating, especially considering the fact that Nicola and I both had boyfriends, and Cheryl was supposedly brokenhearted. We just couldn't believe they'd done it. They'd seemed so genuine, but we were well and truly duped. We were even more stunned by the fact that one of them was saying that Cheryl had tried it on with him in the room – it just wasn't true. In fact, that was probably the furthest thing from her mind after everything she'd been through. They were clearly not the sweet, affable guys that we took them for. It was mortifying.

I think the whole incident was an indication of where our heads were at the time. We weren't thinking logically or acting sensibly, and we were behaving in a way that we would never have done in the UK. At the time, we all just needed to let loose – especially Cheryl. Nicola and I wanted her to have a bit of freedom for a few days and have a good time. I have to say we did laugh about it a lot when the story broke. What a bunch of idiots we must have looked. Luckily, I'd told Justin the whole story as soon as I got home, because as far as I was concerned it was all perfectly innocent. Otherwise I could have been in big trouble.

Eventually, Cheryl gave Ashley another chance and

they tried to repair their marriage, but further down the line yet more stories surfaced of infidelity on his part. I remember thinking, God, no! I cannot bear for her to go through this again. I think I would rather have gone through it myself than have to watch her suffer like that again. In the end, so many stories were flying about that she didn't know what was true and what wasn't any more. She had to walk away. She was far too strong and proud to be treated so badly by someone who was supposed to love and protect her.

This time Ashley left their home in Surrey, and after that Cheryl was literally under siege there, barricaded in with all the press and media camped outside. To me, it seemed inhumane that this was allowed to happen – someone being fair game just because she's famous. I know as well as anyone that when you become a so-called celebrity, you have to give up a certain amount of freedom and any anonymity, but when someone is at such a low and painful point in her life, why do some people want to make it even harder? I didn't really understand it. I've never enjoyed reading about other people's misfortune, and I don't find it interesting. Why would anyone take pleasure in raking over the break-down of someone's relationship while it's happening? Let them breathe. Give them space.

I went to stay with Cheryl because I knew she was

living like a prisoner. I remember thinking they're never going to leave her alone now. This is never going to end. It made me very grateful that my relationship with Justin has always been so strong, and I've never had to go through anything like Cheryl did. The whole thing made me realise that the level of attention and intrusion that Cheryl suffered was on a different scale compared to the rest of us. I had such admiration for her and the way she dealt with it all.

21

It's About Time

Passions wasn't the only big Girls Aloud TV moment in 2008. *The Girls Aloud Party* was a Christmas spectacular with songs, sketches and special guests, including the Kaiser Chiefs and James Morrison. We knew what an amazing opportunity this was for us – a full hour on prime-time TV, dedicated to us and our songs. It was coming hot on the heels of our fourth number-one single, 'The Promise', and our top-ten album, *Out of Control*.

On the first day of camera rehearsals, Nadine was about three hours late and the producers weren't happy. We all felt embarrassed but, to be honest, we were getting used to it by then. It's funny because whenever a situation blew up like that, we always wanted to protect the integrity of the band. Regardless of anything that was going on between us, we wanted to carry on making good music, and we all cared a great deal about our fans and what they thought. Over ten years there have been quite a few stories about massive bust-ups within the band, but the truth is that we weren't at one another's throats all the time. Yes, there were issues, but most of us were very good at biting our tongue, even when things got tough. You can't have a blazing row with someone one minute and then step out on stage all smiles the next. It just wouldn't have worked, and our number-one priority was keeping the band together. Luckily, we are all savvy and professional enough not to let one silly row get in the way of what we were supposed to be doing, and *The Girls Aloud Party* turned out to be a great success and a fantastic end to the year.

At the start of 2009, 'The Promise' was nominated for best single at the Brit Awards. We'd finally been recognised for our success and hard work, and I guess we all felt like we'd earned it. A fair few people had come after us and then disappeared, picking up a Brit along the way, but we'd always missed out. Surely it was our turn now.

For us five girls, winning the Brit was an acknowledgement that we'd been right about 'The Promise'.

Polydor hadn't wanted to release it as a single. In fact, Colin Barlow had warned us that it could ruin our career. I remember being at Xenomania with Nicola and Cheryl on the day we first heard the song, and we fell in love with it straight away – and that was just the backing track with no vocals. Once we'd actually recorded it, we were certain it was going to be massive. There was something special about 'The Promise', and we all felt it. Polydor thought that another track stood out during the recording of the album – 'The Loving Kind', which was written for us by the Pet Shop Boys. We liked it, too, but for us there was just no comparison with 'The Promise'; it didn't come anywhere close. But everyone at Polydor was insistent that 'The Loving Kind' should be the first single from our new album. I'm not sure if it was because they thought that the Pet Shop Boys connection gave it credibility, but we thought it sounded a bit like 'Call the Shots', only not quite as good. We decided between us that we had to stand our ground about this one.

'It *has* to be "The Promise",' I told Hillary. 'You need to let them know that we're not budging on this one.'

Hillary agreed with us, but with the record company so adamant that we were wrong, I think she was starting to doubt herself. Even Peter, who was now general manager of Polydor's pop label, Fascination, thought that we were wrong about the choice of single. Then Hillary got a call from Polydor telling her that releasing 'The Promise' as a first single from the album would be 'career suicide' and that they weren't going to do it. As a group we'd never been short of an opinion, but we had never point blank defied our record company. On this point, though, we were firm. We simply couldn't go ahead with something that we were so sure was wrong, and we decided that we had to take drastic action.

At the time I was in Cannes with Cheryl, performing my duties as her guest judge on the judges' houses section of *The X Factor*. That was something I enjoyed doing, although I did find it very tough, judging these poor young kids. I couldn't help but remember that Cheryl and I had once been in that incredibly vulnerable position ourselves. I kept my sunglasses on throughout the filming, just in case I got too emotional.

I should probably have been enjoying *The X Factor* experience more, but all this arguing about the choice of single was dragging us both down. We told Hillary to make it clear to Polydor that if they went with 'The Loving Kind' as the single, we'd refuse to promote the album, and that was that. Hillary was worried about our relationship with the label suffering, so Cheryl and I suggested a meeting with all concerned the moment we got back from Cannes. That way we could put our point across calmly, without all the angry exchanges back and forth through our management.

So Nicola, Cheryl and I went to put our case forward – the three of us who usually took the reins when it came to decision-making and pushing forward our vision of the band, especially by that point. I sometimes think that if it hadn't been for the drive and ambition the three of us shared, Girls Aloud would have ended much sooner. I sometimes envied the fact that Nadine and Sarah were able just to turn up and get on with their jobs, because I think that would have meant a lot less personal stress over the years, but that's not me. Everything I have ever done in my life I have tried to do wholeheartedly, and whether it was waitressing, teaching or a performance, I have always tried to make it the best it possibly could be, and give it my all. It's a quality I'm proud of, but it means that I often put a lot of pressure on myself.

Once Cheryl, Nicola and I had had our say at the meeting, Colin and the team at Polydor finally – through gritted teeth – agreed to release 'The Promise' as the first single from the *Out of Control* album. It entered the UK charts at number one. Of course, this last-minute decision about the single had meant that the video, which was set in a 1960s drive-in movie theatre, had to be put together very quickly. In fact, it was such a rush that our usual stylist, Victoria Adcock, refused to work on it because she didn't have enough time to get all the clothes together. Luckily, another stylist, Frank Strachan, stepped in and had a genius notion of how to create those fabulous shimmering gold dresses you see in the video, very quickly. He bought the material and wrapped it around our bras and pinned it all up at the back, then stuck a belt around it. They weren't really dresses at all, just pieces of fabric. We had to learn the choreography on the spot, because we had no time for rehearsals. In the end, it didn't matter because the video turned out brilliantly. One of our best, I think.

At the Brits we performed the song in a Busby Berkeley style routine that was one of the most glamorous concepts Beth had ever dreamed up. We started behind a tasselled curtain, holding pink, ostrich-feather fans, and as the song kicked in, we descended a staircase that was decorated with bright lights, accompanied by our dancers, who were in white top hats and tails. We wore the tiniest of gold outfits, which were little more than beautiful leotards with a fringe around the bottom. Luckily, we were covered up with our ostrich feathers for most of the number.

When Alan Carr announced 'The Promise' as the winner of best British single later that night, we all went completely nuts, leaping up from the table with excitement. Our boyfriends were with us, as were all of our Polydor family, Hillary and Angela, who'd been Hillary's right-hand woman ever since we started with Shaw Thing. Everyone was totally elated, and we couldn't get up on the stage quickly enough. When we finally got there, I was the first to speak, thanking the public and our fans for voting for us, and then thanking Shaw Thing Management for looking after us. I also thanked the team at Xenomania for writing such an amazing pop song. I have to give Colin Barlow his due. He did come over to us afterwards and have a laugh about the arguing we'd done over the record, and he admitted that he was wrong about it and we were right, just as we had been about 'Love Machine' a few years before. There really were no hard feelings between us.

After I'd finished my little acceptance speech, Sarah got on the mic and yelled out, 'It's about time!' She was right – it *was* about time.

22

You're a Liar, Ronan!

I didn't know Gary Barlow all that well, so when he called to tell me he was organising a charity walk up the highest mountain in Africa, I was nonplussed. I remember thinking to myself, OK, that's nice, Gary, and you're telling me this because . . . ? Even the phone call made me feel nervous. In fact, the very word 'mountain' sent chills down my spine.

'What do you think, would you be up for something like that?' Gary said.

Really? I mean, really? I was sh***ing myself, quite frankly. No. I didn't think this was something I was going to be able to do at all.

'Er . . .' I said.

Climbing a mountain was about as far away from something I would choose to do as it was possible to get. If you asked any of my friends, they would be sure to tell you that I'm not even that keen on walking from the car to the shop. I'm quite lazy in that respect, and all I ever do is moan about my feet hurting when I have to walk anywhere.

'I can send you an information pack to look over,' Gary told me. 'See what you think.'

I agreed that I would look into it if he sent me the info. I really had no idea what it would entail, but as it was for Comic Relief, which was close to my heart, I had to give it some thought at least. The idea was to raise as much money as we could to buy malaria nets to protect some of the hundreds of thousands of children who are in danger of contracting the deadly disease every year.

Despite my misgivings, I began to have a niggling feeling inside me. Ever since I'd done the Comic Relief trip to Africa in 2007, it had been bugging me that I hadn't followed it up with anything really positive. I wanted to do more to help in some way, and maybe this was it. Over the next few days, the more I thought about it, the more I started to convince myself that I should do it, despite the idea terrifying the life out of me. I told myself that the fact that it scared me so much was the very reason to do it. After all, why would people sponsor you for thousands of pounds to do something that was easy, or that you enjoyed doing? There was no point in that at all. To raise the kind of money that was needed to do some good, I was going to have to put myself out there and go the extra mile. So, after going round and round in circles in my head over the next couple of weeks, I decided that I was doing it. I had to. After all the good things that had happened to me, and all the luxuries I'd been afforded through being in the entertainment industry, this was my chance to give something back.

When I told the rest of the girls about it, they could hardly believe their ears.

'You're crazy. I don't know why you're even thinking about it,' Nicola said. 'Why would you even do that to yourself?'

She's famously terrified of heights, so she really couldn't imagine anything worse. Cheryl, on the other hand, had been through quite a lot of pain and upset in the past year or so, so she wasn't really scared of anything. But it had been a tough time for her, so I was surprised by her reaction when I asked her to do the climb with me, more in hope than expectation.

'I really don't want to do it on my own,' I told her. 'Will you do it?'

I think Cheryl could see how nervous I was.

'OK, I'll do it with you,' she said, confidently.

'What?'

I could no more imagine Cheryl Cole walking up a bloody mountain than I could me, to be honest. I only had to cast my mind back to an incident in Greece, when we were filming for *Girls Aloud: Off the Record*. Drew had encouraged us all to walk up to a restaurant that was at the highest point in Greece, with supposedly fabulous views. It was a really long, steep hike and we were all in heels, having had no previous warning of this two-mile trek. We'd all been unhappy about it, but Cheryl was fuming. She was cursing and swearing all the way up, and loudly asking anyone who would listen to her, 'What's the f***ing point of this? Does anyone really give a sh*t if we see the peak of Greek?' As far as I was concerned, there was no way Cheryl was going to walk up Mount Kilimanjaro, but I was wrong.

'I want to do something good and worthwhile,' she said. 'It'll be good for us to do something together.'

So that was pretty much it. We met up with Gary at Cheryl's house and started making plans. Of course, Gary is always so laid back and he made it seem like the easiest thing in the world.

'Oh, it'll be fine,' he assured us. 'We'll see some animals and all that. It's just a walk.'

Gary wanted as diverse a group of people as possible so that the sponsorship money would be coming in from a number of different avenues. Obviously, with the Girls Aloud fanbase being so big, there was potential to pull in a lot of sponsors and for us to raise a lot of money for the campaign. We both knew we'd made the right decision, but we still had no idea what to expect. Over the next few weeks I was very anxious and I didn't get a lot of sleep. People sometimes died climbing up mountains, didn't they? And I'm not exactly what you'd call an outdoorsy person at the best of times, let alone a mountaineer. I even hate camping.

Clearly, I needed to take this challenge very seriously and do some proper training. A friend of mine, Nicole Abbott, is a personal trainer, and she took me on seven- or eight-mile walks around Hertfordshire while I carried a backpack to get used to carrying weight over long distances. I had to prepare myself as much as I possibly could if I was going to endure what was to come, and all those walks with Nicole made me feel better, slightly alleviating my fear about the trek the more I did.

When we arrived in Tanzania in the little plane we'd taken from Nairobi, I was feeling nervous but also quite excited about the climb. The good news was that I liked all the other people who were taking part, and I knew quite a few of them. As well as Gary, Fearne

Cotton was there, Ben Shephard, Alesha Dixon, Ronan Keating, Chris Moyles and Denise Van Outen. The only one I was a bit unsure of at first was Chris, because he'd been quite rude about Nicola on his Radio 1 breakfast show in the past, but I was hoping that we could put that behind us. During the climb, Cheryl and I both told him how awful we thought his comments were. Chris agreed that he'd been out of order and apologised, and I was glad that we'd put the whole episode to bed. There was no room for bad blood if we were going to be hanging off the side of a mountain together.

That first evening we stayed at a hotel and it was a very strange night. I don't think either Cheryl or I got a wink of sleep. We felt utterly daunted by the whole thing – even though we were there and it was much too late to turn back now. There were just so many questions and so much information being thrown at us. Have you packed this? Have you prepared that? Do you understand all the information about how serious the altitude sickness can be? There was so much to take in; it was no wonder I lay awake all that night, fretting.

The next day, when we all gathered at the start of the walk, ready to go, I remember feeling very lonely, even though there were nine of us. I wasn't going to have the use of my phone to call or get emails or messages, and I just felt so far away from my family. I'm a bit of a softy when it comes to leaving Justin and my family, and I silently thanked God that Cheryl was there. She was going to be the only connection to my real life while we took on this scary challenge.

I can't say I wasn't terrified, because I was. In contrast, Ben and Fearne were incredibly excited about the whole thing and had wanted to do something like this for years. Cheryl, Alesha and Denise were a bit more like me – they'd agreed to do the walk because it was for a good cause, but they weren't especially thrilled about it. I'd not met Denise before, but I liked her straight off, although she was quite different from the person I'd expected. Denise always came across to me as such a big personality – musical theatre star, super confident. When you get to know her, though, she's a really chilled out, calm woman, and she was a good person to have around.

Alesha was great, too. She didn't have a partner to share her tent with, since there was an odd number in the group, but Cheryl and I didn't like the idea of her sleeping on her own, halfway up a mountain. So we offered to make our tent a three-girl affair, which would have worked out fine if we hadn't spent so much time gossiping into the night and not getting enough sleep.

The other problem was that the anti-altitude sickness tablets that we had to take made you want to wee constantly. Literally every ten or fifteen minutes one of us would be getting up to go to the loo and waking up the others.

For the first few hours of the walk everyone was in high spirits and everything looked really pretty with plenty of greenery and flowers. I remember thinking this is fine. I can do this, no trouble. There were a few little hills here and there but nothing too horrendous, and as far as I could tell I had no symptoms of the much talked-about altitude sickness, which has been known actually to kill people. We had a medic with us, and Sherpa mountain guides, who were wonderful. The head guide, Raj, was a veteran of many mountains and a virtual machine when it came to climbing. The Sherpa guides carried our tents for us, while we carried our own water supply in our backpacks, together with lots of energy bars to keep us going, our toiletries and our clothing. You have to have quite a few layers of clothing when you're climbing, because the climate is so dramatically changeable. It was quite a lot to carry and I'm pretty sure I couldn't have managed a tent as well. Cheryl's backpack was as big as she was, so she definitely couldn't have managed any more.

When we reached the first camp we were informed

that a British paparazzi photographer had followed us up, and that put us all on edge because at first we really had no idea who he was or what he looked like. Obviously, the camp wasn't private, so we knew he was staying among us, and all of the girls in our group were petrified that he might have been snapping photographs of us squatting behind a bush or a rock when we went to the toilet, which is what we all had to do while we were walking. That was one particular 'nicety' you had to get used to very quickly. If you needed to go, you just went wherever you were – there were no toilet facilities until you got to the camp, where the guides could set up a makeshift Portaloo. It was pretty disgusting, because whatever spot you found to use, other people had been there before you. You can just imagine! The threat of a photographer following us all the way up Kilimanjaro documenting all this definitely put a damper on the first night. It made us feel like we were being watched, and the climb was tough enough without having that added pressure. Eventually, after much drama, we managed to get the guy removed from our camp, but we couldn't stop him from climbing the mountain and consequently we had no idea whether he was going to be following us or not.

Every morning the Sherpa guide who was assigned to us girls popped his head into our tent to wake us up.

'Hellooo! Hellooo! You want coffee?'

His name was Davis, and he turned out to be such an amazing help and comfort to me as the climb got more difficult.

The first couple of days weren't too bad, though. Yes, there were some steep slopes to conquer, and we were walking for twelve hours a day, but on the whole, everyone seemed to be faring pretty well. All the training I'd done had paid off. My legs felt fine and I actually felt pretty good about how well I was doing. Night times were the problem. Three in a tent was quite a tight squeeze, and what with all the chattering and one of us constantly jumping up for the toilet, there was a fair bit of sleep deprivation going on. Aside from that, sometimes the altitude was making breathing difficult, and I was quite scared to shut my eyes and go to sleep.

By the third night we were quite high up, and the altitude sickness really started to kick in for some people. We were warned that this was the point where it might happen, and sure enough, Alesha began to get very emotional and started to cry all of a sudden. Becoming over-emotional is one of the early physical symptoms of altitude sickness, but at the time Cheryl and I couldn't work out why Alesha was so upset or what was wrong with her. We all rallied round her and were soon told what was happening. By the time we set up camp that night, she seemed to have calmed down quite a lot.

As the night wore on it started to pour with torrential rain, and on top of that, someone was keeping the entire camp awake with their extraordinarily loud snoring. Chris Moyles later swore up and down that it was one of the cameramen, who were documenting our climb for Comic Relief, but I'm convinced it was Chris himself. Our tent was lively that night, as per, with the three of us girls gossiping about anything and everything, like we were on a sleepover rather than a tough hike up the tallest mountain in Africa. It was fun getting to know Alesha. She has a lot in common with us, coming from a girl band herself, and I warmed to her quite quickly. The three us were all such chatterboxes, but eventually that night we decided we'd best pipe down. There was enough noise going on with the rain and the snoring without us adding to it.

Suddenly, as I was drifting off to sleep, I heard Denise outside, sounding quite hysterical.

'Fearne's collapsed,' she said, as I clambered out of the tent into the rain to see what was going on. 'She was just going to the toilet but I found her on the floor outside the tent. I've dragged her in out of the rain, but can you stay with her while I go and get the medic?'

I left Alesha and Cheryl and rushed over to Fearne and Denise's tent. Fearne was conscious but delirious – not with it at all – and it was quite scary to see just how severe the altitude sickness could be. Eventually, Denise came back with Raj and the nurse, and Fearne was given the injections and medical treatment she needed. Raj ended up staying in their tent to make sure Fearne was OK, and I went back to Cheryl and Alesha in a state of shock.

'She did not look well at all,' I told them. 'I really hope that doesn't happen to any of us.'

Fearne was actually quite ill for the rest of the climb, and I wondered if she was going to make it all the way. At several points on the journey she was pretty much ready to give up because she wasn't getting any better. Luckily, she's a strong character, so she managed to battle her way through, but climbing a mountain is a hard enough thing to do as it is, without feeling like you're going to vomit every step of the way.

As we neared the next camp the following day, we passed someone with serious altitude sickness. We were now at nearly 4,000 feet, and the man was being stretchered down the mountain in a real state – delirious with bulging eyes and lungs filling up with water. He was clearly in a critical condition. Immediately, Raj and one of the other guides dashed over to the guy, and they ended up accompanying the party all the way back down the mountain to help look after him. Once the guy was delivered to intensive care – just in the nick of time by all accounts – Raj came all the way back up to meet us again at the next camp. I really don't know how he did it. By then we were all scared of what might happen because we'd seen it up close. I kept telling myself to listen to every single thing I was told by the Sherpas and the medic really carefully. I certainly didn't want anything like that happening to me.

Cheryl and I were still both OK but we continued to take the anti-sickness tablets, just to be on the safe side, despite them making you wee constantly, and I mean constantly, and causing a tingling sensation in your fingers and toes, which could be quite unpleasant at times.

The next point we reached was the Barranco Wall, which is one part of the trek that requires serious climbing rather than hiking, and at that point I almost started to laugh.

'No chance,' I said, my jaw dropping as I looked up at the 300-metre vertical climb in front of me.

I couldn't see myself getting up there, and I certainly couldn't see Chris Moyles, who was quite hefty at the time, managing it. Another problem was that Gary had a really bad back. He'd been popping medication throughout the entire trek, just to get him through. As it happened, though, I surprised myself. Once I started off, I got a real buzz climbing the rock. It was a lot more fun doing some proper climbing than walking for miles on end, and I loved it. I felt a real sense of achievement when we all got to the top of it. That was definitely the best day for me in terms of experience.

After that, it was miles and miles of the bleakest terrain you could ever imagine, and that part of the journey was especially hard. Nothing survived that high up, and at times it felt like we were on some barren planet in another universe – there was absolutely nothing to see. I remember the despondency on everyone's faces as it dawned on us that we faced hours of walking through nothing until we got to the next camp. Everyone was tired and struggling, and none of us knew if Fearne was going to make it. Cheryl and I had a bit of a 'moment', sitting down on a rock together and crying our eyes out. The expression on Cheryl's face was one I knew very well and it mirrored my own feelings. It said, 'I'm done. I want to go down.' It said, 'This is bloody awful.' Again it hit me how far away from Justin and my family I was, and I felt utterly distraught.

The camera crew came over and tried to film us, but neither of us was in any mood to be filmed.

'Let's not do this now,' I said. 'Give us a minute. We need to get ourselves together, and we need to be on our own.'

The cameraman obliged, and so Cheryl and I sat there on that rock, trying to encourage one another to go on, reminding ourselves why we were there, and of how far we'd already come.

That night as we neared the camp, exhausted and miserable, we suddenly heard the most beautiful and reassuring sound. The Sherpas, who had reached the camp before us, were all singing at the tops of their voices to spur us on to complete the journey. I'd been in a dark place that day, and the sound of the music and those gorgeous African songs seemed like salvation. It changed everything and gave us something to head towards. It was a wonderful moment. When we finally got there, the Sherpas all looked so happy, and they cheered as each one of us arrived. The last person to reach the camp was Fearne, and everyone was so over-joyed that she'd made it we all virtually broke down in tears. I remember Gary hugging me, and I was so happy that I'd pushed myself to go on. Yes, it was hard but we'd all made it.

Later that night, however, I started to feel quite ill and I got very emotional. That's how the altitude sickness gets you. My head felt like it was being squashed by a ten-ton weight and I became disorientated and anxious. I felt alone again, and the fact that I couldn't contact my loved ones at home sent a feeling of panic running through me.

It started when we all sat down for some food and I couldn't find Cheryl. Raj told me she was resting, but she'd been projectile vomiting for the past hour. He hadn't wanted to scare me, and he wanted me to eat and have a rest myself without worrying about Cheryl. When I finally found her, she was in a real state, which unnerved me. Then later that night, when I couldn't find my phone, I completely lost it. It's not as if I could have used it anyway – there was no signal – but the fact that I thought I'd lost it made me freak out completely. It was all very dramatic and over the top, but altitude sickness just makes you lose all sense of reality.

'Where's my phone, it's got everything in it,' I sobbed, hysterically. Even though I couldn't use the damn thing, it still had all my photographs of my family and Justin on it. It was at least some sort of link to my real life and to the real world, which felt so very far away. I was inconsolable, and every time somebody even tried to speak to me I burst into tears. Now it was Cheryl's turn to try to calm me down in her own inimitable, no-nonsense fashion.

'You're acting totally bizarre,' she said. 'You need to get a grip and calm down because you're scaring me. This is not you. You would never be like this normally.'

I'm usually in control, but at that moment I felt like I was losing my mind, becoming more and more vulnerable with each minute that passed, like I was breaking open, and yet Cheryl stayed so strong. I was laughing one minute and crying hysterically the next. Cheryl, meanwhile, kept trying to pull me back from the brink.

'Kimberley! Kimberley! Pull yourself together. Who *is* this person? You're gonna have to calm down. I've got a bad head!'

It's laughable when I think back on it now, but at the time it really wasn't funny. God only knows what Alesha must have thought of the two of us. She was caught in the middle of it all.

Eventually, I was able to use the special phone that the guides used for emergencies. I called Justin at home, where he was happily playing computer games with my brother, Adam. It just seemed so weird to me that they were at home in a normal environment, doing normal things, and here I was in the most abnormal situation imaginable. I don't think they could understand why I was so upset, but speaking to Justin and knowing that everything and everyone back home was OK made me feel so much better. When all was said and done, though, it wasn't the best night ever, what with Cheryl being sick for hours on end and me having a mental breakdown.

During that night we both got up to go to the loo at the same time, and we ended up sitting on the ground outside the tent together while everyone else was sleeping. There we sat, just looking all around us, trying to take in the ridiculousness of having to get up for a pee in minus God knows how many degrees in the middle of the night up a bloody mountain. It was completely random, but quite a special moment for the two of us. We were both so grateful to have one another, and being there in that situation really brought it home to us. We decided that although the climb had been much worse and scarier than we ever imagined it could be, we just needed to push on and get on with it. We'd come too far to go back now. The funny thing was that Cheryl and I had both assumed that we knew everything there was to know about one another and there was nothing left to learn. And then we climbed a mountain together and found out that wasn't the case. We both saw very different sides of each other on that journey. She'd seen me lose control and turn into a vulnerable child, and I saw strength and resolve in her that I never knew she had. She walked up that mountain like a bloody gazelle. I was the one who'd done weeks and weeks of training, and she strode up it, no trouble.

I was a mess by the time we got to the last leg of the journey. By this time, I was so run down, and I looked like the Elephant Woman, with a mouth covered in cold sores.

'Me lips! I can't feel me mouth,' I announced to Cheryl in the tent in the middle of the night. They were horrible, open wounds, and in the absence of anything else, Cheryl sprayed perfume on them in an attempt to dry them up. This turned out to be unbearably painful, and not a very good idea. What we didn't realise was that when you're at that high altitude, wounds don't heal, so I just had to put up with these terrible sores all over my mouth. What with that and all the insect bites, I was in a right state. I remember Ronan coming up to me while I was on the verge of tears yet again.

'Are you all right?' he said.

'Yeah,' I sniffed, 'but me lips are really sore, look at me.'

'Ah sure, you look great!' he said in his chirpy Irish accent.

You're a liar, Ronan, I thought. A f***ing liar!

Finally, it was summit night – the last push to the top of the mountain. This part of the journey has to be done in the dark, because the sun and daylight conditions make the ground too soft and it can be unstable. This was the night that we'd all been waiting and preparing for, and everyone was geared up to go for it. It was one last walk, and one of the hardest – extremely steep, dark and minus thirty degrees. I put on every single article of clothing I had with me.

We were all supposed to go for a few hours' sleep after dinner but instead, Alesha, Cheryl and I ended up having a sing-along session in our tent, belting out every song we could think of that related to climbing a mountain or achieving something momentous. 'Ain't No Mountain High Enough' was, of course, one of the numbers we sang, and soon enough we could hear Denise and Fearne joining in from their tent. When we eventually started the long climb to the top I realised just how hard it was going to be. We were strung out in one long line, because that's all the path would allow, and all I could see was a twinkling caterpillar of lights up the hill in front of me – the beams from everyone's head-torches.

For the seven-hour climb in the pitch black Raj stayed close. He seemed quite worried about me and I must say I didn't feel well at all, so I kept stopping to drink some hot tea, which made us fall back from the group somewhat. Then I had to go to the loo, which isn't the easiest thing to do at minus thirty in the dark, I can tell you. Afterwards, I managed to get my knickers back up, but I literally couldn't pull up my trousers because my hands felt like they were frozen solid. Poor Raj had to help me, which was quite embarrassing, but by that point I was past caring.

One of the cameramen was getting sick by now, stumbling around while he was trying to film us, and then we met an older couple coming down, who'd had to turn back just an hour from the summit because one of them was so ill. I was suddenly determined. No chance! NO f***ing chance! There was no way that I was going back down again. I was going to get to that summit if it killed me, and by then I actually thought it might. But the main thing that kept me going that night was having Davis there. He'd been like my own personal guide for most of the trip, and every time I got despondent he would spur me on. 'Hakuna matata,' he'd say, which is a Swahili saying, meaning 'there are no worries'. I don't think I would have got up there that night if it hadn't been for him. He was dragging me up from under the arm by the end of it.

As the sun came up I was finally nearing the summit of Mount Kilimanjaro, around the same time as Gary and Ben. Fearne, Cheryl and Denise were the first to get there, while it was still dark, and they were now on their way down again because it was so cold up there. When I got to the top, the sun rose above the clouds and I was in awe of the view. A huge and beautiful glacier lay right next to us, and the panorama was completely amazing. I'd seen nothing like it before. That being said, the actual summit was just a flat area with a little wooden sign on it. I'm not going to pretend I didn't feel slightly let down by that! My main feeling was one of relief, and I wondered how my family were going to feel on hearing that I'd made it to the summit. Believe it or not, my phone suddenly found a signal while I was up there, and I received a text from my sister saying that she'd got engaged. It was quite an odd place to receive happy family news, but it couldn't have been more perfect. So I sat down with the Sherpa guides on top of Mount Kilimanjaro, and they rubbed my hands to keep me warm, while singing their wonderful African songs to me. It was a fantastic sight to take in, an amazing experience, and I'll never forget it.

One of the best things about the whole event was meeting the wonderful Sherpa people who guided us so brilliantly throughout the climb. Getting to know them was a real privilege, and I have so much respect for their knowledge and what they do. During the trek, Ronan had his thirty-second birthday, and as a surprise,

Emmanuel – who was a Sherpa cook – came into the dining area with his crew, carrying a great big chocolate cake. They were all singing like a choir and wearing red noses. That underlined what very special people they are. The Sherpas seemed to like me, too, and I remember at one point one of them asking Gary, 'How many cows for Kimberley?'

'Oh, mate, she's worth quite a bit,' Gary said in his usual matter-of-fact fashion. 'I don't think you've got enough cows for Kimberley.'

They were all so lovely, and utterly amazing.

A little while later, Gary, Fearne, Ben, Chris and I travelled to Uganda to make a follow-up documentary about how some of that money was spent and the distribution of the malaria nets. While we were there, Chris Moyles and I were asked to appear on Ugandan TV to talk about our experience and the importance of raising money for nets. This turned out to be one of the funniest TV experiences of my life. The TV studio itself was pretty basic – like somebody's living room with a camera in it – and without any sort of brief or rehearsal we just went live on prime-time Ugandan TV. Chris and I took it in our stride and assumed that it was going to be pretty straightforward. The presenter would ask us a few questions, and we would talk about our amazing achievement and get to feel good about ourselves for raising so much money for a worth-while cause. It was all going fairly smoothly until the presenter, Alan, started firing questions at us.

'Why did you choose Kilimanjaro?' Alan asked, as if it was a really bad idea to climb the highest mountain in Africa. Then he turned to Chris with a look of disbelief. 'Did YOU climb the mountain yourself?'

Chris's face was a picture, and I wanted to laugh.

'Do I not look like I could climb a mountain?' Chris asked, wide-eyed.

Alan asked us about the nets themselves, which threw the pair of us into a complete panic.

'So, you're going to show us all how to put a mosquito net up properly?'

'Kimberley is,' Chris said, quick as a flash and pointing at me.

Of course, we had no idea what we were doing, but the TV crew had already set up a bed in the studio and they were all prepared for a live demonstration on the correct way to erect a malaria net. Chris looked at me and I knew exactly what he was thinking: Bloody hell, we're going to have to blag this, aren't we? I smiled sweetly at Alan.

'Demonstrate,' I said, nervously. 'We'll try.'

Unfortunately, I got the giggles straight away, which was pretty bad timing given the seriousness and importance of what we were doing, but I just couldn't stop myself. Chris, meanwhile, kept making sarcastic comments, which was making me laugh even more. I tried as best I could to make it through the demonstration.

'Am I doing it right, Kimberley?' As if I knew.

'Er, well, you secure the net to the top of the pole and . . . er . . . even it out on your side as best you can, Chris, because they're all made to fit different sized beds.'

I didn't know what I was doing as I flapped about like a maniac with that bloody net, and it got worse when the presenter started asking us serious and detailed questions about the construction of the net. What were they made of? What chemicals were they treated with?

'Er . . . Er . . .'

We didn't have a clue. In the end, Chris got on the bed under the badly erected net.

'I'm now safe from the mosquitoes, and you two are not safe,' he told Alan and me, and we eventually crawled under the net with him.

'So no mosquitoes now,' Alan said. Even he was giggling by then.

The minute Chris and I left the studio we both burst into fits of laughter, and later that evening we saw it repeated on the fuzzy TV in our hotel. Gary, Ben and Fearne watched it with us, and we all fell about – it looked such a mess. God knows what the viewers must have been thinking – the programme was called *Health Focus* of all things.

All nine of us who went on the climb reached the summit of Mount Kilimanjaro, and we raised around £3.5 million for our cause. It was by far the hardest thing I've ever done in my life, and the sense of achievement was amazing. I'd done something I never in my wildest dreams thought I'd do. I'd climbed a mountain.

23

Hanging on for Dear Life

Although I'd had an incredible experience in Tanzania, by the time I got back I was very unwell. I just didn't feel myself – like I was a shell – and all I wanted to do was sleep. My emotions had been firing all over the place during the climb, and no matter how hard I tried, I couldn't seem to get back on a normal footing again once I was home. I felt like the whole experience had completely changed my life, and that I could never look at the world in the same way again. I constantly felt weak and I kept getting dizzy every time I stood up. I began to wonder if the altitude sickness I'd suffered in Africa was having some kind of lasting effect. I was sure something was wrong, and it got to the point that I was scared to be left on my own. I asked Justin to check on me while I was asleep in case I never woke up again. It felt like I was almost passing out rather than sleeping normally. I seemed to be unconscious the whole time.

In the end, I went to the doctor to have some tests done, and he told me that my blood pressure was very low and that I needed to rest. The trouble was I didn't really have time for that. For a start, all nine of us who'd done the climb were invited to attend a special party with the Prime Minister, Gordon Brown, at 10 Downing Street. He'd made a pledge to match the money we'd raised on the climb and donate it to the charity, which was fantastic. I felt quite privileged to be invited to meet the Prime Minister, especially in order to be commended and thanked for something I'd done.

Number 10 was just how I'd imagined it would be – very traditional, with big fireplaces, family pictures and antique furniture all around the place. I've been there several times since then, but this was really special. The only trouble was I was still half off the planet and getting dizzy spells the whole time. To combat this constant dizziness, the doctor suggested I wear compression stockings, which helped keep my blood circulating properly. I must say it wasn't the most fabulous I'd ever felt at a soiree. What with the surgical stockings and a face full of cold sores, which I still hadn't got rid of, it was really quite grim.

Eventually, I ended up having tests on my heart and all sorts, but nobody seemed to be able to find anything too sinister. That didn't stop my mum and the rest of my family worrying about me, and they were constantly turning up at my house with care parcels of food and general sustenance. On top of all this, I had no time at all to get myself better before we were jumping head-long into promotion for our new single, 'Untouchable'. The promotions department at the record label scheduled an appearance on *Dancing on Ice* only days after Cheryl and I got back. Hillary added it to the diary, and for that I could have happily killed the lot of them. Then I found out that a couple of days after that we had the video shoot scheduled – it wasn't good. I remember being at the studio where *Dancing on Ice* was filmed and I felt utterly miserable. I sat there remembering the advice that Raj had given us on the day we'd left Tanzania after completing the climb.

'Don't do too much for the next few weeks, girls,' he told Cheryl and me. 'Let your body get back to normal. You've put it under a lot of pressure and now you need a bit of rest.'

Yeah, right! That couldn't have been any further

from what was actually happening, but that's how it always was in Girls Aloud. You just kept going no matter how you felt. It was like a rollercoaster that you couldn't jump off. During that week, though, I felt as though I was being abused and I was furious with Hillary for putting such major things in the diary so soon after we'd got back. Looking back, it wasn't really her fault. I don't think she or anyone realised just how hard that trip was going to be on us, and more than anything she was just so relieved that we'd come back safe and sound. She'd been up every night while we were away, watching the live camera feed online – just to make sure nothing bad happened to us. At the time, though, neither Cheryl nor I gave a crap about performing on television or doing the video. We just needed to sleep.

The worst part about the *Dancing on Ice* slot was that at the start of the song, we were hanging on wires, as if suspended in mid-air. Well, I could barely stand up, so the last thing I felt like was being hung from the ceiling and dangled over an ice rink in a Grecian goddess frock while Torvill and bloody Dean skated about underneath me. It was hell. We weren't even in the right costumes that night, because the ones we'd had made looked like something you'd wear on Halloween. Black and red nightmares! Cheryl and I were amazed that nothing had been done about it while we were away.

'Why the hell hasn't someone sorted something else out?' I wanted to know. It was just the usual GA drama, but at the time I guess I was pissed off at everyone because I felt so tired and ill.

Right after that we were straight into rehearsals for the 'Out of Control' tour, and although I'd started to feel a little bit better, my body was still trying to tell me to slow down and I knew it. Sure enough, my hip gave out after a week of choreography rehearsals and I was in agony. For the next week or so I just had to sit and watch because I couldn't move. Cheryl also got into difficulties because of all the strain she'd put her body under climbing the mountain. This made the whole rehearsal period quite a difficult time for both of us, and we had to take a physiotherapist with us on the tour to help us out when we needed it.

Mountaineering injuries aside, being on tour can be really dangerous. Yes, it's an amazing experience and we almost always had a great time, but if you don't know what you're doing on that stage, you could get hurt quite easily. When we were doing the technical run-through for the first night of our 'Greatest Hits' tour, we'd had quite a terrifying few minutes while rehearsing our spectacular opening number, which was

'Something Kinda Oooh'. The idea was that all five of us would be lowered on a mechanically controlled platform all the way down from the top of the arena, dressed in fabulous military outfits. The platform itself was secured on four chains, which hung from each corner, and all that was holding us girls on the platform was a bit of seatbelt through a loop – nothing major. So up we went to run through it all with the proper timing, and as soon as our musical director, Joseph, started the music the platform started to come down. Nadine wasn't too keen on being up that high, and Nicola is absolutely terrified of heights at the best of times, but my attitude is usually one of 'oh, don't worry, it'll all be fine'. Suddenly, though, I realised that only one side of the platform was being lowered, and before we knew it we were all hanging on for dear life as the bloody thing dangled, completely lopsided, high over the arena. The band, meanwhile, were going hell for leather and had no idea what was going on, even though we were all screaming our heads off. I looked over at Nadine, who was saying a prayer, and then at Nicola, who was clutching on to me in absolute terror.

'Stop the f***ing music!' Cheryl screamed into her microphone, but it just went on and on.

Once the platform was finally levelled out and lowered, Beth, who devised the whole idea, was quite as traumatised as we were. She'd planned it all so meticulously, poor thing, and usually stuff like that goes pretty smoothly.

'Right! We're not doing that,' she announced as we clambered off the platform in a right old state. 'I'll find some other fabulous entrance for you, don't worry, girls.'

Once we were back in the dressing room and had calmed down a bit, however, we were each in agreement that any other entrance was going to be a bit crap.

'We have to do this,' Nicola suddenly said. 'We have to make this happen. Let's get out there and do it again.'

Well, if Nicola could do it, we all could, so we marched back out to the arena and did it over again that night in front of an audience.

On the 'Out of Control' tour, we entered on hydraulic podiums, which came out of trapdoors on the stage and rose high into the air as we performed our opening number, 'The Promise'. It was supposed to be a beautiful moment, but on the first night at the O2 in London, I was slightly confused to see that only four of us were rising gracefully above the crowd. Cheryl's forehead was just about poking out above the trapdoor. Her podium hadn't worked and she was still almost completely submerged below the stage. The rest of us valiantly and desperately tried to style it out, but Cheryl's solo lines are almost at the start of the first verse of the song, right after the opening chorus, and we didn't have very long before it was time for her to sing them. The other girls were looking at me as if to say, Where the hell is she? But there really was nothing any of us could do aside from smile sweetly and carry on. When I glanced down, I could see Cheryl out of the corner of my eye. Sure enough, she was giving it loads underneath the stage, but all the audience could see was the top of her head bobbing up and down and back and forth – it was hilarious. She had to sing her part underground before eventually rising up to join us just before the next chorus kicked in.

After 'The Promise', the hydraulic podiums disappeared and the stage blacked out before the next song, which was 'Miss You Bow Wow'. The idea was that while the blackout was happening, we would swiftly rip off the long skirt section of our dresses and throw them down the trapdoor before it closed. Then when the lights came up, we'd be revealed in shimmering mini-dresses for a quick 'hello' before the song started. On the second night of the tour the lights came up much too soon, and we all froze in horror in the most unflattering poses as we tried desperately to struggle out of our skirts. It was like broad daylight on that stage, and I had one of my legs up, half out of my long skirt. I've never felt so horrified to be on a stage in my entire life, and I just wanted to drop down through the trapdoor along with the bloody skirt. It felt like an eternity until the lights went off again and we could finish undressing.

'Somebody's gonna die for this,' Cheryl said to me through gritted teeth. 'We have been made to look like FOOLS!'

By that point in our career, we were so proud of our stage shows, with all their slick professionalism, but on those two occasions we felt as though we looked like amateurs. It was all part of being on the road, though, and, looking back, I would say the times when things went wrong were just as much fun as the times when everything went right. It was all part of being in Girls Aloud.

24

Taking a Break

It wasn't only painful joints and stage malfunctions that were a problem. The 'Out of Control' tour in the spring of 2009 wasn't just the beginning of the end for Girls Aloud – it was almost the end of the end.

There had been a weird atmosphere within the band ever since we'd found out about Nadine's manager, who turned out to be an American guy, Bruce Garfield. It was hard for us to accept her need to separate herself from the rest of us, because at that time none of us had considered a solo career outside the band, and she never once talked to us about it. Now all of a sudden, Bruce was there in our midst – on our tour bus and backstage at the gigs – telling anyone who would listen that he was 'Nadine's manager' and that was that. Well, we already had a manager and that was Hillary. We were a band, not a bunch of solo artists, so what the hell was going on?

We did try talking to Nadine, asking her why she hadn't at least spoken to us about it. I did my best to explain to her how strange it was for us to have someone walking around backstage who wasn't part of our team or Hillary's team or anything to do with Girls Aloud. Nadine said she was sorry and that Bruce was just there to look after her interests, but she didn't really seem to understand our concerns or want to talk about it any further. At the end of the day, there was nothing we could do to stop her from having her own manager, and although we all felt a little disrespected, there wasn't much we could do about it.

By the time the 'Out of Control' tour was off and rolling, quite a wedge had developed between Nadine and the rest of us – it was sad. The four of us were close, but she had become detached, and she was now living permanently in LA. We'd known for some time that her loyalty didn't really lie with us as a group any more, and we also knew that we couldn't force her to stay. I would never want to do that anyway. If she wasn't happy in the group, she had every right to leave, the same as any of us did. Nadine had been in the band since she was sixteen, and I think that she just wanted to be free to do her own thing, and I could understand that. That being said, it didn't make for a great working relationship, especially when we were thrown together every day on the tour bus and in various arenas around the country. For a long time, the rest of us had felt that she was holding us to ransom, and with the constant whispers of Nadine's imminent solo deal, we felt as if she was calling the shots, and that the band's future was in her hands.

So what was the answer? Surely the best thing for the band was to have a break from one another so everyone could do what they wanted to do for a while. After all, while we were recording the TV series, *Passions*, we'd all gone off and done different things. I'd gone back to my musical theatre roots and loved it, and Cheryl had danced in a video for the American recording artist, will.i.am, which led to her performing as a guest vocalist on his single, 'Heartbreaker'. She was also juggling her job on *The X Factor* with all her Girls Aloud duties. Sarah, meanwhile, had landed herself a part in the new *St Trinian's* movie, *The Legend of Fritton's Gold*, and she was due to start filming later in the year. Maybe it was the right time for us to dip our toes in the water and discover what else was out there. On the other hand Girls Aloud were the biggest they'd ever been – we were on a real high. Sometimes when

I thought about the prospect of a hiatus, it just seemed crazy at this point in our career, and I knew that Nicola was very much of that opinion. She simply couldn't see the sense in us taking a break. She was always the baby of the band and I felt a bit guilty because the decision was sort of forced upon her.

With all this uncertainty about the future, day-to-day life on the tour could be a bit strained, to say the least. As far as I was concerned, it didn't feel like it was about being in a group any more, and because I was in a really strange place after Kilimanjaro, I just felt deflated and unhappy. That's not to say it wasn't one of our biggest and certainly one of our best tours as far as the actual show went. Our fans were as wonderful as ever, and our individual performances were really strong . . . but I didn't enjoy it as much as I should have done. Looking back, it doesn't feel like I was there, because I was worn down and my heart wasn't in it. In the past, I'd always tried to hold everything and everyone together in the band, but now I didn't see the point. It wasn't going to work any more, and I was exhausted by the thought of even trying to make it work. That's why the idea of a break appealed to me, I suppose. Luckily, there were three of us to take all the important decisions, because I really couldn't have coped otherwise. Nicola, Cheryl and I were always the ones who had to steer the ship, and that was even more apparent now. Sarah usually went with the flow, and it was often hit and miss whether she'd turn up for a meeting or answer an email, and Nadine never seemed interested.

All this amounted to a lot of pressure on my shoulders, especially when I had to think about choreography, vocals and performance as well. It was a very sad time, because at that stage I couldn't discount the possibility that there would be no more Girls Aloud once the tour was over. Even though we'd only ever used the phrase 'taking a break' publicly, I wasn't sure if we would come back. I've seen it happen to bands before. They drift apart, go off and do different things, and before you know it that's the end of them.

One of the biggest and most exciting things we ever did as a band happened just before we took our break – supporting Coldplay at Wembley Stadium in September of 2009, along with Jay-Z. Chris Martin had made no secret of the fact that he was a bit of a Girls Aloud fan, saying some very positive things about our music in the press. We all felt this was a great compliment, especially given the fact that they could have asked almost any artist in the world, and it meant a lot to all of us. I think Chris's enthusiasm for our music, along with the Arctic Monkeys performing a cover of 'Love Machine' on Radio 1's 'Live Lounge', gave Girls

Aloud a credibility that we hadn't expected. We'd gone down brilliantly at the V festival in 2006, but this was on another level entirely. Suddenly, we didn't have to be a guilty pleasure any more. Even the more trendy music papers, such as *NME*, wrote good things about us. By the time we took our three-year hiatus, Girls Aloud were no longer seen as just another girl band and not to be taken seriously. We were looked upon as a credible pop band who made well-crafted records and who were actually quite cool. Chris definitely played a big part in that.

'Thanks for doing this,' he smiled when we saw him at Wembley on the day.

'No, thank you for asking,' we told him.

We could hardly believe we were there, on the same bill as Coldplay and Jay-Z. It was an incredible moment, stepping out on that stage to a packed, cheering stadium – something I'll never forget. That day was also quite poignant because we all knew it was the last thing we were going to be doing together for a while, so there was a certain amount of sadness, too. I remember just trying to take it all in. I thought about where we'd started as a band, and about just how far we'd come. There we were on the stage at Wembley, one of the biggest pop bands in the country, and yet we were about to step away from it all. It was an emotional moment.

25

On My Own

So what the hell was I going to do now? How was I going to cope with all this free time on my hands after seven years of jam-packed diaries? Why was nobody telling me where I was supposed to be and what I was supposed to be doing, and what was I going to do for work? To be honest, I wasn't really sure that I even had a career outside Girls Aloud – it was all a little bit scary.

Almost immediately, I got my first solo endorsement deal, as the new face of high-street fashion chain New Look. I was in good company. Previous 'faces' included Drew Barrymore and Alexa Chung. I had been nominated by customers on the New Look website as their top choice of 'modern-day icon'. There had been a lot of outrage in the press about stick thin, size zero models gracing the catwalks at various fashion shows, and women had apparently nominated me because they felt that I had a 'real' figure and quality that girls love. I wasn't sure about all that, but I was very happy that the campaign was to promote a positive and healthy body image. Given the weight issues I'd had as a teenager, it was a real compliment.

As a performer in the public eye, I've always felt that it's important to relate to other women. It's all well and good being a sexy pop star whom all the boys like, but the positive response I get from women means a lot more to me. The modelling itself was really good fun, and it's certainly a lot easier getting through a photoshoot when there's only one of you. The other positive thing about doing the campaign was that it made me realise that there really was life outside Girls Aloud. Landing such a major job straight out of the band gave me the financial breathing space to think about what I wanted to do next, and that was quite a relief I have to say. I never wanted to be in the position where I had to do something just for the money.

Even so, the first few months of the band's hiatus was a very strange time, and I wasn't sure that I was ready for it. I was so used to the comfort and security of being in a five-piece band that the thought of putting myself out there alone scared the life out of me. I needed to find my feet and get comfortable on my own, but after seven years of being in a group it was tough. So what should I do? It was hard to know where to start.

Luckily, lots of opportunities started to come my way. At first it was mainly presenting jobs, and although I hadn't previously considered presenting as an option, I thought I might be good at it. One of the jobs I did was a 'live from the red carpet' show before the BAFTAs, and then I was given a pop-music show, *Suck My Pop*, for the VIVA channel, which I hosted with Will Best. It was a fun show, and a good way for me to test the water as far as TV presenting went, but I don't think I was passionate enough about being a TV host when it came down to it. I didn't feel like a performer any more, and didn't find it fulfilling enough. I needed to try other things – but what?

I'd been offered the chance to cut a solo record, but I knew I didn't want to do that. Cheryl had done it and been amazingly successful, but I didn't think it would work for me. The thought of going back to the beginning and finding a sound and a direction that suited me did not appeal in the slightest. I was happy with what I'd achieved in the world of pop within the band, and I really didn't have any burning desire to show people what I could do as a solo pop artist. I did, however, manage a top-ten chart position, with a featured vocal on rapper Agros Santos's track, 'Like You Like'. He was one of Gary Barlow's new signings, and Gary asked me to sing on the record as a favour. I had a lot of fun recording the track and making the video, but I knew in my heart that I wanted to move away from pop and discover new horizons.

The good news was that I was never short of offers, whether it was more presenting or endorsement campaigns. I even got the chance to do some acting again, appearing in the kids' movie *Horrid Henry* as Prissy Polly. One thing was leading to another, and although some of the jobs paled in comparison with my days in Girls Aloud, slowly but surely I was building a career outside the band.

In the midst of all this I got the shock of my life after I returned from a week's holiday with my family. Hillary called me with the scariest news in July 2010.

'I'm sorry to have to tell you this, Kimberley,' she said, 'but Cheryl's got malaria.'

I couldn't believe that Hillary had actually said those words, and a cold rush went through me – I felt sick. As the news started to sink in, I felt panicky. Having been to Africa for the purpose of raising money to buy malaria nets, I knew first-hand just how bad this viral disease is, and how deadly. I'd seen people who had it up close and it was horrific. I was with my mum and my sister when Hillary called and as soon as I relayed the news we all just started to cry. Then I pulled myself together and called Cheryl's mum, Joan, who was beside herself.

'It's not good,' she told me. 'It's really serious.'

Cheryl had been on safari with her friend Derek Hough, and the strain of malaria she'd caught was a particularly bad one. She was critically ill. At one point, the doctors told Joan that she should prepare herself to say goodbye. I just couldn't believe what was happening. How does a person who'd climbed Kilimanjaro to raise money to buy malaria nets, go on holiday and catch one of the most dangerous strains of the illness herself? You couldn't make it up. The worst part about it was that nobody could go to the hospital to visit her because she was so ill. I was stuck at home with this awful black cloud hanging over me, and I couldn't function. I was terrified. All I could do was stay in constant contact with Joan, and if there was anything even slightly positive to report, she would call and let me know. Nicola and I tried to support one another through it as much as we could. We were on the phone almost every hour of every day, and thank God we had one another.

Some people may have thought that the whole thing was overdramatised in the papers, but if anything, it was underplayed for once. Cheryl's lungs were filling up with water and she could barely breathe, so the doctors decided to give her a blood transfusion, hoping that might give her body a kick down the right path. Even when she started taking a turn for the better, it was very slow progress, and sometimes a case of two steps forward and one step back. It took them ages to find out exactly what the strain of the illness was. Thinking about it now, I'm glad I didn't see her in that state, because I don't think I could have handled it.

When she finally got out of hospital, she came to stay at mine, and when I first saw her, I felt as though I hadn't seen her for twenty years. The two of us just threw our arms around one another and burst into tears. It was such a weird feeling. Suddenly she was there again, and better, after seeming so far away for all those weeks. I'd never had someone so close to me fall that seriously ill before, or come that close to losing someone who was such a big part of my life. She's seriously made of steel, that girl, I swear.

At the start of 2011, I felt like it was time to sit back and take stock of my life. I needed to figure out where I was at, and what was important. In the end, I decided not to do anything for a while and to take advantage of the free time to search for my dream home. I'd been thinking about it for a while, but I just hadn't had a minute even to look at any properties. Now I had some down time, which was perfect.

Justin and I found somewhere we loved, and the minute we got the keys and started fixing the place up together, I had a massive revelation. I was happy. Very, very happy. It was such an amazing feeling, not having anything to organise or stress over. All I had to think about was making a beautiful new 'forever' home for the two of us, and I absolutely loved it. I ended up taking a few months off to renovate the house. Every day we would get up and strip wallpaper or paint walls, and although we were both working really hard, it was total, mind-numbing bliss, and very therapeutic. I guess my contentment must have been infectious, because Cheryl came over to help me with the decorating. She was going through a tough time, dealing with all the drama surrounding the US version of *The X Factor*, so she was just glad to get away from it all for a while. It's funny, neither of us wanted to be out in the eye of the public at that time, so it felt good to be doing something so incredibly normal.

Just as we finished the house, I was called into action as the birthing partner for my sister, Sally. Her husband Joe was more than keen for me to be there to help them out, and I was honoured to be asked. Sally was two weeks overdue by that time, so Joe took her into hospital to be induced. Once that had been done, he was told it could take up to twelve hours to start working, and that he should go home. Not long after he got back to my place, however, Sally started texting us, clearly in a flap. 'You need to come to the hospital now – it's starting already. Come back now.' Sure enough, she'd gone into labour straight away, but the nurses seemed to be leaving her to it, and in her next text she sounded quite distressed. 'I'm in pain, and I haven't even got a pillow.' Both Joe and I were really worried, but by that time it was late at night, so nobody was allowed in to see her.

'Sod that,' I said to Joe. 'We're going!'

We drove the thirty minutes to the hospital, and I snuck past the nurses into the ward, and darted into her cubicle with a pillow I'd brought from home. As soon as Sally saw me she burst into tears, she was so relieved to see a familiar face. She'd been having quite strong contractions, but the nurse had told her it was nothing to worry about and ignored the fact that she was in distress. I know for a fact that isn't the norm in a maternity unit, but Sally was very unlucky with the experience she had. It was awful. I was soon asked to leave as it was after visiting hours, but we hadn't been back home for long when Sally was texting again. 'Seriously, you need to get here now. I'm close. I know I am. Please come back.'

When we got back to the hospital we waited for someone to call us, and by the time they did she was already 6 centimetres dilated and in full labour.

'Sh*t!' Joe and I both exclaimed, as we walked in on a scene that to me looked like something out of *The Exorcist*. Sally later told us that she thought we looked like Jane and Michael Banks from *Mary Poppins*, standing there next to her bed – two little kids staring in absolute wonder. Only she could think of a musical reference at a time like that. If ever I'd wanted to see something to put me off having kids for life, there it was. The labour had come on so strong and so quickly, it was 0–100 in no time, and there was no time to give her an epidural. Sally was going psycho with the pain, and neither of us wanted to be the one to tell her that she was too far gone for any pain relief. She had to do it all completely naturally, and when she had no energy to push, I yelled words of encouragement at her.

'You've got to push, I can see the head. I can see it!'

At one point I actually thought I was going to pass out. I had to sit down because I felt unsteady, and Joe looked at me as if to say, Don't you dare faint. She'll bloody kill you! It was quite a traumatic thing to witness, though; I won't lie. At one point, the baby got stuck in the birth canal, and then they lost his heartbeat. The midwife had to do a vacuum extraction using a ventouse, which is a suction device used in the event of a difficult birth, and once he was finally out, he wasn't breathing at all. Normally, the midwife would put the new baby straight onto his mum, but instead he was whipped away to be resuscitated. I can't put into words how terrifying and awful those next few moments were. The thought that Sally's baby, my little nephew, might not make it was just too much even to contemplate.

'Please cry,' I said under my breath. 'Please, please cry.'

For a minute it didn't look as though he was going to, but then suddenly we heard his little cry and I completely lost it, bursting into tears of joy. People describe many things as amazing, but the birth of a baby truly is.

Once I'd stopped crying, I left Joe and Sally to have their moment while I went to call my mum and Amy and then meet my brother and Justin, who were waiting in the car park. Justin said I looked like I'd been through the most horrific experience imaginable, and I was adamant.

'Guys, no! Never! Never, ever am I doing this, ever!'

It was incredible how much love I had for Billy from

the minute he was born. It was almost like he was my own, and the whole family felt the same. He's two now, and still the joy of all our lives. After that experience, however, my sister vowed never to have another one.

'Don't ever, EVER let me do this again,' she said, looking as though she might kill me if I did.

I guess you just forget the bad stuff where kids are concerned, don't you? As I sit here writing this book, she's pregnant again.

26

Eight Shows a Week

However much I'd loved being part of Girls Aloud, I still had a real hankering to star in a West End musical. That dream hadn't changed since I was a kid. By the time the offer of an audition for *Shrek the Musical* came along – for the part of Princess Fiona – I'd grown in confidence and felt finally ready to take my shot at a West End show. Mind you, it was still a daunting prospect. This would be the first big part I'd had in a musical since I was a young teenager, and it was a lead role.

One of the things that scared me was the idea of routine. When Hillary told me that the run would be six months minimum, which isn't that long for a West

With Hillary in the big apple, filming for The Passions of Girls Aloud.

'Lovely Lady?' trying on my costume during Passions.

Justin with his daughter, Chloe, at the first Girls Aloud tour.

Glamming it up with Hills, Cheryl and Nic at the Brits.

A Prince and two showgirls! Deana Morgan and me meeting Prince Charles for our work promoting the breast cancer Haven.

One of the beautiful babies I met on our return to Africa to distribute Malaria nets.

We thought we knew one another, then we climbed a mountain together!

Me and Chezza: All smiles before summit night on Kilimanjaro.

Chris Moyles and me in our outstanding debut on Ugandan TV.

As Princess Fiona in Shrek The Musical, with Nigel Lindsay.

A quick wig change! With my two gorgeous wiggies, Stefan and Linda, on my final night in Shrek.

Performing the Viennese Waltz on Strictly, with Pasha Kovalev.

Backstage at Strictly.

Celebrating with Justin, at the after party for the Tangled Up tour.

A birthday dinner for Chezza's 30th in Malibu.

What happens in Vegas!

End lead, I got the jitters. I couldn't imagine being in the same building every night, doing the same thing at the same time. My life had never been so regimented and the whole idea seemed completely alien to me. But then I looked over the script, listened to the cast recording, and watched some clips from the Broadway version on YouTube, and I fell completely in love with both the part and all of the songs from the show. I knew I was going to take the plunge and go for the audition. The problem was I hadn't auditioned for anything in almost ten years – not since *Popstars* – and I knew that I was going to be walking into a highly competitive and professional environment. The people casting the show certainly weren't going to make any concessions for me just because I'd recently stepped out of a famous pop group. I needed to be able to hold my own on a West End stage for eight performances a week, and be brilliant. That was the bottom line, and it was terrifying.

The audition was in Covent Garden, at the office of David Grindrod, who was the casting director. I sat nervously waiting for a while before going in to sing my prepared audition piece, which was 'I Know it's Today', one of the more difficult songs from the show. I hadn't sung anything like it for quite some time, and although I was well rehearsed, I knew that my voice wasn't quite up to the standard that it should have been for an audition like that. When I walked into the room, a seated pianist was there, ready to accompany me, two directors – one English, one American – and an assortment of producers, all looking at me in anticipation. It wasn't a warm environment at all. In fact, I felt quite uneasy as I took up my position, ready to give it my all. As I opened my mouth to sing I actually had no idea what the hell was going to come out of it, I was that nervous, but off I went anyway, hoping against hope that my voice didn't let me down when I really needed it. Once it was over, I breathed a huge sigh of relief, knowing that my audition, although not stunningly perfect, had been pretty damn good. After that I read a scene from the script and then it was, 'Thank you very much, goodbye!' And I was out the door.

It had been a long time since I'd had to suffer the dreadful anxiety of waiting for the 'callback' phone call, and it hadn't got any easier over the years. When the news was positive, I was over the moon, despite the fact that there was a condition attached. 'Can you please ask Kimberley to come a little less glamorous for the recall,' was the request from the casting agent. I was mortified. Had I really marched in there like a pop star, dressed up like a dog's dinner? I didn't think I had at the time. It was just a simple dress, with my hair and make-up done nicely. I guess actors and actresses are running in and out of auditions all the time, and casting directors are used to seeing people who are dressed casually. That wasn't my life, though. I'd been preened and styled and made up for every professional thing I'd done for the past ten years. As far as I was concerned, I was just making an effort. OK, I thought, jeans and a T-shirt it is, then.

The next audition was more of a workshop with some of the other actors, plus we tried out a few different keys for some of the songs to see what suited my voice. That day went really well, but even after they decided that they wanted me, I had to audition all over again in front of a camera, so that the producers over in America could watch it. They also had a say in whether or not I got to play Princess Fiona.

When I eventually got the good news telling me that I'd got the part, I was at a family barbecue, which soon turned into a celebration. I hadn't felt so excited about something for ages. Yes, the audition process had been nerve-racking and intense, but I was glad that I'd gone through it because it reassured me that I still had it in me to fulfil my dreams. There was life outside Girls Aloud after all.

I was taking over the role of the ogre princess from Amanda Holden, who was pregnant, and I had about two weeks' rehearsal because they wanted me to start as quickly as possible. Two weeks is not all that long, especially when you're the only new cast member, and for most of the time it was just me and the director, or me and the musical director. It was quite intense. As well as that, there were costume fittings and prosthetic fittings and everything else that was needed to get me ready for my opening night. In fact, it was only in the last few days of rehearsal that I actually got to do any acting with the other cast members at all. Despite all that, I absolutely loved the experience of *Shrek* from the minute I walked through the door. I got such a buzz from the fast pace, the daily rehearsals and from singing musical theatre songs again. I felt as if I'd come home. I remember thinking to myself, *This is what I do!* As much as I loved being in a pop band and singing great pop songs, I just knew that my voice was made for this, and it made me happy.

I suppose it made me realise how much my confidence as a singer had been knocked while I was in the group. You don't always get to show off what you can do in a live situation, and so I lost the knack a little bit. Now I was standing onstage in a theatre, rehearsing my parts and singing my heart out – on my own – and the feedback I was getting from the cast and directors alike was really positive. I suddenly remembered the reason I started singing in the first place: because I loved it and I was good at it.

Once again, I worked with my singing teacher Mary Hammond, and the company employed Mary King, who was on hand to help get my voice up to scratch. She told me things about my voice that I didn't even know, and I learned so much from her in just one week. Mary was really good at problem solving, and if there was a tricky hurdle that I struggled to get over, vocally, she was always able to help me find a way. It was invaluable technical experience and I would never have learned all those theatrical tricks had I not joined the company.

I threw myself into the part wholeheartedly. In fact, I became slightly obsessive about it and drove poor Justin mad with my constant warbling around the house. I don't think he really knew how crazy I was about musical theatre until I started on *Shrek* and it was a bit of a shock to him. I wanted to be the best that I could possibly be, and I wanted to prove that I was worthy of having been given the role. I had a lot of respect for musical theatre performers, and I didn't want the other actors thinking she's going to be sh*t because she's just a pop singer. It was just like when I was a kid, practising with my sister all the time, and it suddenly dawned on me that something wonderful had happened. I'd got *that* feeling back – the one I always used to get when I sang as a child. It was a pure love and enjoyment of singing without any strings attached. Just excitement. As soon as that feeling came back to me I realised just how long I'd been missing it. I'd never had it during my time with the group. I don't know why. Perhaps it was because all the singing I did then was so fragmented – the bitty method of recording, the quick TV appearances, the one or two lines here and there. It's not that I didn't love it, but there was something much more liberating, and simpler, about this. It was precisely why I'd started singing in the first place.

When it came to my opening night I was dead excited finally to be getting out there. By that time I'd rehearsed the part to within an inch of its life, and I felt like I could do it in my sleep. As well as most of my family and Hillary, Cheryl and Nicola were both there on opening night. They were quite surprised to find me calm right before the show.

'How are you not a complete wreck?' Nicola wanted to know.

'You seem weird. Why are you all right?' Cheryl added.

They were so used to me being a bag of nerves before I did anything big, but on that night I knew what I was doing. I had first-night butterflies, yes, but nothing like the terrible stage fright I'd suffered in the past. Sharing the stage with Nigel Lindsay, who played Shrek, as well as Richard Blackwood and Nigel Harman, was just wonderful, and the entire cast was so supportive. The whole atmosphere surrounding the show was magical for me. I was in my element.

My family were, of course, all very proud, and when my grandma and granddad came to see the show, my grandma went completely over the top.

'Oh my God, it's amazing, Kimberley. I loved it!' she said.

Granddad was his usual reserved self as far as my performance went, bless him. It was a case of, 'Yes, that was nice,' but that was about it. I remember at the time being a little bit hurt by it, because I was sure that he was going to be really impressed and proud of me – it was the West End, after all. He knew what a big thing that was, and he'd never seen me do anything like that before. Still, I knew that was just his way. He struggled all his life and maybe he found the idea of me having such success a little bit hard to take in, so I tried not to dwell on it for too long.

It's hard work when you're performing in eight shows a week on a West End stage, especially doing the same thing night after night. Every new audience has paid to see the same show, and I was very aware that I had to be on top form the whole time. Musical theatre is about consistency and stamina, delivering the same performance every night, which is not really the way we do things in the world of pop. With a pop concert you normally go with the flow of the audience and the journey of the gig. Yes, you usually do the same songs, but each night can be very different, depending on the vibe of the crowd and the venue.

I put quite a lot of pressure on myself every night while I was doing *Shrek*. I knew that people would be coming to see me with a certain degree of expectation, because I was well known, and I didn't want to let them down. For a start, my social life went completely out of the window. When you're on in a theatre every night from six until eleven in the evening, your window for socialising doesn't really work with anybody else's, apart from the people you're working with. And even then the schedule was such that we didn't have the time or energy to go out partying after the show. Part of the job was being responsible and looking after yourself, and there was no way I could have done that show on a hangover – although I did once try. I foolishly went out drinking with some friends the night before one show and it wasn't good. There was a show on the day after my big thirtieth birthday bash at the Westbury Hotel, but I was sensible enough to have booked the day off. Unfortunately, the other cast members who celebrated with me had to go on for a Sunday matinee. There were a few stories of people being sick in the wings, and desperately trying to haul it together for the show.

During my run in *Shrek*, I did, of course, have my share of mishaps. The entrance for my first song was supposed to look very dreamlike and Disney-esque. I came out at the top of a tower from between two clouds, which were made of wood and run on tracks operated by two stagehands. Now these clouds could be extremely temperamental, and one night I had an incident that became known as cloud-gate. A few times one or other of the clouds had come too far off its track and almost knocked me through the window of the tower, but on this occasion, the cloud hit me so hard that I spun around in a circle and was revealed with my back to the audience, breathlessly trying to get my first note out.

One night during the marriage scene, my veil got caught in the altar as I was walking away from it, and my head was unceremoniously yanked backwards. Nigel Lindsay had to improvise and rip the veil off my head so I could make my exit. Worst of all was the time when I'd just finished a tap dance with a bunch of dancing rats. During the number I had to rip off my long skirt to reveal a tiny little mini-dress, and then I put the long skirt back on for my next song, 'I Got You Beat'. On this particular night I had a stand-in dresser who forgot to set my long skirt in the correct place, so I had to go on and do the song – which entails me burping and farting and lifting my leg in an ogre-like fashion – still wearing the tiny mini-dress. It just looked so wrong and I was dying inside, and the fact that Nigel Harman was behind a nearby tree, pissing himself laughing, didn't help matters, either. Still, I just had to grit my teeth and get through it. It was bloody embarrassing.

Despite being knackered most of the time, I loved walking into that theatre every day. It was such a buzz, and one I'd really missed. The people I was working with got me through as much as anything. The cast was fantastic, and my backstage team – Stephan and Linda, who did my wigs, and Divs, my dresser – have become good friends since the show. I didn't think it was possible for me to get that close with another group of people outside the band, but we really did become like a proper little backstage family over those eight months.

My last night was more like a pop concert. An army of Girls Aloud fans were in the audience, screaming every time I walked on. It was a great way to bow out and, of course, I was very emotional. Dean Chisnall, who had taken over in the role of Shrek by then, made a very touching speech, and I was all over the place, green ogre make-up everywhere. Dean was a lovely guy and he knew that I'd really put myself out there when I took the role of Fiona. There's no getting away from the fact that if you come from a well-known pop band, the audience have a preconception of you, and I sometimes felt I was being overly scrutinised or judged because of it. That being said, *Shrek* was a brilliant experience for me. I'd been part of something special, and I'll never forget it. I was in the cast for eight months and I probably would have stayed longer . . . if there hadn't been such an important reunion looming.

27

Something Old,
Something New

In October 2011, just after I'd started in *Shrek*, we all decided that we were going to have to sit down together to discuss the Girls Aloud reunion, if there was ever going to be one. We'd originally planned to take a year off and now, two years plus down the line, it was time to decide exactly what it was we wanted to do. It was the band's ten-year anniversary the following year, after all.

Nadine was in LA, but the rest of us decided to meet at my house, see where our heads were and make some firm decisions. Personally, I wanted to gauge how much the other girls wanted to give to the reunion because

I really had no idea. It wasn't as if I hadn't seen them all individually – I'd seen quite a lot of Cheryl and Nicola, socially, and Sarah and I still had the same management – but sitting down with our Girls Aloud heads on was another matter entirely. Luckily, it all went smoothly, and as we sat talking over the various possibilities in my living room, everybody seemed to be on the same page.

One thing that concerned Cheryl, Nicola and me was Sarah's health. She'd had such a rough time of it, and we all knew that she was frail. She'd broken up with her fiancé, Tom, and it had hit her hard, and we all knew she'd been partying hard as well. She was suffering from depression and addiction to alcohol. Cheryl was particularly worried that throwing Sarah into a whole load of promotion, and possibly a full-on tour, might just elevate her problems. None of us wanted to push her into something that was going to make her ill or send her off the rails any more than she seemed to be already. She had to be in the right state of mind and the best of health above anything else. At one point during the evening, Sarah dropped a bit of a bombshell. 'I'm going into rehab,' she told us. 'Tomorrow.'

We were surprised to hear the news, but we were also really proud of her. She was doing this not only for herself, but also for the band. She wanted to get better so that she'd be OK for the tour, and that meant a lot to us. I could tell that she was terrified at the prospect of it, but I was relieved that she'd finally realised that she needed to do something – I'd been worrying about her constantly. Even though we hadn't been working together, I could see from a distance that something was very wrong. That night she looked a bit like a broken woman, so we knew she'd made the right decision. She was going about as far away as she could get – to South Africa – in an attempt to get well again.

After a couple of hours chatting, we decided that we would do a greatest hits album, including a few new songs, plus a full tour, provided Sarah was well enough and Nadine was up for it. We also came to the conclusion that if we were going to commit to doing a tour, it was going to have to be the best one ever. At the end of the meeting we tweeted a picture of the four of us together, just for the fans. It wasn't until the following April that all five of us got together in a London hotel room finally to get things moving. That was the first time we'd all been in a room together since the last gig we'd performed, so it was kind of a big deal, and I have to say it was a little bit strange.

Although I was excited that we were finally going to make it happen, turning our plans for a Girls Aloud comeback into a reality, I was also uneasy. For me, it was like going back in time, and it stirred up memories of how bad things had got when we'd gone our separate ways three years before. I hadn't set eyes on Nadine since the split, and although I knew her so well, she seemed very distant from the rest of us. So much had happened since I'd last seen her. We'd had totally separate careers on separate continents, her sister had had three kids, and I'd become an aunt. In the old days we would have spoken about these events and even shared them, but now I felt disconnected from her. It was weird. I think we all knew that we had a bit of rebuilding to do before we went any further.

When we all sat down, along with Hillary and Sundraj, the mood among all the girls was very upbeat and positive. I suppose, if anything, the meeting was just a bit more businesslike than in the old days. We weren't just a gang of girls who were in a pop group together any more; we were five women who'd all gone away and had careers in our own right. Some of the girls had their own albums, Cheryl had been on *The X Factor*, and I'd been in a completely different groove with the musical theatre stuff. The good thing about it was that we all wanted the same thing out of a reunion. We wanted to create some great new music that the fans would enjoy and that would sound and feel like Girls Aloud music, and we wanted to make the tour the biggest and best it could be. It wasn't about making money, it was about going out on a high and doing something amazing to say thank you to our fans. It was also about saying goodbye – for all of us.

After the meeting it was all systems go. There were venues to be booked and studio sessions to coordinate, so there was a lot to organise if we were going to have an album ready for the Christmas market. The five of us were really excited about getting out there again, so we put the plans in motion to get back into the studio and record some new material as soon as possible. Nicola had blossomed into a talented song-writer, and she'd been writing quite a lot down at Xenomania, so there were already some fresh song ideas waiting for us.

However, it wasn't as easy as just walking into a studio and singing. It was actually really hard to find our sound again after almost three years apart, both for us and for the team at Xenomania. The fact that it didn't come easily cemented the idea in my mind that it was all coming to an end. I would never have wanted to be part of something that felt forced or unnatural. I wanted to remember Girls Aloud as a fantastic place in time, and something that was amazing.

Maybe part of the reason it took a bit of time to come together was because we all had other commitments. I was still doing *Shrek* when we started recording, so I had to cram in my recording sessions in the midst of singing eight shows a week in the West End. For this reason, we didn't all hang out in the studio together when we were recording, like we did in the early years. It had been that way for quite a long time, I suppose. Gone were the days when you sat in the lounge waiting for your turn while one of the other girls finished recording. Nowadays we were all too busy to sit around for hours on end and the recording had to be worked around our individual schedules. That being said, I was in the studio with all of the girls, individually, at different points during the recording, and I was still willing to put in all the hours God sent to make the songs as good as they possibly could be. It was the same process as it always had been at Xenomania. We recorded a whole heap of songs just so we could pick the absolute best ones from the sessions.

The song that was eventually picked to be the single was 'Something New'. It wasn't my favourite of the songs we'd recorded. Maybe my tastes had changed and I'd outgrown that kind of song. I don't know. I would probably have chosen one of the other new songs, 'On the Metro'. Choices for singles are rarely unanimous, though, not when there are five of you, plus record label and management, so you just have to respect the opinions of others. At the end of the day, 'Something New' *was* probably the right choice for a comeback single because it did so well. Unfortunately, we missed out on the number-one spot, being beaten to it by Olly Murs, but after a three-year break, number two wasn't too bad at all.

Before we launched into a new batch of promotion for the single, Nicola and I decided that we needed to sit down with Nadine for an honest and frank discussion. The rest of us had grown and changed so much during the three-year break, and I was hopeful that Nadine had, too. But if we were all going to be working together again, and getting back into the mentality of being in a group, certain things needed addressing. When we suggested a casual meet to Nadine, she saw the sense in it. This way we could talk about any worries we had, and lay to rest any past resentments. It had to be done for all our sakes, including hers, and, among other things, we talked frankly about the way she'd behaved towards us before the break, and her constant lateness. After working in the theatre and on movies I'd got used to people being punctual, professional and respectful of one another's time, and I didn't want to go back to the way it had been before. Now we had to be on the same page, and I wanted Nadine to know how I felt.

The meeting at Hillary's house turned out to be quite therapeutic. The thing about Nadine is that she lives in her own little bubble. I don't think she even realised that the way she behaved could sometimes be detrimental to the rest of us. She just wasn't always very aware of the people around her. When we sat down and told her how we felt rather than getting into a blazing row with her, she was quite receptive and apologetic about the way she'd behaved in the past. She told us that it was just the way she was, but she shouldn't have expected the rest of us to pick up the pieces and she was sorry. It was funny – the things that bothered me about Nadine's behaviour seemed so trivial when I thought about it. Then I remembered all the times I'd sat in a car outside her house for forty-five minutes to an hour, waiting for her to get up and get ready. I felt very disrespected back then, and I didn't want to feel like that again. The other girls were in agreement. If we were going to do this, we *all* had to be respectful of one another.

Our idea of clearing the air appeared to do the trick. Nadine seemed genuinely excited about the upcoming reunion, and she took it just as seriously as the rest of us. It was certainly a marked difference from the way she'd felt at the end of the previous tour, and I was happy about that. Things were going to be a lot easier if we were working together to make this happen. Still, it was never going to be easy, coordinating the five of us. We each had other commitments, so it was always going to be a struggle to get us all together. Then, in the midst of it, I decided to do something completely crazy, agreeing to become a contestant on one of the BBC's biggest shows, *Strictly Come Dancing*.

It wasn't the first time this idea had come up. The BBC had asked Hillary if I'd be interested in doing it quite a few times in the past but it had never felt right. Being in Girls Aloud had always been so full-on and intense, work-wise, and there was always something going on in the run-up to Christmas, when *Strictly* goes out. I'd never been able to consider it seriously before, although it had always appealed to me. I'd watched the show every year and I loved the idea of it. Justin would catch me watching it with child-like excitement in my eyes. 'Leave it,' he'd laugh. 'You're not doing it.' And I'd be thinking, I will do it one day, whether you like it or not.

The only reservation I had about doing *Strictly* was that it's a reality show, so the public vote for you to stay or go. It's partly a popularity contest at the end of the day, and I didn't want to have come this far in my career only to discover that people didn't really like me that much, did I? That would be awful. I had no reservations about the actual competition or learning the dances. Appearing in *Shrek* had suddenly unleashed a desire to throw myself into new things and push myself. I was itching for the next challenge to come along, and maybe this was it. When Hillary asked me about it, I went with my gut reaction. 'God, I really want to do this,' I told her.

Then I thought about it a bit more and it just seemed impossible. How the hell was I going to manage all those intense dance rehearsals at the same time as I was embarking on major promotion for a new Girls Aloud single and album? It just wasn't realistic. In fact, it seemed like total madness. I had to say no and just concentrate on the job in hand.

Still, the idea of doing *Strictly* kept niggling at me – I just couldn't let it go. In the end, I ran it past the girls, who all agreed that I should most definitely do it.

'You'll be in your element,' Nicola said. 'You'll absolutely love it. If you can do it, go for it!'

The BBC really seemed to want me, so they were very accommodating as far as rehearsal times and filming were concerned. 'We appreciate she's got a lot going on,' the producer told Hillary. 'We'll try to make it work around that.'

Hillary thought long and hard about it and then

called me. 'I think we could make this work, you know,' she said. 'It's physically do-able – if you don't mind working your arse off till Christmas.'

So that was it. I was doing it.

28

Strictly Knackered

The first thing we had to do was the trailer for the show, which was being filmed in a secret location. I didn't even know who else was taking part when I walked into the room to meet everyone – none of us did – but I was thrilled when I discovered that my good friend Denise Van Outen was one of the other contestants. It meant that I'd have a partner in crime to hang out with, and also to share the experience with. Since Kilimanjaro, Denise had been a bit of a mentor to me. She's a little bit older and she seems to know the entertainment business really well. At the start of my three-year hiatus from Girls Aloud, she'd encouraged me to get out there and try some new things, including musical theatre, and she'd also pointed me in the direction of a few people whom she thought might be able to help me. Denise could see that it was a bit of a weird time for me and I think she just wanted to help. She pushed me to go for things, and I'm so happy and grateful that she did. Having her with me on *Strictly* was hopefully going to make the journey a little bit easier.

Once the trailer was done we were off and rolling and it was non-stop till Christmas. I got into the groove of it fairly quickly, and felt confident I'd made the right decision about doing the show. For a start, I was really happy with the professional dancing partner I'd been assigned. Pasha Kovalev was a calm, chilled-out sort of guy, which suited me fine, and from watching him on the previous year's show, he seemed to have a good temperament and be a skilled teacher. He was also a good fit for me because, as he's Russian, he didn't know anything about me, or Girls Aloud, especially as we'd been out of the limelight for the past three years. It might sound silly, but when you're in the public eye and you've been known throughout the entertainment industry for ten years, it's quite nice to start something new as just two people working together towards the same goal. We got straight down to dancing. Pasha wanted to find out what I was like and how good I was, so he put me through my paces with basic steps and walks. It was quite embarrassing at first, having never done any sort of ballroom dancing, but after a while I began to loosen up and told myself just to have fun.

First off, we rehearsed in groups, which gave us all a taste of what the competition was going to be like, and I was already looking forward to getting out there in front of the cameras and doing it. To me, it seemed like such a nice group of people, and we all thought the experience was going to be a really good laugh. Once we were assigned our professional dancing partners, we were told to rehearse as much and as often as we wanted to, and that we had three weeks to master our first routine. This seemed like ages, but God did I need it. Luckily, Pasha was brilliant.

I didn't imagine it was going to be easy, but I didn't realise how complex all the different moves and disciplines of a ballroom or Latin routine actually are. It's one thing watching it, but doing it is another matter entirely. I thought that, because I could dance, I was going to pick things up just like that, but the way I saw the moves was very different from what they actually are. During those first three weeks, I had to work really hard to make our first routine look even remotely like a cha-cha-cha, but when it finally came to the live show, I felt quite confident. Seconds before we were due to go on, however, I turned to Pasha in panic.

'I can't remember it,' I said. 'I can't remember a single thing you taught me. Where do we start?'

It was the first time Pasha had seen me as anything other than cool and confident, and he looked at me as if to say, Is she for real? Once the music started I was fine, but it was quite a strange moment and it happened to me throughout the series. I was perfectly fine during rehearsals and then it all went to pot when I was about to go on. Luckily, we weren't being judged that first week and nobody was going home, so the pressure was off a little bit.

The second week was a different story altogether. Pasha and I had rehearsed the foxtrot thoroughly, and we had a really good connection. Just before the performance, though, I got 'the fear' and it all went wrong. Nicola and Nadine were in the audience that night, and Nicola told me later that as soon as she saw my face she knew I was terribly nervous, and she was right. I knew it wasn't going to be good before I even started, and it was basically because I didn't know it well enough. For the first live show we'd had a whole three weeks to learn the routine, but this time we'd had just five days. All the time I was dancing I felt as though I was outside my body, watching myself, and I was dying inside because it just felt so bad. I remember my thoughts as Pasha led me, awkwardly, around the floor. 'Oh my God, oh my God! Did you really just stand on his toe?'

I'm such a perfectionist, so for me it was a nightmare. I wasn't prepared, I messed it up, and consequently the judges were underwhelmed – especially Len Goodman, who was quite aggressive with his critique. 'I thought it was limp,' was his opening comment. 'There was no conviction and you were hanging on. Our expectations are high; you've got to do better than that, girl!'

In truth, I agreed with him. I wanted to turn round and say, 'I know, Len, what a mess! That was sh*t, wasn't it?' Still, it upset me. I felt as though everybody expected me to be brilliant just because they'd seen what I'd done in Girls Aloud over the years, but contemporary choreography is a completely different discipline from the kind of dancing I was doing on *Strictly*. And besides that, I usually had a lot more time to rehearse when I was doing routines with the girls. Suddenly, the pressure was mounting, and the thought of getting another battering from one of the judges was unbearable. By the time I did my post-dance interview with Tess Daly I was really upset, and it was all I could do not to cry. Pasha tried to snap me out of it.

'It was really good,' he said. 'You need to give yourself a break; you've got so much going on.'

Looking back, I can see he was right, but all I could think about at the time was how brilliant I was going to be the following week.

Things got a little better until week six when we were doing a Viennese waltz. We'd loved learning this routine, and I loved the song we were dancing to – 'A Thousand Years' by Christina Perri, which is from one of the *Twilight* films. During the dance, besides messing up part of it, I caught my heel in the net underskirt of my dress and ended up hopping around like a bloody rabbit. That part of the routine was supposed to look refined and elegant, like the figure of a ballerina turning gracefully around on a jewellery box, but unfortunately it all went a bit wrong. Still, we actually got decent marks from the judges, and overall we were happy, but we ended up in the bottom two that week, and consequently had to dance for survival. I don't think that did my confidence any favours, but luckily, we won the dance-off.

It turned out to be much harder than I'd imagined, juggling all my commitments, and at one point I didn't think I was going to get through it. From the moment the show started, *Strictly Come Dancing* completely took over my life. I was rehearsing with Pasha all day, every day, and by the time I started rehearsals for the Girls Aloud TV appearances to promote the single, I was already in the full swing of the show. By then, I was completely hooked, and I became obsessive about mastering every different ballroom and Latin dance for Saturday's show each week. I just wanted to get better and better, but there never seemed to be enough hours in the day to do all the things I had to do. It was also really hard to switch both my body and mind back to the kind of contemporary choreography I was doing with the girls, because it was so very different.

Alongside *Strictly* rehearsals, I was cramming in Girls Aloud rehearsals for *Children in Need*, the Jingle Bell Ball, *Graham Norton* and also a performance of the new single on *Strictly*. That's just a few of the things the band had to do, and in the middle of it there was a video to shoot. The only way I could fit it all in was by dashing back and forth between the various rehearsals. Sometimes Pasha would come with me to the Girls Aloud rehearsals, and while they took a break, the two of us would rehearse our *Strictly* routine for that week. Then, after the girls had finished for the day, Pasha and I would stay late and rehearse some more. Sometimes I was dancing from eight or nine in the morning till nine or ten at night, which was exhausting, especially as I was trying to cope with learning two completely different routines that were poles apart in both style and content. The girls would laugh at me when I couldn't remember which 'hat' I was supposed to be wearing at what time. The dances I was doing for *Strictly* were like nothing I'd ever done before, and it was so much harder than I'd imagined it would be to keep up. At times, it really messed with my head, and there were a few moments when I thought I was going to lose it completely.

By the time we reached week seven, which was the *Children in Need* special, live from Wembley Arena, I was mentally drained. That week Pasha and I were dancing the samba, and as well as the rehearsals for that, Girls Aloud were preparing for their first big TV performances of 'Something New'. One of them was on *Strictly*, which meant I had no time to rehearse the two group ballroom numbers for that week. I just had to blag it. I think some of the other contestants thought, What is she doing? Is she mad?

On the night I think I coped with it quite well, but I did feel the pressure and I knew I'd taken on too much. I didn't seem to have time to process all the information that was coming my way, so as well as the physical exhaustion I felt as if my head was going to explode. To perform confidently, I need to know exactly what I'm doing, and that week it was just too much. I was determined not to be beaten, though, and I made up my mind to do each different thing I had to do as well as I could. I refused to let the girls down, and I wasn't going to let myself down, either.

On the week we did the jive routine – week nine – I actually did break down. I was so excited to be learning this particular dance, but physically it's probably the hardest of the lot. The rehearsals were going OK, but I was struggling. I just didn't feel as though I had anything left. I remember thinking that if the jive had come a bit earlier on in the series, I might have been all right – but right then I was dying. Denise was rehearsing in the room next door to me and she was feeling the same that week, so when I was on a break, I'd pop next door to spur her on, and then she'd do the same for me. It was a massive help having someone yelling enthusiastically at you while you were going through the routine for the hundredth time.

There was one particular trick in the dance where I was supposed to bend down and pull Pasha's leg around me, which was quite a complicated move. When it came to this part of the dance during the dress rehearsal, I started to go down to the floor but then I just fell. I was suddenly just lying there in heap on the floor in the middle of the dress run – I couldn't move. I remember looking at the floor and thinking, I'm not meant to be on the floor right now, but I didn't have the strength to get back up, and I didn't want to, either. In all my years of performing, I'd never felt that exhausted.

'I can't do it,' I said to Pasha. 'I just can't do it.'

Pasha was great, and he got me back up on my feet, practically carrying me through the rest of the dress run. Once it was finished I broke down like some hysterical lunatic. I couldn't stop crying.

'Come on, let's go outside,' Pasha said.

He's a calm and private person, and he knew that I wouldn't want everyone to see me like that, but I could see that the producers were worried. When we were outside in the BBC Star Bar, I was sobbing like a small child.

'I really can't go on any more,' I told him. 'I thought I could. I thought I was superwoman but I'm clearly not. I can't even feel my legs any more, let alone lift them up. How the f*** am I going to be able to manage the jive?'

I suppose it didn't help that I felt as though I'd been criticised quite a lot by the judges, and my points didn't seem to be getting any better as the weeks went by. What else could I possibly do? I was working my arse off, wasn't I? Pasha wasn't having any of my self-pity, however, not a drop of it.

'Look, you're a professional,' he told me, firmly. 'Of course you can do it. You will get through it because you've got to.'

He was right – there was no point moaning about it.

After all, it was me who thought I'd be able to do it all. Nobody forced me to enter one of the most physically demanding competitions on television while I was in the midst of a Girls Aloud reunion. Pasha's words of encouragement were exactly what I needed to snap me out of it. Somehow, when the music started for the actual performance, I managed to rise to the occasion, even though it seemed like the fastest bloody jive ever to have been performed on *Strictly*. I cursed Pasha under my breath for choosing 'Land of a Thousand Dances' as our music. Couldn't he have chosen something a bit slower, for God's sake?

To be honest, it wasn't the greatest performance we'd done and one of the tricks still went wrong, but luckily the points were good enough to take us through to the next round. After the show I marched straight up to the BBC bar.

'I need a drink,' I said. 'Somebody get me a drink!'

I needed to let loose. I didn't give a sh*t that I had another full day of work to do the next day; I just wanted to relax and have some fun. Louis Smith, the Olympic gymnast who eventually won the competition, laughed about it with me the following week.

'You were a bit worse for wear,' he said. 'Man, you were so funny. I've not seen you like that before.'

I didn't care, though. I needed to get some perspective

on what was going on my life. It was just a TV programme at the end of the day – a dance show. It was supposed to be fun, not life or death.

I wish I could give myself a break occasionally, and accept that everything can't always be perfect. You meet people in life who are so confident that you think they must be bordering on delusion, but I sometimes think that I could do with a little bit of that. I need encouragement to fire me up, rather than criticism, which just makes me crumble.

After that terrible week, I picked myself and gave myself a good talking to. 'You've just got to be better than you were the previous week – that's all you've got to do.' That's how I tried to rationalise the whole experience. As long as I was improving each time, I was doing OK. I told Pasha that my main objective was to know exactly what I was doing within the dance. His way of learning was to go over every step meticulously before moving on to the next bit, but I wanted to learn the basic routine and then refine it. That way at least I would know where I was supposed to be and what I was supposed to be doing at all times, even if it wasn't completely perfect.

That worked for us, and as the weeks went on things started to get better. We loved coming up with the music and the concepts for our routines, and each week we tried to become different characters to keep it fun and interesting. By the time we got to the quarter-final – where we did a fusion of tango and cha-cha to 'It's Raining Men' – I was feeling more confident again, and that was the week we scored the first perfect forty of the series, with a ten from every judge. The crowd were up on their feet, and even Len Goodman gave us a standing ovation. It was such a great feeling, and I needed it. I was just so tired. It really couldn't have come at a better time.

For the semi-final, Pasha and I did a charleston, and he decided to put in a move where we did three consecutive cartwheels while attached to one another. I wasn't convinced. 'Really?' I said. 'Do I strike you as the athletic, sporty type?'

During the first few practices of this difficult move, I somehow managed to pop one of my ribs out of place – it was agony. For a while it felt as if I'd been winded, and I couldn't breathe properly. It was such a big week in the competition, but we couldn't practise any of the lifts because I was in too much pain. Pasha had to call in a friend of his, Colin, who was used to this kind of injury through working closely with the army. He somehow managed to pop my rib back into place, and after that he was on standby at all the rehearsals. After each run-through I'd go over to Colin so he could

331

manoeuvre my rib back to where it was meant to be. He was like some sort of ballroom guardian angel. It was all worth it, though. Pasha and I got a perfect score for that dance, too, and that spurred me on to the final.

After everything that had happened, I was really quite calm for the whole day of the final. Pasha and I had come such a long way together on the show, and I'd improved massively along the way. That was enough for us, really. I'd had a fabulous time, and when it came down to it, I just wanted to feel that I'd done myself proud and got something positive out of the *Strictly* experience, which I had. So that night I just went out there, let loose, and enjoyed myself. And I didn't at all mind not winning. I was more than happy to finish as joint runner-up with Denise. We'd been on the *Strictly* journey together every step of the way.

Once *Strictly* and all the pre-Christmas Girls Aloud promo were over, I took some much-needed time off for Christmas at my place. I'd invited all my family, but I could hardly get my head around actually organising anything. There was no way I was going to be able to get everything ready, prepare all the goodies and cook a big Christmas dinner. I was just too knackered. In fact, I hardly even knew it was Christmas at all I was so exhausted, and I'm generally the annoying, overly festive one in our family – full-on decorations and tons of pressies, with three Christmas trees in the house. I'm like Mrs Claus! This time I hadn't even had time to buy any gifts for anyone, but luckily Nikki helped me out with the shopping. Meanwhile, Sally and Joe stepped into the breach as far as organising the day was concerned. 'All we want you to do is lie on the couch while we feed you up,' Sally ordered. 'We're actually quite worried about you.' My only task was to look after my nephew Billy while they went off to the kitchen to get the dinner ready.

It was quite a different Christmas for me that year. Usually it's all about the tradition and presents and everything that goes along with the day, but right then it was all about reconnecting with my family. I hate feeling detached from everyone, as I had been over the previous few months. I'd submerged myself in *Strictly* and Girls Aloud to the point that I didn't even know what my own sisters were doing from week to week. I'm just not used to that, coming from such a close family. It felt as though I was being too self-involved, and I didn't like it. Having them all there on Christmas Day was brilliant, despite the fact that it felt very weird for me to be lying around with nothing to do, nothing to learn and nothing to rehearse.

On New Year's Eve, Justin and I decided to have an impromptu party at our place, and invite our guests to stay over. Nicola said that she hadn't made any plans for New Year and that she was coming along, and I also invited Kelli Young, from Liberty X, and her husband, Sparx, who was in Triple 8 with Justin, plus Sally and Adam with their partners. My old friend Alix came with her husband, and so did my dear friend Jenny. The three of us girls, along with Sally, meet once a week for dinner, and have done for years. We like to think of it as our 'Sex and the City' group. It's a tradition I inherited from my mum. Thursday night was always her night out with her girlfriends and now I do the same – except with my convoluted schedule the designated night changes from week to week.

Whenever I'm out with the girls from the band, it can be hard to let loose completely, because there's always the danger that you're going to get snapped by a photographer while making an absolute fool of yourself. When you're in the comfort and privacy of your own home, however, it's much easier to relax – perhaps too easy. At one point during our New Year's Eve party, I remember Justin giving Nicola's boyfriend, Charlie, a sideways glance.

'Look at these two jokers,' he muttered as Nicola and I chatted away, becoming more and more animated the more alcohol we consumed.

'This is gonna go very wrong, I can see it,' Charlie warned.

They were right. The next thing I remember was Nicola and I being mortal drunk and somehow throwing red wine all over a couch that Justin and I had spent £3,000 on. Then I vaguely remember Nicola dragging me out into the street to do 'Auld Lang Syne' in a circle, but I think it was about 2 a.m. by that point, so about two hours too late. I'm sure my neighbours must have loved that. Poor Justin had to strip all the covers off our rather large sofa and put them in the washing machine before he went to bed, as I was fit for nothing. When they came out completely clean the next day, I said to him, 'I love you more for that than for anything else you've ever done.'

I must admit to feeling a little bit smug and very relieved on the morning of 1 January, when Kelli and Sparx had to get up at 6 a.m. to see to their twins, and Sally had to drag herself out of bed for Billy. I just stayed in bed and slept.

My Christmas gift to my family was to take all of them for a fantastic New Year holiday to Barbados, where I'd rented a gorgeous villa big enough for everyone. When we left on 2 January, our house was still an absolute tip from the party and I was still horribly hungover, but it was well worth it.

29

Good People Get Nervous

Dickon Stainer from Decca Records had come to see me in *Shrek* one night, and suddenly an idea was hatched for me to record an album of well-known musical theatre songs. This was a dream come true! I loved being in the studio and recording, but I didn't want to make a solo pop record, so this was perfect. I said yes as soon as Dickon pitched the idea to me.

The team at Decca were amazing, allowing me to choose the songs I wanted to record and working alongside me to get the best results. I started off with a shortlist of numbers that I loved, and then I sat down with my A&R guy, Tom Lewis, to talk through them. Tom was great, and almost all of the songs I wanted to do, he agreed with. I wanted to be challenged musically, but I also wanted to record songs that I had a connection with, such as 'Somewhere' from *West Side Story*, which I'd sung as a child, and 'I Still Believe' from *Miss Saigon*, which is one of my all time favourite musical songs. I'd never had that sort of creative control in the past, and so this felt much more real and straightforward to me than I'd been used to. I was going to be singing songs that I wanted to do, in the way that I wanted to do them.

I chose to work with two Swedish producers, Per Magnusson and David Kreuger, who were based in Stockholm, and who had worked with everyone from Leona Lewis to Il Divo, Josh Groban and Katherine Jenkins. They were great at delivering classical style for a more mainstream audience. This was important to me because I didn't want to alienate Girls Aloud fans by doing something that they might not appreciate or expect me to do. My aim was to introduce some of the fans I already had to musical theatre but to stay with a commercial pop sound.

I went to Stockholm to record the album *Centre Stage* in the summer of 2012, with Hillary popping over once or twice to keep an eye on how things were going. I stayed in a very pretty and artistic area of Stockholm from where I could walk to the studio each day, and once I was there I felt very relaxed. After all the hard work and madness of *Shrek*, getting away from London to record was actually like having a break. Yes, I was working, but there was very little pressure and I had to concentrate only on giving the best performance that I could in the studio.

The process of recording was very relaxed and easy because Per and David really understood what I was trying to do with the album. We took one day for each song, and I felt very much at home singing those songs in that environment. I've always been at my best when I'm in the recording studio, and most days I was happy to sing away until midnight, or at least until my voice gave out. While I was there, I met Swedish singer-songwriter Fredrik Kempe, who performs both opera and pop. Fredrik had an idea for us to write a couple of original songs for the album and the results were wonderful. 'Dreams Can Learn to Fly' is one of my favourite songs on the album, and the fans absolutely love it, too.

Doing the album led to quite a few duets and performances with some unexpected singing partners. Towards the end of my run in *Shrek*, I sang with Ronan Keating at the Olivier Awards, and then I sang with Alfie Boe on a recording of the Queen song 'One Vision', which was recorded especially for the British Olympic and

Paralympic team during London 2012. It was a huge compliment to be asked to sing with Alfie. He's one of my idols within the classical and musical theatre world, and we had great fun working in the recording studio together. He was nothing like I'd imagined, though. For some reason, I always expect classical singers to be sensible and serious, but Alfie was quite laddish and a bit of a joker, and that made him very easy to work with. We performed the song together at an Olympic gala event, 'Our Greatest Team Rises', at the Royal Albert Hall in front of the Duke and Duchess of Cambridge. My mum is a big fan of Alfie's and she felt very proud to be at the Albert Hall watching me perform with him.

I also performed the single from *Centre Stage*, 'One Day I'll Fly Away', at the 2012 National Television Awards, but that went horribly pear-shaped. The awards were held at the O2 Arena, and it was my first big solo TV appearance. Needless to say, I was feeling the pressure. I'm always much more at ease doing live gigs, when I don't have to worry about what the TV cameras and the sound are doing. Performing live on television is a lot scarier, because you're often at the mercy of the people who are hitting the buttons and pushing the faders. For a start, the show wasn't set up for me to have an orchestra, so I had to use a track. It wasn't ideal, but the soundcheck went well so I felt happy and positive about the following night's performance.

On the day, though, I was terrified. It was one of those times when my nerves completely took over and I felt as though I was having some sort of attack. I hadn't experienced fear like that in a very long time. For some reason I just couldn't shake it and it got worse as the day went on. It's a hard thing to explain to someone who's never experienced it, so I called Cheryl, who is one of the few people I know who understands what it's like to feel that scared of stepping out onto a stage or in front of a camera. By that time I was in a bit of a state.

'I can't breathe properly,' I said to her. 'My chest is tightening – what is this? I've never experienced anything like it.'

I wasn't sure I'd ever had a panic attack before, but I think I might have been having one on that day – it was vile.

'Just try and calm down,' Cheryl said. 'I've been there so many times. Don't you dare let this mess you up. I've just seen you in *Shrek*, and I want everyone to know how amazing you are. Please don't let the fear ruin it for you.'

I think some of my acute nervousness stemmed from the realisation that I really was out on my own now.

I'd just come out of *Strictly* and my profile was fairly high, so I thought that people expected much more of me as an individual than they ever had before. Suddenly I knew how Cheryl must have felt going out as a solo artist after being in Girls Aloud for so long. She had all the same anxieties that I did, and now I knew why.

After speaking to Cheryl I had a little conversation with myself. 'You can do this in your sleep! Don't worry. It's just TV – just get on with it.'

My sister Amy came along to give me a bit of moral support. 'It'll be fine, you'll be fine,' she said, smiling cheerily at me in the dressing room. I later found out that she'd called Sally because she was so worried about me. 'She's not in a good way,' Amy said. 'I haven't seen her look this scared for a long time.'

Hillary was also trying to reassure me that it wasn't a big deal, but she knew how important it was, and we both knew that it was going to happen anyway and there was sod all I could do about it.

'Is there any way I can not do this?' I asked Hillary as the moment of truth drew closer. I was deadly serious.

'I'm afraid not,' she said, solemnly.

I would have done anything to run out of that building.

When it came to the actual performance, I was so on edge I think I was running on pure adrenalin. I was happy that I'd actually managed to walk out onto the stage. Then as I moved towards my start position, the most horrible loud crackling noise came through my in-ear monitors. At the same time, the music on stage was quiet and all I could hear was this awful crunching. I had no idea what was going on and my first thought was, Oh my God, what am I going to do? I kept thinking to myself that someone was going to sort the sound out, and that it was all suddenly going to kick in, but it never did, not through the entire song. I was basically singing over almost nothing. What was even worse was that the sound that was being broadcast was just horrendous. There had been a problem in the sound truck, which meant that I was singing full out over a weedy sounding backing track. The music through most of the song was barely audible, and my voice was just booming out with no musical support from the orchestration. I couldn't believe that I managed to haul it together enough to get out there, only to be stitched up by the ITV sound department.

I did get a bit of stick from the media, and some publications seemed to revel in the fact that I didn't do as well as I might have. That's not unusual, I suppose, but it's still a bit of a downer. Hillary had people from ITV calling her all week to apologise, saying that they couldn't believe something like that could have happened.

I could, though. I knew there was a reason why I'd had a bad feeling about it. What can you do? At the end of the day there's no point making excuses about it or complaining. You just have to take it on the chin and try to do better next time. No one is ever going to judge me as harshly as I judge myself. I asked Denise Van Outen how she always stays so calm when she's performing. She never seems to look nervous. She told me that she always gets nervous, but tries to use her nerves in a positive way.

'I believe that nice people get nervous before they go on,' she said. 'The only people I've ever met who don't get nervous are either arrogant or deluded. The reason good people get nervous is because they don't want to let their audience down.'

The good news was that once it was all over, I didn't fall to pieces, as I might have done in the past. I think I'd finally got to the stage where I knew what I was capable of, and that if I'd done it the next day, it probably would have been perfect. I'd done enough on my own now to know that I *could* do it. Still, after that night I'll always take my own sound team with me when I do live TV – just to be on the safe side.

30
Ten

On the day we did the press conference to announce the record and the 'Ten' tour in October of 2012, I was really worried about Sarah – we all were. She was terrified about going out in front of the press and TV cameras again, especially as there had been so much speculation in the media about whether or not she was getting herself back together after her time in rehab. She'd had a couple of drinks to calm her nerves, which didn't help matters. Sarah can be a bit unpredictable when she's nervous and upset, and as it was such an important event, we were all very anxious about her state of mind. The only thing we could do was to be as supportive as possible and hope for the best, but she really was in a bad way. I went over and spoke to her just before we were due to go on stage.

'Are you all right, Sarah? How are you doing?'

That was all it took to tip her over, and she started to cry.

'I haven't done anything like this for so long,' she said. 'I'm so nervous.'

She was so daunted by the whole thing, and I completely understood that. Of all of us, she had the most to prove. Sarah wanted to let everyone know that she *could* do it, and that she was back on her feet again. She wanted to get out there and show everyone that she was fine, but she didn't seem it. Luckily, the rest of us were all pretty calm, so we resolved to help her through it as best we could.

We waited in the wings as Nick Grimshaw from Radio 1 prepared to introduce us to the assembled press, TV and media people, but suddenly Sarah was really freaking out.

'I can't do this,' she said. 'I can't do it.'

The tears were starting again and I really felt for her but this wasn't the time for sympathy or sentimentality. If she stepped out in front of the cameras in that state, she'd just have to deal with a whole new batch of negative press stories the next day, and then she'd feel even worse. Being hard on her was the only way.

'You can do this,' I said, firmly. 'You have to. You've done it a thousand times, and you can do it now. We'll take the brunt of it for you. All you need to do is go out there and smile.'

Sarah nodded and pulled herself together just in time. She was still very nervous all through the conference, but she got through it. After all she'd been through, each new thing we did as a band over the next few weeks was a big achievement for her. It did make the whole day of the press conference very stressful for the rest of us, but that's the way it is sometimes when you're in a group. If someone isn't in such a good place, it's up to the rest of the group to rally round as best they can.

I was aware that Sarah was still quite frail, and sometimes it was pretty hard going being with her. She was very nervous about getting back in the saddle as a live performer after three years, and I could see that she was struggling. Sarah had never been particularly confident about the choreography side of things, and now she was even more out of practice. I felt for her. After all, Sarah never signed up to be a dancer but she was always such a great singer, and that's all she ever wanted to be. Unfortunately, Girls Aloud had become a very visual group over the years and choreography was part of the package. It was obvious to all of us that her confidence was at an all-time low. At the first proper gig we did, which was Capital Radio's Jingle Bell Ball, alongside Pink, the Wanted and Rita Ora, we could tell that Sarah didn't have the routine down properly, and I wondered how well she was coping. There were times when I even wondered whether a whole, full-on tour was the right thing for her to be doing – it became a bit of a moral dilemma. Of course I wanted the tour to happen and for it to be amazing, but not at the expense of Sarah's wellbeing. It worried all of us. We tried to keep her spirits up and to help her through it as best we could.

Despite the odd teething problems, the preparations for the tour went really well. We had two 'glam squads' now, which made getting ready for gigs and TV appearances a lot faster than it had been in the past, and our amazing stylist Alison Elwin pulled together all our different looks for the show. Being the stylist for Girls Aloud is quite a tall order – trying to please five girls, with all their different tastes and body-shapes, is no easy task, although there wasn't really any competition between us on that front. You might think that we'd all have different ideas about what we wanted to wear and how we wanted to look after doing things on our own for so long, but after ten years in the band we all knew that what worked for us as individuals might not be what worked for us within our Girls Aloud roles. We were all pretty much on the same page while we were choosing our looks for the show – the camper and more over-the-top and glamorous, the better. We even had Vicky Gill, who was the head of costume for *Strictly*, make some of our costumes, because the girls all loved the costumes I'd worn on the show so much.

Little by little it started to come together. When rehearsals for the tour got under way, we were all excited, and I found it liberating to be dancing and singing with the girls again. Sarah worked her arse off during rehearsals, and it paid off because she gradually got back into the swing of it. There was a feeling of great energy in the room and a sense of pride in what we'd achieved and what we were about to celebrate – ten years of being one of Britain's biggest pop bands.

At first I wondered if it might be difficult – five women who had all had different careers with varying levels of success, now coming back together into a pop group they started out in as teenagers – but it wasn't hard. Once we were back in the dance studio rehearsing together, it was as if the last three years had been wiped away and we were all back where we belonged. This was Girls Aloud, so all our other incarnations went out of the window. I hoped that this feeling and momentum would carry us all right through to the end of the tour, but unfortunately that wasn't the case.

By the time we got to the actual shows, some of the old problems and niggles we had with Nadine started bubbling to the surface again. Nothing had really changed. This meant that the closeness we'd built up during the rehearsal period quickly fragmented. Nicola, Cheryl and I have always remained close, and I think that we'd have been friends even if we weren't in a band together, but I'm not sure that would have been the case for me with Nadine or even Sarah. That's not to say I don't care about them or respect them. They're both just very different from me and I don't always understand where they're coming from. So as much as we were together every night on stage, we didn't spend time all together off stage. I suppose you choose the people you want to spend time with because they're the people you get on with, and who bring out the best in you. It would be the same for someone who worked in an office with four other people. They might all work well together day-to-day, but it doesn't mean that they'd necessarily all be best friends outside work. You are always going to connect with some people more than others, but when you're in a girl band that's in the public eye, things tend to be well scrutinised and can be blown out of proportion.

On a day-to-day level everything was just how it should have been. When you're on tour, you can't really do anything else but be on tour. That life takes over and becomes the norm. You don't have a lot of time to do anything but sleep and get ready for the next show, and you don't really have to think about much besides getting from place to place and then stepping out on stage and giving the best performance you can possibly give. For me, the hard graft of the tour seemed a breeze after doing *Strictly*, because after all that dance training I was in really good shape and able to cope with the physical demands that a Girls Aloud show throws at you. That being said, I constantly felt as though I was in the middle of a whirlwind, and I was so thankful to have Nikki around to help me through it. She was my saviour throughout the 'Ten' tour, just as she was through all the madness of *Strictly* and my solo album campaign. I didn't have time to draw breath a lot of the time, so I needed her more than ever. She's incredibly sweet, very patient and nothing is ever a problem, and luckily she's remained part of Hillary's management team at Shaw Thing since the band split as my own personal assistant.

Sarah coped brilliantly with the demands of the tour, despite all of our worries. She worked really hard and was on top form at every show, which was quite an achievement, given how frail she'd been at the start of it all. I really hope she continues to get better now we're not together any more, because I do worry about her after all that's happened. The good news is she seems to be a lot stronger now, so I'm hopeful that she's come through the worst of it.

In the middle of the tour, my granddad was taken into hospital. He'd not been well for a while but it was suddenly more serious. He was admitted with breathing problems, but it turned out a few other things weren't working as well as they should have been, either. Fortunately, we had a day off in Manchester, so I was easily able to drive back to Bradford for a visit. I hadn't seen him for ages, and he lit up when he saw me. I spent a lovely few hours with him, and although I knew he was very unwell, I convinced myself that he was going to get better again. 'I'm not ready to go,' he told me. He was a month off of his ninety-third birthday, but as far as he was concerned he still had a lot to live for.

Not long after my visit, he took a turn for the better, and the news from the hospital was that things were looking good. However, one morning towards the very end of the tour, when we were in Belfast, I got a short phone message from my mum – 'Can you ring me when you're up?' I knew straight away why she was calling. Mum wouldn't normally call me in the morning while I was on tour, because she knows how tiring the shows are. I knew exactly what I was going to hear when I spoke to her, and I was right. My granddad was gone.

That night I had a show to do, so during the day the girls were all with me, and I cried it out with them as much as I could. Grief is a very odd thing; it comes in waves. You can't possibly cry solidly for an entire day and night, and so I thought I would probably be able to find some strength to do the show that night. I'd get through it for him, if nothing else. I was fine until we got to the song 'Untouchable', at which point we'd travelled on a moving platform from the main stage to a second stage, right in the middle of the arena. Suddenly, I couldn't do it. I went to sing my line and nothing came out, and unexpectedly the tears came, pouring like a waterfall. I simply couldn't control what was happening; it was pure emotion and just too raw. The lyrics I sing in 'Untouchable' didn't help, either. In fact, they couldn't have been worse.

I remember the fans around the stage looking at me and probably wondering what on earth was wrong. Meanwhile, the girls were all trying to squeeze my hand at every possible moment, trying to give me the strength to get through the song, as was Kieran, the guy I dance with. I couldn't do it, though, and in the end there was no point in trying. I just sobbed my heart out.

I was a mess for the rest of the show. I'd never had to perform feeling like that and now I realise that it was too soon after the fact. I shouldn't have pushed myself. I was already feeling shaky and emotional because it was the last couple of dates and therefore the end of Girls Aloud. What with that and my family preparing for the funeral of someone we'd all loved so desperately, it was a very weird and sad week.

As soon as the tour finished I went back home for the funeral. It had already been a week of huge upheaval, what with both the tour and the band ending, but by that time all I really cared about was saying goodbye to my granddad. Thank God I'd made that journey to the hospital in Bradford, because that was the last time I ever saw him. If we hadn't been where we were on that particular day, I might not have been able to get there. I wouldn't have been able to bear that. On that day at the hospital he told me the same story he always tells me, which is his favourite memory of me. He'd driven me to a speech and drama festival in Ilkley when I was about nine. I was doing a performance there, and while I was sitting in the car waiting to go on and recite my piece, some joyriders crashed into the back of us and smashed his car up. Typically,

I still went ahead with my performance, and afterwards he took me to a little café where he bought me a scone with cream and jam.

'Can I really have a whole scone all to myself, Granddad?'

To me, it was the most amazing thing ever; I'd never had an entire scone just for me. We just didn't have that kind of treat when I was little, so it was a big deal.

'If it means that much to you, you can have two,' he said.

He told me that story whenever I saw him as he got older. I guess it meant a lot to him, and now I'll never forget it, either.

After the funeral, my mum told me that on the day he died she'd gone to the hospital to say her last goodbye. While she was there some of the nurses came over to talk to her.

'Well, we've been hearing all about your daughter Kimberley,' one of them said. 'Your dad never stopped talking about her.'

My mum was quite taken aback, because it just didn't sound like him. It turned out he'd spoken to each of the nurses individually.

'Do you know who my granddaughter is? Kimberley Walsh! Keep it to yourself, though, I don't want anyone else to know.' After he'd told one nurse, he'd wait till the next one came along and then tell her the same thing. 'My granddaughter is Kimberley Walsh – but don't tell anyone.'

I always thought I knew exactly how my granddad saw me, which was as just as one of his grandchildren, no different from the others. I thought he wasn't all that impressed with all the things I'd done, and I was fine with that. It turned out that he was impressed, and hearing that made me smile and cry all at the same time. He'd given me one extra little thing, even though he was gone. He was really proud of me after all.

31

The End and the Beginning

During the tour it became clear that being in Girls Aloud had changed, and I made my peace with the fact that it was coming to an end. At times it felt like being in some strange time warp, as if I was getting up and living each day in the past rather than the present. In so many ways I loved being back with the girls, but in truth it was purely nostalgia – a group of great friends reminiscing about days gone by, but instead of doing it around a table with a bottle of wine, we were doing it every night in front of thousands of people. I remember thinking that Sarah must have felt the same. She seemed very emotional all the way through the tour, but I think she needed Girls Aloud to come to an end as much as I did. There wasn't one night when she didn't struggle through 'I'll Stand By You', watching all those precious moments that had been captured in time, flickering on a screen above us. She needed a fresh start, too. We'd all been through such a lot during our time in the band, but I think Cheryl and Sarah had gone through the most drama and upheaval in their lives. That part of the show always seemed to affect them the most, and that was no real surprise to me, I suppose. It just wouldn't have felt right for us to stay together and make new music after the tour had ended. This was just one last, fabulous walk down memory lane for the sake of our fans, who had always been so loyal and wonderful.

Nicola, Cheryl, Sarah and I tore ourselves apart about how we were going to announce to the fans that Girls Aloud was finally over. All five us knew that it was going to end, which is why we'd agreed to do one final tour. An hour before the very last show, while we were still working on the official announcement, Nadine point blank refused to agree to any kind of press release, but we had to let the fans know somehow. We didn't want them to go away believing that there might be another album or another tour next year. We owed them that. 'Ten' hadn't been advertised as a farewell tour because we wanted it to be a celebration of our past achievements, rather than cashing in on 'the end of Girls Aloud'. That's why we'd really pushed the boat out on the production. We wanted to make it a show to remember for our fans.

In the end, we made the announcement on Twitter – on TwitLonger – which we thought would be a nice direct connection to the fans: 'Dear Alouders, we just want to say from the bottom of our hearts thank you!! This tour has been an amazing experience and the perfect chance to say thank you for being on this journey with us through a decade. It has far exceeded any of our dreams and we hope we are forever your inspiration and reminder that dreams really do glitter!! Your love and support will stay with us forever but we have now come to the end of our incredible time together. Love you lots.'

Some people thought that we'd got it wrong, making the announcement on Twitter. A lot of the fans were angry that we hadn't put out an official statement, but our hands had been tied, and we could never have held it together to make that sort of announcement on stage during our final show – emotions were running far too high. Also, none of us wanted that memory recorded for posterity – the moment when the band was no more. It was too sad, and we knew it wasn't what the fans wanted to hear. There was no way we could end our last show like that. However, the four of us were all in agreement that we needed to let our fans know, and that's why we decided to tweet the news. You can imagine our surprise when Nadine went public, saying that she had no part in our decision to split, and that she wanted the group to keep going. It was quite a hard piece of news to swallow because she never said any such thing to the rest of us, and splitting up was what we'd always planned.

The highlights of the tour for me were the shows at the O2 Arena in London. The crowds were so brilliant. I'd never seen anything like it. The atmosphere was totally electric every night. All our shows up and down the country were amazing, but each of the O2 shows felt like a big party rather than a gig. The fans were just revelling in the nostalgia, sharing the end of the journey with us. Those shows have given us brilliant memories to walk away with, and I'll always cherish them.

For me, the end of Girls Aloud is simply the start of something new. There are so many things I want to do and I'm lucky enough not to have to panic about my future. I just want to take my time and enjoy whatever new challenges come along. Throughout the past eleven years, my family, my friends and Justin have remained more important than anything and that's never going to change. On Mum's sixtieth in July 2012, I threw a big party for her at our house and the whole family came. After she'd opened her gifts, Justin drove around the corner in the brand new car that I'd bought for her. It had a big red bow on it, and when she opened the door, the music system was all set to blast out 'Happy Birthday' by Stevie Wonder. She loved it, and I feel very grateful that I'm able to do things like that for my family from time to time. I'll never forget the smile on my granddad's face when he saw that brand new car. He'd never been able to afford one himself, and I think he was just happy to know that his daughter was always going to be OK, whatever happened. It's such a special memory.

I'm also aware of how precious my relationship with Justin is. It seems to be quite rare in the entertainment industry for a romance to survive as long as ours has, and that's something I'm proud of. I guess I've had the best of both worlds. Having been a part of the industry, Justin knows how it works, so he's very understanding of the pressures and the demands that I've had to face. On the other hand, the fact that he's no longer part of it is probably what helps keep us together. If the two of us had both been away all the time, with constant clashes of priorities and commitments, who knows what might have happened? Justin took a step back from the limelight without any bitterness or regret. He hadn't come from a performing background, as I had. His band, Triple 8, had evolved more organically. The band was something he and his friends had wanted to develop, rather than him having a burning passion to be a singer. After the band finished, he went on to work for Sally's husband, Joe, at his promotional company, Pod, and now he's running the property company that we've started together. His new passion is renovating houses, which is something I love, too, and we hope to build the business together.

I don't think there's any doubt in either of our minds that we're going to be together forever, and I'm sure one day we'll get married. I think Justin wants to achieve a bit more professionally and find his own feet, financially, before he proposes, which says a lot to me about the kind of man he is. He's also *very* laid back, like his dad, so it might be a while! What's far more important to us right now is children. Justin has Chloe and we both love her to bits, but we're both getting extremely broody now – although he wouldn't admit it publicly. Whenever there's a baby around, they're completely drawn to Justin. He's a natural around them and he loves it. To be honest, I don't really know what we're waiting for, so I don't think it's going to be too long now before my nephew Billy has some cousins. Watch this space!

32

What Happens in Vegas . . .

In June of 2013, Nicola and I travelled to LA to celebrate Cheryl's thirtieth birthday along with ten of her nearest and dearest. She'd rented the most unbelievable house in Malibu, and planned a whole weekend of celebrations, including a trip to Vegas on a private plane to see Beyoncé at the MGM Grand, followed by a DJ set by Calvin Harris at Hakkasan. The house itself was stunning – overlooking the beach, with a large pool and a beautiful garden – and it was two doors up from Julia Roberts. The place was currently up for sale for $24,000,000. Of course, Cheryl had gone all out because she wanted to treat everyone and make it the best experience ever.

The barbecue on the day of her birthday was a real spectacle. Cheryl's PA, Lily, had helped her organise beautiful food and a great DJ, and on top of that she'd hired a couple of 'mermaids' to swim around in the pool; plus there was a girl in a see-through bubble, a bit like a hamster ball, tumbling around the place. We partied all afternoon, and once the sun had gone down, Nicola and I read the birthday poem we'd written with the help of our friend, Terry. It was a funny and very personal tribute to our eleven years as friends, and although Nicola was a bit the worse for wear by the time she read it, there wasn't a dry eye in the place. When we gave Cheryl her gift – a heart-shaped ring from Chopard, with three diamonds – she was in bits all over again. The diamonds represented the three of us and our close friendship. We'd been through so much together, and although Girls Aloud was now something in all of our pasts, the closeness and bond that we shared was very much a part of our future. It's something that will last forever.

Of course, there's one final Girls Aloud drama I have to mention. You knew there had to be one. When it came to the trip to Vegas, everyone was, of course, very excited. Cars were booked to collect us at 10 a.m. to drive us to a small airport where we'd board our very own private jet. Nicola, by some miracle, was ready half an hour before we were due to leave, and I was all ready and organised as usual. Cheryl, however, was still in her pyjamas. I could see there was no way we were going to leave on time, which was pretty much the norm.

'We might as well go upstairs and do some present wrapping,' I said to Nicola. 'We've got loads to do.'

As well as the ring, we'd bought her thirty other little gifts, all personalised, including biscuits, candles, lollipops and a dressing gown. All those still needed wrapping, so we had plenty to keep us occupied while we waited for Cheryl to get ready. We were well into the task by twenty past ten, but I was aware that time was getting on and if we didn't leave soon, we were going to be really late for the plane.

'It's twenty past,' I said to Nicola. 'Surely she must be ready by now.'

'Oh don't worry,' Nicola said. 'She was still in her pyjamas. They'll shout for us when it's time to go.'

By half ten I was very concerned.

'It's really quiet out there. Really quiet.'

Nicola listened for a moment.

'Shall I go and check?'

'I think so, yeah.'

As soon as Nicola walked out of the bedroom she bumped into some random English guy whom she didn't know from Adam.

'Er . . . who are you?

'I'm one of the party planners,' he said. 'I'm here to get ready for the barbecue tomorrow.'

'Oh!' Nicola said. 'Well, where *is* everyone?'

'They all left about twenty minutes ago,' the guy said.

'WHAT?'

There were four or five cars ordered. Everyone must have piled in with their luggage and driven off assuming that Nicola and I were in one of the other cars. They'd left us behind. We were home alone! Not only did we have no idea where the private airport was, but there was zero phone signal in the house. You either had to tear down to the end of the beach to get a full signal, or go right to the very front of the house to get even a hint of one.

The next ten minutes had to be seen to be believed. Nicola and I ran around the house like something out of the *Benny Hill Show*, waving our phones in the air in an attempt to get a signal, and screaming. Nicola was laughing like a mad woman, just as she always does, and I was yelling instructions at her as we went.

'Quick, run down that end! Try over there!'

We tried to call Lily, we tried to call Cheryl's brother, Gary – nothing!

'Sh*t sh*t sh*t! What are we gonna do?'

We couldn't believe that an entire group of people

we knew had driven off without us, not even noticing that we were missing. Finally, we got through to Gary.

'Where are you?' I asked, breathlessly.

'I'm in the car behind you,' he said.

'No you're not. We're still at the bloody house!'

'What are you talking about?'

'Yeah, we're still at the house. You've left us.'

We knew it was too late for them to come back and get us, or for us to order another car, so we had to beg the party planner to take us to the airport. Thankfully, he agreed, but he had a tiny sports car, so I ended up jammed in the back like a sardine. He raced us there, and after another ten minutes' mad panic when we couldn't find the right gate, we finally got there. It was pure drama. When we boarded the plane, everyone was pretending to be asleep – even the pilot joined in with the piss-taking – and for the entire weekend nobody let us forget that we were almost left at home alone like Macaulay Culkin. Still, we'd made it to the plane at last, and we were overjoyed when it finally taxied along the runway and took off into the perfect, blue Californian sky.

Of course, that was just the start of a whole new set of amazing experiences for my two best friends and me, and I know there'll be many more. But that's another story . . . and you know the old saying – what happens in Vegas stays in Vegas.

33

The Last Piece of the Puzzle

24 February 2014

The traffic was horrific. Floods in Swiss Cottage or something, so tailbacks forever. It had to be the worst traffic I'd ever sat in, travelling into town from our place, I was certain of it. Justin was his usual relaxed self as men always seem to be in these situations, but I was getting more anxious by the second. I'd been building up to it all week.

'Why are you stressing? It's all going to be fine, and if there *is* a problem, we'll deal with it as and when it happens.'

I knew he was right but I couldn't wait for it to be

over. Then I'd be free, finally, to tell people what was going on and to let myself relax and be happy. Not long now.

Still we weren't moving, and by this time I was freaking out, having a *total* drama. We were definitely going to be late now and miss it completely.

'Just stay calm,' Justin said . . . calmly. How do men do that?

'No. You don't understand. I've been waiting three months for this. If it doesn't go ahead today, then . . . I can't cope. This is the day when I was supposed to find out.'

'Yes, but worst case scenario we could do it tomorrow and everything will be fine.'

'No,' I said. 'It won't be. That's not an option.'

As far as I was concerned, this was happening. And it was happening today.

It hadn't been all that long, really – just a few months. By October 2013 it was clear that Justin and I had both come to the same conclusion, and were asking ourselves the same question – what are we waiting for? When you're in the sort of profession that means you don't really know when, what or where the next job is going to be, it can sometimes seem as though it's never going to be the right time to think about having a baby. I'd certainly thought about the idea of becoming a mum when Girls Aloud took a break at the end of 2009, but back then there had been so many opportunities for me to grow as a performer in my own right and at the time I felt like I needed to do that. I wanted to do everything that I possibly could – achieve all those dreams – so that when I did decide to have a baby, I could be completely selfless and dedicated. Looking back, I'm sure I made the right choice at the time because the experiences I had doing *Shrek* and *Strictly*, not to mention recording my own album, are some of the best of my life.

Now, for the first time in ages, I didn't really have anything set in stone workwise and I knew it was the perfect time. I could at last do this without stressing or worrying about what was coming up or how I was going to make it all work. Yes, there was one big plan on the horizon – a brand new show with my good friends Denise van Outen and actress Kara Tointon. We'd all loved doing *Strictly* and wanted to dust off our dancing shoes again, so our idea was to put together an all-singing, all-dancing extravaganza starring all three of us. I was certainly excited about the prospect, but I also knew it would take some time to get together. I was sure I'd be able to go ahead with it if we just pushed it back by a few months, and I knew the other girls wouldn't mind either. Yep! It was time.

One of the things that really cemented things in my mind, once Justin and I had decided, was our amazing trip to Australia towards the end of 2013. I was invited to be a guest panellist for a few days on ITV2's *I'm A Celebrity Get Me Out Of Here! Now!* and Justin and I decided to make a holiday of it. Justin had never been to Australia before and I hadn't seen much of it, despite having worked there, so the plan was to do it all in one go and see as much as we could in the time we had. Melbourne, Sydney, the Gold Coast, Brisbane – we always have a fantastic time together and this was no exception. We knew it might well be our last holiday with just the two of us, so we really went all out to enjoy it. After a week, though, we both felt something was missing. As lovely as it was, we were ready to share it all with a little one and we both knew it. The two of us would be mucking about on the beach or doing handstands in the pool at our gorgeous villa, yet we were both imagining how much more it would mean if we were doing it as a family. It was a real turning point for me.

The thing was I'd been on the pill for many years, and I had no idea how long getting pregnant would take. I imagined it might take ages, so I just carried on with my life as normal, not really thinking about it too much.

Leading up to Christmas I seemed to be working non-stop. I was doing a campaign for the fashion company Very, which involved a lot of photo-shoots and press days, so it was quite intense. I'd chosen clothes from their line to bring together in my own capsule collection, which I then modelled and promoted. It was a lot of fun, but hard work, and I really didn't have time to stop and think about very much else in the run-up to the Christmas holiday.

Over Christmas there were signs that something might be going on, but I didn't put two and two together. On a couple of nights I woke up absolutely boiling. I just lay there thinking, 'I can't possibly sleep in this heat. What's going on? Has someone turned the heating up in this house because it's far too bloody hot!'

In the end I just assumed my period was due as that kind of hot flush was often a symptom. When Justin's family visited over Christmas, I cooked lunch, but when I finally sat down to eat, I was sweltering hot again with a face like a tomato.

'Are you OK, love?' Justin's mum, Jo, asked, looking slightly concerned. 'Maybe you should step outside and get a bit of fresh air.'

'No, it's fine, I'm fine; it's just a very hot oven!'

I clearly remember her looking at me as if she knew

something might be happening. Mums have those intuitions, don't they? They know the signs. Meanwhile, I still had no clue that I might be pregnant.

Christmas came and went, and on New Year's Eve we threw a party at our place. Luckily, most of my girlfriends already have kids, so they all bailed out early and none of us went too crazy with alcohol. It was then that I realized I was two days late, but I put it down to the fact that I'd not long stopped taking a contraceptive pill and probably my body had not quite adjusted yet. Still, I did mention it to Alix, who got rather excited.

'Oh my God, do a test,' she said breathlessly. 'Do a test now!'

Sally and Amy both had the same reaction, but I brushed it off. I didn't want to get all excited only to end up disappointed. I'd just wait a few more days to see what happened.

'Just do a test, you weirdo. How can you bear to wait?' Amy said.

In the end, the peer pressure got to me and I decided that I would do a test on New Year's Day, once everyone had gone home and Justin and I were at the house on our own. I'd never done a pregnancy test before – never had any scares or false alarms – so I decided to get one of the posh ones that tell you in writing, rather than just indicating the result with a little blue line. It either says pregnant or not pregnant, and it also tells you how many weeks. With this test it was possible to get a false negative, but it wasn't possible to get a false positive. And it was positive! Pregnant: two to three weeks.

I immediately started giggling, nervously. I couldn't believe that it was there in front of me in black and white. It all seemed so easy.

I walked out of the bathroom and broke the news to Justin and he was – you guessed it – calm. Very happy . . . but calm. For the next few hours it was all a bit weird. We were both excited but I'm not sure either of us really believed it. I kept thinking I should do another test, even though I knew there was no point. When I broke the news to Sally, she burst into tears, and my mum, always the picture of calm, literally jumped up and down. My dad, Adam and Amy were over the moon with the news. Everyone around me, in fact, seemed to be bursting with joy, whereas I was a bit astonished by the whole thing. Yes we'd been trying, but for some reason it was all still a bit of a surprise, albeit a lovely one. I also think I was a little bit scared of getting too excited as it was very early days, but that's just my nature.

So what did I do next? I had no idea if I had to start taking supplements or eating, or not eating, certain foods. What was I supposed to do?

I have quite a close relationship with my doctor, Meemee, so I went to see her straight away. After checking me over and letting me know that everything seemed to be as it should be, she told me that I needed to decide which hospital I wanted to have the baby in as soon as possible. I'm in the very fortunate position of being able to go private, which means I'll be able to have the same doctor looking after me from start to finish, and for this reason I was told to book in for an early scan at a clinic in Harley Street. I felt a little bit odd that day because the scan showed that, although there was definitely a baby, there was no discernible heartbeat.

'Don't panic,' the doctor told me. 'It's very early days and we can't always detect a heartbeat before six weeks. Everything looks perfect, but you'll have to come back again next week.'

I didn't fret too much, but at the same time I couldn't get too excited, either. At the following week's scan, however, the baby's heartbeat was pounding away like crazy and I immediately burst into tears. I'm not usually prone to being over-emotional, so I really don't know what came over me. I guess it was a potent mixture of joy and relief. The baby was there and I could see it. This was real and it felt great.

After that, all the classic symptoms appeared. I felt

continuously nauseous, tired and *very* hungry. In fact, I was so hungry it got to the point when I'd be driving home from somewhere and find myself unable to resist the sudden compulsion to stop for fast food . . . as soon as possible. I'm sure if anyone had seen me sitting in the car ravaging a KFC Twister they'd probably assume I hadn't eaten for a few weeks – it was that bad. Meanwhile, I was still waiting for that 'happy glow' I kept hearing about to kick in.

At first, Justin had been adamant that I shouldn't tell anybody else until we were over the three-month mark. Obviously, we told his mum and dad and sister, but we didn't even tell his daughter, Chloe, because he felt it was too big a secret to expect a fifteen year old to keep. If she'd made a mistake and let it slip in front of one of her friends, it could easily have got out before we were ready, so although it was a hard decision, we didn't want to put her under that kind of pressure.

'And no telling Nicola or Cheryl, either,' he said.

What? No, please . . . I can't do this! Keeping it from the girls for three months was going to be the hardest thing of all.

After that second scan, however, the doctor seemed sure that my pregnancy was textbook and that the chances of anything going wrong were quite small. This was a lovely thing to hear and made a huge difference to the way Justin and I thought about everything.

'Oh, go on! Let me tell the girls,' I pleaded.

Justin knows how close I am to the two of them, so in the end he gave in. After all, Cheryl and Nicola were the last people likely to blurt out something publicly. If there was anyone we could trust, it was them. The trouble was Cheryl was away in Cape Town on a holiday that she seemed to keep extending. I kept texting to find out when she was coming back but I was getting impatient. 'I'll be back soon,' was all she kept saying. I couldn't possibly tell her big news like that over the phone.

Once she was home, I dashed over straight away, but when we sat down and she started raving on about how fabulous her holiday had been, I wasn't sure whether or not to tell her my news at all. Cheryl told me that she'd felt so relaxed and free in Cape Town; she'd been partying and having more fun than she'd had in ages. It had been a revelation and she seemed thrilled to be back to her old self and enjoying her life after all the drama of the past couple of years. She said she was happy with the way things were now and that she didn't think she was ready to settle down and start a family just yet. It was suddenly abundantly clear that the two of us were in a totally different place at that point in our lives. I was very happy that my friend seemed to have found her feet again, but at the same time I was wondering if I should perhaps put my big news on ice for the time being. Maybe it wouldn't be quite as well received as I thought.

'So what's going on with you?' Cheryl asked, eventually. 'Any news?' I nodded and smiled.

'Yeah, there's news.'

Cheryl just looked at me, her eyes widening, and I didn't have to say another word. She just burst into tears and threw her arms around me, hugging me tightly for about ten minutes. She was literally shaking, and then she just pretty much cried for the next hour, she was so happy. The two of us had grown up together and talked about a moment like this so many times over the years, and now it was actually happening. I could not have hoped for a more wonderful reaction.

After that, Cheryl was just dying to tell Nicola, but I wanted to be the one to do it. I knew I'd have to organise a girls' dinner as soon as possible or Cheryl was going to burst. She wasn't going to be able to hold that sort of information in for long. That Saturday night the three of us went for dinner at a restaurant, but once again I was pipped at the post before I could get the words out.

'So what are we having, girls?' Nicola asked Cheryl

and I as she sat down at the table, up for a good night out. 'Have you ordered the cocktails?'

'Er, I'm just going to have a soft drink,' I said. Well, that's not me and Nicola knew it immediately.

'What? What's going on?' She said, eyeing me intently. 'Is there news?'

When you're as close of the three of us are, sometimes you don't even need words.

'Yeah,' I said. 'There is.'

Poor Nicola had to contain her hysteria because we were in a public place, and at first she didn't even quite believe it.

'You're talking the piss,' she said. 'Come on, tell me the truth.'

Then Cheryl got all teary again and Nicola knew we were on the level. After that, they both started asking if I could organise a special scan, just so they could come, and what was the due date, so they could clear their diaries and make sure they were sitting outside my hospital room when he or she was born. It was a very happy evening.

After dinner we were all so excited that we decided to make a night of it and head to cabaret nightclub The Box, in Soho. I knew I wasn't going to be able to party with the girls like I normally would, but I was sure I'd enjoy myself anyway.

'Oh, it's fine. I'll come. I don't need to have a drink to enjoy myself. It's fine.'

Nicola and Cheryl were on a bit of a mission to party, though, and once they were off and running it dawned on me just how hard it was to be the only sober one in the group. I suppose it was a good thing, really. It was just after Christmas and, like most people, I'd over-indulged. It certainly wasn't going to hurt me to have a dry night out for once. Still, Cheryl and Nic went a little wild that night, fuelled by all the excitement, and so I got some good practice in, being the mother hen who looked after them.

Keeping the secret from everyone else for the next couple of months wasn't exactly a walk in the park, especially as I thought the people close to me might suspect. For a start, my stylist, Nisha, must have wondered why on earth she had virtually to cram me into my outfit for the BRIT awards in February. It wasn't like I was huge but I'd definitely noticed myself thick-ening around the middle. She must have been thinking, 'Crikey, you need to lay off the pies for a while, love!' Then there was Lisa, who was doing my make-up.

'What's goin' on with your skin?' she yelped at me, noticing the unsightly rash around my chin. 'You never have bad skin.'

'Oh yeah, I think it's because I've come off the pill; it's all gone a bit crazy,' I said, as casually as I could manage.

I knew I couldn't keep it up for much longer.

Then there were the times when I was away from home working and Nikki was with me. We always had a glass of red wine with dinner after work and I knew she was wondering why I didn't fancy one. It was far easier to get away with the not drinking thing when I was in a big group. I had dinner at The Ivy one night with Denise and Kara. We'd met up to talk about ideas for our new show. Hillary and a few other friends were there, too, and that night, when the wine came round, I just let the waitress pour it for me and then didn't touch it. With everyone noisily chatting around the table, nobody even noticed.

Still, it wasn't until after the twelve-week scan that we could finally go public with the news, and I for one couldn't wait. That's the reason I was so anxious, sitting in such a horrendous traffic jam that day on the way to the appointment. Not only would I know for sure that our baby was OK, but I could finally tell the world that I was pregnant. It was a big day. Still, the traffic wasn't getting any better. In the end, Justin phoned ahead to tell the receptionist at the clinic that we were going to be late, and she said it was fine – OK, breathe,

breathe – and eventually we arrived, saving me from a possible heart attack. It wasn't over yet, though.

This twelve-week scan was the important one – the Nuchal scan, which helps determine the chances of conditions such as Down's syndrome. For many women, it's the first time they see their baby or hear their baby's heartbeat, and although I'd been lucky enough to have early scans, it was nerve-wracking nonetheless. I'm a bit of a realist. I'm not one of those people who takes everything in her stride and thinks, this won't happen to me. No, I'm the opposite. As far as I'm concerned, it could happen to me and, as I said, I'd been anxious for the whole week leading up to the scan. I wanted to know that a) my baby was still alive in there, and b) he or she was going to be born healthy.

First, they take a blood sample and then you go in for the actual scan, and that's the first moment when we saw something that actually looked like a baby. It was a real person in there, and right away I swore it looked just like me.

'Shut. Up!' Justin clearly wasn't convinced. 'How can it look like you?'

I knew, though. It was the profile and the way that it was sitting, with its lips pouted. There was just some-thing about the bone structure that made me feel like I was looking at a little mini-me. Meanwhile, the doctor who was doing the scan said she couldn't really get any measurements or a proper reading because the baby wouldn't stay still. He or she was literally doing somersaults in there, and it was weird because although I could see it jumping about all over the place on the screen, I couldn't feel a single thing inside my body. Still, for the first time we could really see our baby and hear its heart beating at the same time – it was amazing. One by one, the doctor ticked things off her list, while I waited with bated breath to find out what she could see.

'Heart looks fine, stomach looks fine, and the baby has ten fingers and ten toes.'

Absolutely everything was checked, and at the end of it she told us that it all seemed completely normal and as it should be. The blood test results were all good, too. Our baby was healthy.

Once outside, I felt like doing a musical heel click and shouting at the top of my voice, 'I'm free! I can actually let it all out!'

I'd found it quite difficult, keeping everything under wraps. I'd desperately wanted to tell my extended family, my cousins and my friends, but once you start to open things up and tell more people it's very difficult to keep a lid on it, especially when you're in the public eye. It would only take somebody innocently tweeting a message of congratulations and that would be it – everyone would know. At the end of the day, I wanted to be the one to tell the world that we were having a baby, because I was excited about it, and I wanted to be in control of the news rather than having endless media speculation. We decided that it was best if I made a simple announcement on Twitter: 'Justin and I are so happy to let you all know we are having a baby!!! Couldn't wait to share our lovely news with you all.' That was it. Done.

The next few hours were completely mental. I was flooded with so many lovely messages from every direction. Fans, friends, people I knew, people I didn't know, and lots of celebrities and people I'd worked with, too. The announcement of a baby really does bring the joy out in people. It was wonderful, one of the happiest days of my life, without a doubt.

Whether our baby turns out to be a boy or a girl, our little one is certainly not going to be short of playmates. My best friend Alix had her first son, Miller, in September 2013, and a day later my sister Sally give birth to her second son, Alfie. That was a mad couple of days – a whirlwind to say the least. I had a private gig for the Variety charity in the midst of it all, so I dashed in to see Alix's new baby on the way to the sound check, then later rushed in to see Sally, who'd ended up giving birth while I was in the middle of the sound check. Then after all that I tore back to get myself ready to do the show that same night. They were both gorgeous, healthy babies, though, which is the most important thing, and what every parent hopes for.

Our new arrival will also be lucky enough to have an amazing big sister in Chloe, and just before the twelve-week scan we felt we could finally tell her. I'd been a little bit anxious about what her reaction would be. I was sure she would be happy but she'd lived her whole life without any siblings and we knew it was going to be a big deal for her. Justin encouraged me to say the words when she came down to stay with us during the half-term holiday.

'I think she'd like to hear it from you,' he said.

'We've got some news,' I said, nervously, as we all sat down together. 'You're going to have a little brother or sister.'

I think she was slightly in shock at first, and I'm not sure she actually believed me, but once it sank in she was over the moon and very excited. She went to bed with a big smile on her face and then spent the next few days talking to the new little person inside my tummy. Chloe is wonderful with kids and I'm pretty certain she'll be spending a lot more time with us once the baby is born.

Of course, Justin and I have talked about marriage but as far as we're concerned, nothing has really changed. Our relationship is as loving and strong as any married couple's and we would never have let the fact that we haven't tied the knot stop us from having a child. Saying that, I do want us all – one day – to be a family with the same name, and I know it will happen when the time feels right. So far, for Justin and I, getting married hasn't felt like the be all and end all. It's far more important to me to have my baby at the right time, and on top of that I quite like the idea of our child being a part of the special day when it finally happens. A wedding is often a celebration of two people coming together – a public declaration of their love – but Justin and I have been together for so long that everyone knows how much we love one another. For me, a wedding would be more like honouring what we've already had for so long, and celebrating the family that we already are. I can't see us going for a big white wedding, either. Something personal and small is more our style. One of the reasons I didn't want to get married during my time with Girls Aloud was because it would have all got too big and impersonal. I'd have found myself having to invite the world and his wife, just so I didn't offend anyone – 'Ted' from the record company and somebody else whom I don't really know, but who had done this or that for the band. That's just not us. I want our wedding to be a big party full of the people we love. That's how I imagine it.

Luckily, I now have the luxury of being able to do things my way. I'm looking forward to the brand new experience of being a mum, and also to giving myself the time to sit back and think about what I want to do next in my career. It's a bit of a weird one because I've tried my hand at so many things, but there are still a few dreams out there to realise. More than anything I love performing live and being on stage, especially in some kind of musical show. That's what I'd love to do more of; in fact, I've still got my heart set on playing Evita – that would be the ultimate role for me.

After everything I've done it feels good still to have new ambitions, but I've had so many amazing experiences and been so incredibly lucky that anything else is a bonus. However much things have changed for me over the years, one thing has remained the same, and that's my passion to get out there on stage and perform. Deep down I guess I'm still that same little girl who sang show tunes in her bedroom . . . all those years ago.

Index